D1268238

A Hot-Bed of Musicians

A Hot-Bed of Musicians

Traditional Music in the Upper New River Valley–Whitetop Region

Paula Hathaway Anderson-Green

THE UNIVERSITY OF TENNESSEE PRESS

Knoxville

Copyright © 2002 by The University of Tennessee Press / Knoxville.
All Rights Reserved. Manufactured in the United States of America.
First Edition.

This book is printed on acid-free paper.

Library of Congress Cataloging-in-Publication Data

Anderson-Green, Paula Hathaway.
    A hot-bed of musicians: traditional music in the upper New River Valley-
Whitetop region/Paula Hathaway Anderson-Green.—1st ed.
        p. cm.
Includes bibliographical references (p.   ) and discography (p.   ).
ISBN 1-57233-180-1(cl.: alk. paper)
ISBN 1-57233-181-X (pbk.: alk. paper)
1. Old-time music—Virginia—History and criticism.
2. Old-time music—North Carolina—History and criticism.
3. Musicians—Virginia.
4. Musicians—North Carolina.
I. Title.
ML3551.7.V8 A63 2002
781.642'09755'7—dc21   2001006276

Dedicated to my husband, Robert Hamilton Green,
and my father, Paul H. Anderson.
Both supported this long-term project,
for which I am deeply indebted.

Also dedicated to the memory of my mother,
Edith Hathaway Anderson, who encouraged me to
do research with her in my youth; my grandfather,
William Byron Hathaway, professor of languages
at the University of Florida, 1913–1943;
and my grandmother, Lula H. Anderson,
who taught me to value family traditions.

Contents

Appendix

Illustrations

Acknowledgments

Many people provided information and advice in the course of my research. I am especially grateful to: Peggy Bulger, now at the American Folklife Center, Library of Congress; Kip Lornell, Office of Folklife Programs, Smithsonian Institution; Alan Jabbour, Ann Hoog, and Jennifer Cutting at the American Folklife Center, Library of Congress; John Burrison, Department of English, Georgia State University; Steve Fisher, director of the Appalachian Center for Community Service and professor of political science, Emory and Henry College; Steve Green, archivist, Southern Folklore Collection, University of North Carolina, Chapel Hill; Dan Patterson, Department of Folklife, University of North Carolina, Chapel Hill; Charles Perdue, Department of English, University of Virginia; Walter J. Waddlington, professor of law, University of Virginia; and his student, Wilton Strickland, now an attorney in Miami; and the staff in the Virgil Sturgill Collection, Appalachian State University Library, Boone, North Carolina.

During the period 1997–2001, Bob Barrier, director of the Writing Center at Kennesaw State University (KSU), helped in myriad essential ways. He provided the place and the equipment necessary for me to complete this book, helped edit and format the text, served as a reader for some sections, sent electronic versions to the publisher, and encouraged me to finish the manuscript. The staff of the Writing Center was unfailingly gracious.

Thanks to KSU librarians Beverly Brasch, Betty Childress, Dewey Wilson, Carolyn Harris, Rita Spisak, and Lorraine Jetter as well as Carolyn Mitchum of Georgia State University Library Reference.

The staff of the KSU Learning Center, led by Valerie Jersey and Janese Thompson, were especially helpful with office supplies and services. Also helpful were Jeanette Eberhart and Kathy Alday.

At DeKalb (now Perimeter) College, Dunwoody, Georgia, Trish Fields, director of the Computer Lab in 1992–96, and the entire staff of the Writing Lab were most helpful.

Andrew Hamilton Davidson, assistant to the photographer, Rhett Turner, deserves special thanks.

Numerous residents of the Virginia–North Carolina area of study helped with information and assistance. Janeta Bonham, a member of the faculty of Oak Hill Academy, supplied family history information, as did Barbara Anderson Carter, Janelle Cooper, Laverne Kiser, and Sylvia Henderson. Edna Greer and Geraldine Anderson Trent offered important assistance, as well as family information. For supplying historical information, I am indebted to Shirley Gordon of the Grayson County (Virginia) Courthouse Foundation; Minnie Wells Hall, Grayson County Historical Society; and Guy and Jane Halsey. Amy Hauslohner, editor of the *Galax* (Virginia) *Gazette*, provided information on musicians. Paul Hiatt of High Point, North Carolina, shared the records he keeps on winners at fiddling conventions. Gary Poe, disk jockey at WKSK Radio, West Jefferson, North Carolina, was an invaluable source of information on the old-time and bluegrass music of Ashe County and checked sources at Appalachian State University Library. David Hauslohner, chairman of the Comer's Creek Foundation and owner of Fox Hill Inn, Troutdale, Virginia, generously provided facilities. ❖

Traditional Music in the New River-Whitetop Region of Virginia and North Carolina

The spectacular land of the "New River" or "Whitetop" area of Virginia–North Carolina is home to a resonant yet haunting and poignant musical tradition still vigorous today. In these Blue Ridge Mountains, vast numbers of musicians and their audiences participate in the music culture.[1] From the colonial period to the present day, this musical heritage has been evolving from its roots in the British tradition into the current Appalachian mix of old-time and bluegrass music. Throughout the year, in jam sessions and fiddlers conventions, the music continues, enriching lives, passing on values, and creating bonds between individuals and groups.

Sitting outside their shop in Rugby, Virginia, in the shadow of Whitetop Mountain, Wayne Henderson and Gerald Anderson talk about the music scene in their home area. "It's a hot-bed of musicians around here," says Gerald (interview by Anderson-Green, Aug. 2, 1994). He and Wayne make and play guitars and mandolins, performing not only locally but around the nation. Wayne has even toured internationally. Most of all, though, they prefer playing in their home territory. Musicians from both sides of the Virginia-Carolina line gather in their shop for jam sessions on Wednesday nights, while similar gatherings take place in homes or stores in nearby areas, such as Troutdale, Flatridge, and Grassy Creek. On these nights in the summer when the Rugby shop's windows are open, people driving by can hear tunes like "Soldier's Joy" and "Ragtime Annie." Other favorite gathering places for music include the rescue squad buildings and local firehouses, where benefits raise money for anyone with a special need. While the crowd circles around to the music of fiddles and banjos playing old-time tunes— "John Henry," "Leather Britches," and more—money is dropped in the hat to help the neighbor. As far back as the days of hoe-downs at the harvest, all-day singings at churches, and musical perform-ances at auctions and political rallies, music always has been an integral part of community efforts in this region.

The significance of this region has been recognized by scholars and musicologists. A leading folklorist, David E. Whisnant, of Chapel Hill, North Carolina, terms this Whitetop region "the center of gravity" for mountain music (*All That Is Native* 186). And Bill Malone of Tulane University states, "The seedbed of southern religious rural music appears to have been in southwest Virginia" (*Singing Cowboys* 28–29). From this area, lasting music traditions spread across the South as a whole, influencing a large regional (and later even a national) population.

Although this recognition has brought no great fame or wealth to the home territory, the musical tradition there persists with great vigor. The highlight of the year is a summer season filled with local fiddlers conventions. This tradition goes all the way back to the earliest fiddlers contest on record in colonial Virginia—that of Hanover County, Virginia, in 1737 (Blaustein 14; Orr 1056 gives the date as 1736). In the Whitetop region today, these gatherings usually are identified by county name, such as the Alleghany County (North Carolina) Fiddlers Convention in July, and that of Ashe County (North Carolina) in early August. The largest and most famous fiddlers convention is in the town of Galax, Virginia, on the eastern edge of Grayson County. This Galax Fiddlers Convention goes on for an entire week between the first and second weekends of August, bringing in over thirty thousand people from throughout the United States and even Canada and Great Britain, all fired with enthusiasm for making and hearing southern mountain music day and night.

These thousands of musicians and followers pour onto the field of Felts Park in Galax every year, pulling their campers and tents into place at the beginning of the week. A visitor from Pittsburgh, beginning to realize the significance of it all, describes what he experiences:

> The size of this gathering boggles the mind; when you first view the grounds, a race track and adjacent parking lots, you can't believe your eyes. Are there really this many old-time and bluegrass pickers and fans willing to brave the summer heat and storms and infamous Galax red mud that sucks the shoes off your feet after a hard rain? The answer of course is a resounding yes, and dedicated parking lot pickers, singers, and dancers are busy into the wee small hours proving it. (Charles Anderson 1)

For many, this week is a homecoming, bringing back those who have taken part in the outmigration, renewing musical friendships and family bonds, reuniting teachers and former students, and even introducing new people to the scene. Sitting around their campfires and grills, older musicians reminisce, telling younger ones about learning tunes from Albert Hash, maybe even showing off one of his hand-crafted fiddles, while nearby grandparents and grandchildren dance the "flat-foot" together as a band plays "Sally Ann." Even in the late twentieth century, Appalachian people cherish their involvement in old-time musical traditions.

Outstanding twentieth-century musicians from this Whitetop region, winners of various regional and even national awards, include Albert Hash, Wayne Henderson, Ola Belle Campbell Reed,

Working hand. Elk Creek, Virginia, 1997. Photograph by Rhett Turner. Used by permission.

and Dave Sturgill. They tell their stories so that others may know the traditions. The lives and careers of these highly acclaimed musicians demonstrate how this heritage is communicated, what its values are, and why it is still being carried on.

Born early in the twentieth century, Albert Hash, Ola Belle Reed, Dave Sturgill, and others of their era represent a bridge generation. They are the last musicians of an agrarian, non-materialistic culture, which can be termed a "folk" culture. They began to perform before, and were playing during, the generation of early Nashville country music, which emphasizes commercial or professional musicians. Despite changes in the music scene of the South and the nation, however, Albert, Ola Belle, and Dave were leaders who carried on the old-time Appalachian music traditions.

In the agrarian life, the best musicians played for their local communities, just for fun. Usually they were unpaid, but sometimes they received a small amount for performing at auctions or sales. Later, when the recording industry began to develop, some musicians in the region eventually began to make more money. At the same time, to some degree at least, they were influenced to shift from traditional music into styles that others thought would get a larger audience. The agents for recording companies preferred to set aside older vocal styles and patterns deemed "too regional" and cater to urban tastes (Blaustein 152).

The old-time music, played among kin and friends, rarely was performed using the dynamic and dramatic devices characteristic of show business; in fact, such would have been considered inappropriate. In a study of traditional singers, Perdue points out that, to one who "never performed for anyone outside her immediate family," an "outside aesthetic" would have had slight, if any, appeal (149). The old-time tradition is conservative; it is based not on originality but on a good command of the traditional repertoire. Creativity is allowed within traditional limits, and singers can display some emotion so long as it is not carried to extremes (Sandberg and Weisman, *Folk Music Sourcebook* 66). To the modern listener, singers sometimes sound out of tune when actually they are singing in archaic scales. The southern mountain music tradition has preserved "the music brought over by the early English and Irish settlers" because, there in the mountains, it "flourished with the least interference from other influences" (Sandberg and Weisman, *Folk Music Sourcebook* 65). The focus is not on the individual singer or performer so much as on the sound and meaning of the music and the camaraderie and fellowship it engenders.

Recording agents were not the only ones who helped to bring about a shift in styles of country music. Even scholars who went into the southern mountains in the early to middle twentieth century to document and record the music there influenced its presentation. For example, a scholarly preference for ballads over instrumental music frequently resulted in string bands and banjo players being overlooked and going unacknowledged. Below, Ola Belle, Dave, and Albert recount their lives and trace their musical development in the context of their home region. In the process, they give a valid portrayal of their Southern Appalachian culture and the manner in which old-time music is presented.

Some traditional musicians, such as Ola Belle and Dave, who moved away from their mountain homes to the urban East Coast, carrying their southern mountain music to a wider audience, did not shift with the winds of commercial popularity. Although, as performers, they were aware of playing to an audience, they nevertheless maintained their tradition. Gradually, as they became conscious of cultural stereotypes concerning Appalachia, they opposed such interpretations and became leaders in preserving the culture. Dave's older cousin, Virgil Sturgill, raised in Kentucky, moved to the East for some years and then returned to the mountains of North Carolina. Virgil, as part of the generation of transition, was especially concerned with preserving the ballad tradition. These musicians deserve attention not only for their talent and participation in Appalachian music, but also for their outstanding leadership in passing on the heritage amid twentieth-century demographic and cultural changes.

Other musicians remained in the Blue Ridge Mountains, maintaining and transmitting the traditional culture. One such musician was Albert Hash, whose work in the Whitetop–New River region was influential in bringing national attention to the out-standing music and craftsmanship produced there. Similar to Ola Belle Reed, Virgil Sturgill, and Dave Sturgill, Albert Hash was keenly aware of educating others. For Albert, this meant devoting special time and attention to the younger generation in his com-munity, teaching both the craft of making instruments and the art of playing fiddle in the old-time style. The current generation in the Whitetop region, including Wayne Henderson, Brian Grim and Debbie Grim, Thornton Spencer and Emily Spencer, and many others, were heavily influenced by Albert.

Both Virgil Sturgill and Dave Sturgill finally returned to live in the Blue Ridge Mountains of North Carolina in their later years, also devoting themselves to educational efforts in music or instru-ment making. Ola Belle Reed has remained on the East Coast, in the three-state area of Maryland-Pennsylvania-Delaware, where she is surrounded by family and has attained fame in music circles outside Appalachia. Even so, she always visited "down home" until she became unable to travel. The home region remains close to her heart as the source of her musical inspiration.

Both those who are just learning the old-time mountain music and those who love it deeply all will benefit from knowing about the lives of these famous musicians of the Whitetop region. Ola Belle, Dave, Virgil, and Albert all are related in some degree. Even more important, they were interconnected in their folk com-munity in ways that supported the lives of individuals and helped to keep traditions alive. Through their stories, we can comprehend the close-knit, meaningful kinship networks and the agrarian cul-ture into which they were born. Here they were raised, learned to transmit their cultural heritage to a new generation, and so emerged as leaders of their people.

The people of mountain communities recognize "distant kin" as well as "close kin," and to them kinship is more than biol-ogy. As a researcher states, "It connotes a kind of social relation-ship between those who share it," based on a feeling of solidarity, "sticking together through thick and thin" (Bryant 129). There is a sense of identity, of equality, as well as a strong feeling that support and love are "given freely and voluntarily . . . that within the group of close kin, people are most free to 'be themselves'"; they also talk about their descent from a common ancestor, recognize "family traits," and feel that they are passing all this on to the next generation (129).

These attitudes are prominent in the conversations of Ola Belle Reed, "Uncle" Dave Sturgill, and Albert Hash. Both Ola Belle and Dave are intensely interested in family relations, and both frequently refer to having swapped music with cousins at many jam sessions. Dave used to make trips visiting kin throughout North Carolina, Virginia, and Kentucky, to get information for the family genealogy he was writing and also to exchange musical styles and repertoire. Ola Belle also emphasizes family making music together. She notes how much kinship connections mattered to those who left their home places to move "up East" during the Great Depression. For example, after Ola and her family had made that transition and reestablished their store in Maryland and then their music venue, Dave Sturgill came to play banjo and fiddle at their New River Ranch, and they recognized each other as cousins. This was one of the important connections that helped Dave make the transition to Maryland and so continue his music.

As each musician tells his or her life story, expressing a deep love of the shared musical heritage, anecdotes about stores, church gatherings, family reunions, and fiddlers conventions demonstrate and develop the main themes of this book. All these artists emphasize that mountain music is indeed the core of Appalachian culture, promoting solidarity and a sense of common identity. To preserve that identity and to convey the values of the Appalachian heritage are the major reasons why Albert Hash, Ola Belle Reed, Dave Sturgill, and Virgil Sturgill performed and taught music, and why Dave and Albert hand-crafted instruments.

Since these leaders acted as mentors, the traditions are still carried on today, in the music and instrument making of people like Gerald Anderson, Brian Grim, Audrey Hash Hamm, Wayne Henderson, Greg Hooven, Emily Spencer, Thornton Spencer, Dean Sturgill, and many others who are introduced in the last chapter.

Currently, these younger musicians are bringing additional state and national recognition to this Whitetop region. There is also an effort under way to develop the Fisher's Peak Music Center near Galax, Virginia, dedicated to the presentation of the region's traditional music in the authentic style of performance, rather than the "pop culture" interpretations of Appalachian music heard elsewhere. Thus even more Americans may begin to discover this old-time heritage in the home region of Ola Belle, Dave, Albert, and so many less famous but still outstanding musicians and craftsmen.

Experiencing this Appalachian music in the context of its natural environment, as it is handed on by the people living there, may bring insight and renewed vigor to people who, amid our urbanized mass culture, are seeking meaning. Knowing the stories of these musicians in the bridge generation can inspire the audience to "carry on." ❖

Ola Belle Campbell Reed: Ballad-singing Banjo-picker

Moving from the southern Blue Ridge Mountains of North Carolina to the mid-Atlantic seaboard during the Great Depression, sensitive, talented, and plain-spoken Ola Belle Campbell Reed has played a major role in bringing traditional, old-time Appalachian music to a broad national audience. In the process, she influenced and was influenced by commercial country music and even, to some extent, rock and popular music. "Her repertoire was broad, reflecting the cultural mix that attends rapid social change and large movements of population" (Whisnant, "Notes"). Throughout these turbulent decades, Ola Belle's music and deepest beliefs have been rooted in the Appalachian culture of her childhood, and all her life she has transmitted this heritage to others.

Ola Belle Reed's voice was described in the *Washington Post* in 1976 as "one of the truest Appalachian contraltos" (Thompson). Indeed, Ola is a powerful singer who can "really belt one out" while expressing a range of emotion. Her repertoire includes both traditional ballads learned at her grandmother's knee and her own original compositions reflecting her mountain heritage. In addition, Ola Belle is an outstanding banjo player in the old-time clawhammer style, having mastered an instrument usually played by men in her culture.

In recognition of her contributions to our society, she has received honors from the Maryland Council for the Arts, an honorary doctorate from the University of Maryland, and finally a National Heritage Fellowship from the National Endowment for the Arts (NEA).

Ola's achievements have been lauded by the country's leading folklorists and cultural arbiters. At the presentation of the NEA award, Bess Lomax Hawes, then director of the NEA's Folk Arts Program, called Ola Belle "a national cultural treasure." Ralph Rinzler, of the Office of Folklife Programs at the Smithsonian Institution, has cited her as "a powerful and articulate interpreter of issues related to the problem of cultural continuity and change." Alan Jabbour, of the American Folklife Center at the Library of Congress, once called her "a commanding social force for her knack of winning audiences, disciples, and adherents wherever she goes." Finally, folklorist Henry Glassie has called her "a spokesman for a maligned culture" and "an artist of the first rank" (Rehert).

Despite all this attention, Ola Belle remains down-to-earth, even "self-effacing" (Hurst). She makes no great claims for herself but merely explains, "I'm a hillbilly and I sing hillbilly music" (Hurst). This heritage, she says, goes back "before bluegrass, it's old." Actually she is deeply knowledgeable concerning Appalachian culture. Over the years she has developed and articulated a critique of the images of Appalachia found throughout American culture. However, her main focus has been, and continues to be, performance as a musician.

Ola Belle's art can be understood best by examining her place in her culture of origin—that is, by recognizing the major forces that shaped her music and beliefs. A descendant of early settlers, she was born in 1916 in Ashe County, North Carolina, one of thirteen children of Arthur Harrison Campbell and his wife, Ella Mae Osborne from adjoining Grayson County, Virginia. Ashe and Grayson are in the upper New River Valley, which during the pioneer era bound several counties in a meaningful community despite the border between the states of North Carolina and Virginia. The New River—geologically one of the oldest rivers in the world—and its surrounding hills had provided pristine hunting grounds for the Cherokees and later a new frontier for Anglo-Celtic settlers in the mid-eighteenth century. With these settlers came a folk music tradition that is considered to be one of America's oldest and richest treasures.

Family History

When a scholar sat down to interview Ola about her life and work, he asked her to begin where she wanted to. Immediately she began telling about her family history (interview by Glassie, 1967). This in itself is indicative of the core of Appalachian culture, awareness of a handed-on tradition in which the individual forms part of a great chain of being. Further, the story she began with suggests a basis for her sensitivity regarding social issues, including her well-known egalitarianism. This was the tale of her father's grandfather, Duncan Campbell, from Lenoir, Caldwell County, North Carolina, the son of a well-to-do businessman.

Ola says that, despite the family's affluence, Duncan was disinherited for "marrying beneath his status." As Ola tells it, the "only thing they gave him was one slave," so he left Lenoir with his bride and the slave and moved westward into the mountains of Ashe County. There he became a tailor and had a large family. The slave stayed with them and later was buried with them in the family cemetery—the only black there. Perhaps he contributed to their musical repertoire, since Duncan's family was recognized locally for great musical traditions and talent. Certainly the black man was accepted as one of the family; later on, Duncan's descendants felt at ease jamming with blacks in the area.

Ola always has expressed admiration for this great-grand-father's determination and values, which placed love above social status. This attitude has had a lifelong influence on her. Henry Glassie has said about Ola: "Her political views are democratic, non-elitist, analogous to those of poet Walt Whitman" (quoted in Soulsman J1). Ola's lifestyle further demonstrates this, as her home always has been open to a cross-section of humanity. Her song lyrics enunciate an acceptance of all people. Her goals have been not only to personify and perpetuate the Appalachian her-itage, but also to recognize that other groups in America also have a valuable cultural heritage. In 1977, to emphasize this, she and her son David made a Folkways album, *All in One Evening,* with a Jewish musician, Kevin Roth, in which they all played dulcimer together, emphasizing the theme that music unifies all people (see discography).

Through her Duncan Campbell line, Ola inherits Scottish traditions, especially in music. Since Ola's father and grandfather played fiddle, it is likely that her great-grandfather Duncan did, too, for he was known to be a musician. According to tradition, the colonists of Scottish heritage especially loved the strains of the fiddle because that instrument can simulate the sound of the bagpipe (Sturgill family interview by Anderson-Green, Aug. 5, 1982; see chap. 4 below; Malone, *Singing Cowboys,* 9). Thus, as these pio-neers came into Appalachia, the fiddle eventually became the most prominent mountain instrument.

The rest of the history of Ola Belle's extended family shows a pattern typical of the Appalachian region. She is a thirteenth-generation American, whose ancestors were Scottish, Scots-Irish, English, Welsh, and German pioneers, along with a few Huguenots. By the mid-eighteenth century, these people had settled deep in the Blue Ridge Mountains, America's first frontier, perpetuating their Anglo-Celtic folk culture through generations.

In the earliest colonial period, some of Ola's ancestors were in New England. Her family history includes settlers of the rising English middle class, who were seeking opportunities in America.

Among these were Rev. John Lathrop, who came to Massachusetts from Kent with a bachelor of arts degree from Cambridge University; and, even earlier, Edward Fuller, a Mayflower Pilgrim. This family history is congruent with research which indicates that population movement into the southern backcountry in the eighteenth century consisted primarily of middle-class people, not "poor whites" being "pushed back" there, as generally is believed (Anderson-Green, "New River"; Beaver 144–45).

Also among Ola's ancestors was a German immigrant, Matthias Weiss, born in Hamburg in 1752 and a weaver by trade, who came to Pennsylvania during the major eighteenth-century German migration there. Matthias then went west and eventually turned southward, following the Great Wagon Road to Wythe County, Virginia. There he married Rachel Bonham, the daughter of Moses and Rebecca Parke Bonham. Each of Rachel's parents had a lineage representing another major stream of migration into the southern uplands. The Parkes were Scots-Irish, coming from County Donegal, Ireland, to Chester County, Pennsylvania, and then eventually into southwestern Virginia, also in the eighteenth century. In contrast, the Bonhams were descendants of seventeenth-century English Puritans who arrived in New England very early; a maternal line descended from the Pilgrim, Edward Fuller.

Fuller's descendant, Moses Bonham, died during the American Revolution on an expedition to Georgia with General "Mad" Anthony Wayne. He left his family living in Wythe County, Virginia, where daughter Rachel married Matthias Weiss. The couple moved a little farther south to Grant, in neighboring Grayson County, Virginia, continuing to work as weavers. In the next generation, their children married into the Osborne, Hash, and other pioneer families there. A son, John Weiss, was noted in local oral history as the first man who built a two-story log house there; people came from miles around to see it and to learn how to build one (Agnes Thomas, Ola's cousin, conversations with Anderson-Green).

Joining the stream from Pennsylvania on the road down the Valley of Virginia were the Osbornes, the Hashes, and other families who had lived near each other in Philadelphia County,

Pennsylvania, before adventuring to the southern frontier (Anderson-Green, "New River"). Ola's mother was an Osborne, so the children always were close to their Osborne and Hash cousins. F. W. Owsley has identified a typical migration pattern: a few family members "moved out together, and when they had reached the promised land they constituted a new community," a "settlement . . . more scattered than they had been in the East"; those who came later usually would be relatives or friends of the early arrivals (Owsley 22). In this manner, these families—Cox, Halsey, Hash, Osborne, Phipps, and others from Pennsylvania—took up land on the Virginia-Carolina border, along the Upper New River and its tributaries: Bridle, Saddle, and Fox creeks in Virginia (then Montgomery County and now Grayson County); and Wilson Creek, which flows in both Virginia and North Carolina. Dave Sturgill, a local family historian and musician, has pointed out that the colonial dividing line between Virginia and North Carolina was not agreed upon for decades, and that settlers thought of the Upper New River as one continuous settlement (Sturgill family interview by Anderson-Green).

These pioneers proceeded to cultivate farms in a wilderness where elevations ranged from 2,500 feet to as high as 5,719 feet at Mount Rogers. The hills were densely covered with black walnut trees, chestnuts, oaks, hickories, white and yellow poplars, and extensive pines. Of course, bottom lands were used for tillage, while sheep and cattle were grazed on the mountains. This agricultural pattern, brought primarily from Ulster and northern Great Britain, continued for generations in western Virginia and North Carolina.

In Ola's girlhood, her grandfather, Enoch Osborne, owned 1,300 acres in Grayson County, much of it high on Mount Rogers, where he grazed sheep and had a cabin. His home, however, was in the valley, near New River (Ola Belle Reed interview by Anderson-Green). Enoch's great-great-grandfather was Capt. Enoch Osborne, a leader in the establishment of the traditional yeoman culture in the Upper New River Valley during the colonial and early Federal period (Williams, "New River Valley," xl). Osborne served first as a magistrate for Montgomery County, Virginia, and later as a justice for Grayson County when it was formed in 1793. Also he was captain of the militia during the American Revolution and a lay leader for the Methodist Church, hosting Bishop Asbury on one of that famous clergyman's journeys through the wilderness. Asbury's journal records: "March 1792. We made an early start for friend Osborne's, on New River, fifteen miles distant. Here we were generously entertained" (Asbury, cited in Anderson-Green, "New River" 423). The congregation Asbury came to visit was that of the Bridle Creek Methodist Church, established by Hashes, Osbornes, and other early settlers at the mouth of Bridle Creek, overlooking the beautiful New River. This church is still in existence today.

Enoch Osborne's wife, born Jane Hash, certainly would have been the one who provided most of the gracious hospitality. The southern colonial homemaker on the Appalachian frontier was as skilled as those of the Tidewater in the arts of entertaining: excellent cooking, friendly atmosphere, musical entertainment, and, finally, comfortable sleeping quarters for guests. Given her husband's leadership roles, Jane Hash Osborne undoubtedly had frequent opportunities to entertain "generously."

Jane was the daughter of another prominent leader, John Hash(e), whose Montgomery County, Virginia, will of 1784 lists Enoch as son-in-law, along with another son-in-law, Francis Sturgill. This grouping demonstrates the kinship connections extant even at the earliest stage of the New River settlement. Into this folk community, in the early twentieth century, Ola Belle Campbell, Albert Hash, "Uncle" Dave Sturgill, and many other outstanding Upper New River musicians would be born (Anderson-Green, "New River").

As W. J. Cash has pointed out, if one placed a pen at any spot in the map of the backcountry South around the year 1800 and drew a circle with a radius of thirty miles, everyone within that circle would have been related by some degree of kinship (Cash 27). Even up until World War II, this would have been true. Certainly people in this Appalachian area had an awareness of kinship (though not always an immediate connection) that created a community marked by shared values and friendships. In

Ola's words, there was "more kinship than you'd ever think about, really," meaning that people took it for granted; however, as she has said, underneath it all, kinship mattered (Ola Belle Reed interview by Anderson-Green).

Another branch of Ola Belle's clan, the Perkins family, contained leaders in the early history of Ashe County, across the river. Unlike the other families, they were Tories who had left New England because of the unpopularity of their views. They entered the frontier around the 1770s, as the first white settlers in the "Old Fields" area of Ashe County. Always willing to speak out for their ideas, the Perkins family members over the generations became leaders in Ashe County in education and politics (Shepherd, *Heritage* 393). Inheriting this legacy, Ola thus learned to be a leader firmly rooted in her values and willing to express her views even when they differed from those of others.

As various branches of Ola Belle's family came into the New River Valley, all contributed to the Appalachian culture there, interacting in farming, craft making, family life, church, and musical entertaining among their relatives and friends.

Musical Heritage

The folk music brought by these early pioneers had vitality and variety: a ballad tradition going back centuries in Great Britain and Europe; fiddle tunes and dances such as reels and jigs; the "high lonesome" sound in singing; and powerful and beautiful hymns. Through her family, Ola Belle learned this Appalachian musical tradition; in her native region today, this musical heritage is still handed on, even now a vital part of the culture. The Upper New River Valley repeatedly has been singled out as one of the richest folk music areas in the Appalachians and, by extension, in the United States. A folklorist writes about the Whitetop section: "For a variety of historical reasons . . . these counties and a few nearby soon became some of the richest culturally in the southern Appalachian region. By the turn of the twentieth century, when modernity had already brought mass culture to much of the rest of the country, the hills and valleys of southwest Virginia were still alive with ballad singers, fiddlers, banjo pickers, and dancers" (Whisnant, *All That Is Native* 186).

These counties Whisnant refers to are Grayson, Smyth, and Washington in Virginia; in North Carolina, the Whitetop area includes Allegheny and Ashe Counties. The folk music found here is primarily of British origin. Research by Cecil Sharp and others has documented that British songs, including those of the English, Scotch-Irish, and Welsh, "lay at the core of the Southern rural repertory." These songs came from all socioeconomic groups in Britain, not only from the lower class. Sharp often collected ballads in the homes of middle- and upper-class families in the Southern Uplands (Malone, *Singing Cowboys* 22–23). Ola Belle's extended family was

deeply involved in this musical tradition in the Ashe-Allegheny-Grayson County region, especially around Grassy Creek, Lansing, and Jefferson, North Carolina; and Mount Rogers, Virginia.

Ola's father, Arthur Campbell, patriarch of the clan, in addition to being a businessman, schoolteacher, and community leader in Ashe County, was also a well-known fiddler. As noted above, from the eighteenth century on, the most important instrument in southern mountain music has been the fiddle. Bill Malone states, "No instrument has been more readily identified with southern whites than the fiddle. Since the fiddle was small and compact enough to be carried in a saddlebag, as the southern frontier advanced westward the fiddle moved with it" (*Southern Music* 8). In the Appalachian region, men who played the fiddle certainly were

Family of Arthur and Ella May Osborne Campbell of Ashe County, North Carolina, 1933. Ola Belle Campbell Reed is one of the middle girls. Photograph from Ola Belle Campbell Reed.

at the center of the culture. Ola Belle says that her father was a great musician who could play the violin in either classical or hoe-down style (interview by Anderson-Green). Folk music was central to dances and entertainment, but classical music sometimes was played in church or as part of school programs. Arthur had a beloved fiddle that had once been repaired by a New River friend, musician, and craftsman, Albert Hash, who lived near Ola's maternal grandparents in Grayson County. After her father's death, Ola stated that she would give that fiddle to be part of a permanent museum collection.

Arthur Campbell and his siblings, Jim, Ellen, and Dockery, along with a friend, Becky Jones, formed a string band and frequently played for neighbors in Ashe County (Ola Belle Reed interview by Anderson-Green). An old photograph shows Doc on banjo and Arthur on fiddle, standing behind the two seated ladies, Ellen with guitar and Becky with banjo. They not only made music with their kin, but also, according to Ola, usually jammed on Friday nights at their general store in Lansing with "colored" musicians, especially the Spurlins family, called "The Little Wonders." These jam sessions encouraged informal swapping of musical styles (Ola Belle Reed interview by Anderson-Green). It was in settings like this that the banjo, originally an African-American instrument, became basic in Appalachian music. (See Malone, *Southern Music* 8 and 165 for discussion of "the complicated question of black-white folk interaction"; see also Winans, "Banjo: From Africa" and "Black Banjo-Playing," for analysis of the banjo-playing tradition in Virginia, showing that style and repertoire were "common stock" for both blacks and whites; also Whisnant, *All That Is Native and Fine,* 244–45.)

In Ashe County, another favorite place where people gathered to play was the Horseshoe Bend of New River, above the falls, frequented by the Sturgills, Campbells, and many others. In addition to these neighborhood gatherings, Arthur and his string band played at events such as medicine shows and sales (Ola Belle Reed interview by Glassie). Although they made some small amount of money at these events, in no way did performance at such events constitute a professional career. Rather, it was done mainly for fun and out of love of the music.

Naturally, Arthur's father, Alexander Campbell, known in the neighborhood as "Uncle Alex," also had played fiddle, despite being a preacher in the Primitive Baptist Church, which did not allow instrumental music. Later he was "churched" for continuing to play—that is, he was put on trial and "turned out." Although he was bitter about it, according to Ola, he then declared, "Today is the day I start to live." He would give up neither his instrumental music or his religious beliefs, proclaiming, "What I will do for people, I'll do from my home, no place else" (Ola Belle Reed interview by Glassie). This example has exerted a strong influence on Ola, who says, "I think he must have been a lot like me." She is deeply Christian but is nondenominational, saying, "What you do to your fellow man *is* your religion" (Ola Belle Reed interview by Glassie). Her grandfather Alex never would belong to another church, but he was widely admired as a musician and as a leading figure in his area of Ashe County (Ola Belle Reed interview by Anderson-Green). People often came to his home to hear him preach there and continued to enjoy his music (Marti 18). (On religious attitudes toward fiddling and dancing in southern culture, see Cauthen 201–14.)

While men carried on the main instrumental tradition in the southern mountains, women were the primary singers. Ola Belle remembers learning from her mother and grandmother both ballads ("Barbara Allen" and "Black Jack Davy," for example) and hymns such as "Wayfaring Stranger" (interview by Anderson-Green; Camp and Whisnant 83). She also recalls visiting at "Blevinstown" across the river, where so many of the Blevins family lived that the neighbors gave the area that nickname. At the church there, Ola as a girl was deeply impressed by a fashionable, slim Blevins woman with a twisted hairdo. When that woman started to sing, "her voice would go till it'd almost blast the ceiling out of the church" (interview by Anderson-Green). In the Appalachian singing tradition, especially in church, women were not expected to be demure or repressed but were allowed to express power and emotion with their voices.

Ola Belle became a prime proponent of this powerful singing style. However, she enlarged the female musical role by becoming an outstanding clawhammer banjo picker as well as a strong singer. By the late nineteenth century, the banjo, introduced into the South by blacks, had been adopted by whites. In this process, in Appalachia the technique for playing banjo was transformed into the "clawhammer" style. A well-known banjo player, Dave Sturgill, explains that, from the viewpoint of the audience, the musician's hand seems to be acting as a "fist whamming" the banjo, since the thumb and finger form a "C" shape, while a highly rhythmic sound is produced (Sturgill family interview by Anderson-Green). The southern banjo tradition, as developed among both blacks and whites, has been thoroughly analyzed by Cecilia Conway. Discussing the clawhammer and frailing techniques, Conway points out that, while there are many "regional and individual variants," it is "along the Blue Ridge in southwestern Virginia and northwestern North Carolina . . . [that this style of playing] is most fully and artistically realized" (*African Banjo Echoes,* 64). This is further evidence that Ola Belle and the other artists treated in this book were born and developed their talents and techniques in one of the richest folk culture regions of the United States.

Gender roles in the South, including the Southern Appalachian Mountains, gave men more contact with people outside the home and more opportunity to interact with blacks. This may help explain why males dominated banjo playing in Appalachia. However, even as a girl, Ola apparently was assertive enough to pick up and try an instrument that appealed to her, even though females did not typically play it. Her father's band included two women, his sister and the friend Becky. As we have seen, Becky played banjo in the band, so Ola had a role model. In one interview, Ola says that she does not remember who taught her to play banjo; somebody loaned her one, and she gradually mastered it, playing first in the home and later in outside appearances, encouraged by her father and brother (interview by Anderson-Green). On another occasion, she stated that Uncle Doc taught her to play banjo, while Aunt Ellen taught her guitar and organ (Marti 18). It is clear that she learned organ first, playing at her grandparents' home, then guitar and banjo. Undoubtedly the home influence was primary in Ola's musical training.

The strong influence of her musical father, uncle, and brother Alex Campbell, as well as Becky, may explain Ola's ability and willingness to ignore traditional gender roles in music. About her singing, a critic has noted, "Her vocal style derives mainly from the male bluegrass singing tradition" (Sandberg and Weisman, *Folk Music Sourcebook* 66). Certainly this style reflects the influence of the male musicians in her family. However, Ola's style also has had other influences, equally significant, such as the forceful singing allowed women in churches like the one in Blevinstown. At any rate, Ola rapidly absorbed techniques from the invigorating musical environment of the New River area, without allowing gender boundaries to limit her development.

Indeed Ola is a creative and gifted musician *within* a tradition, not one who rebels against it. Writing about old-time music, a critic states, "Creativity is manifested . . . within sanctioned limits"; for example, the basic melodic line is not altered or varied, as it is in jazz or classical music (ibid., 58). Modern audiences need to be aware that the traditional singing style does not encourage a singer to be "original" or "dynamic," but instead expects that individual to be straightforward and powerful in a conservative way. Furthermore, audiences may wonder whether a singer in the folk tradition is singing "in tune," when he or she is "very much in tune, but in accordance with archaic forms of the musical scale which are not used in European or contemporary pop music, and so they sound out of tune to the unsophisticated ear" (ibid.).

Finally, it should be noted that traditional singers rarely use guitar as accompaniment because "the guitar, much more than the banjo, tends to pull the singer's voice out of the traditional archaic scales" (ibid.). Further, the guitar was not introduced into mountain music until after 1900 (Lornell 207). In the earlier generations, people preferred to sing without instrumentation; and now many, like Ola Belle, prefer to play banjo while singing.

All of these traditional techniques and approaches Ola learned from members of both her immediate and her extended family throughout her childhood, in singing schools, churches, or just in informal gatherings. Aunts, uncles, cousins, and others in that family were also musicians. Ola's great-uncle, Bob Inghram, of Grayson County, was particularly well known as a singing school teacher, and she refers to him frequently when talking about her girlhood. Families were large yet close-knit, relatives liked to play instruments with each other, and music helped hold the kinship network together. At the same time, the family was passing the music on to each succeeding generation.

As Ola said to a journalist, "I learned most of my songs just from hearing other people play them. I learned a lot of the old gospel songs, banjo numbers, sit-down pickin' tunes. I've known 'Pretty Polly' since I was a girl. The version we had back in the mountains was very old. You just grew up with those things. I didn't get my songs out of no books" (Mullinax). In addition to experiencing the music being sung and played at home and in church, Ola and her siblings were taken to festivals and other events that featured traditional Appalachian music. Ola remembers her brother, Alex, recalling that the family attended the famous White Top Folk Festival in 1933, when Eleanor Roosevelt, as First Lady, was present. Alex said, "Everyone talked about that for quite a while." Undoubtedly such occasions heightened an awareness of the value of their musical heritage.

Close to Nature, Close to People

While all this music making was going on, in order to support his large family, Ola's father both owned a store and worked as a schoolteacher in the town of Lansing, North Carolina. In addition, during the summer he farmed, assisted by his children. During the winter, the family lived in town, but in the spring they moved to the "old home-place" on their family land bordering New River. Ola says they moved out there when the cherry trees were in bloom (interview by Glassie). This home was a large, two-room log cabin far removed from neighbors. Ola remembers how the father and children worked in the fields during the day; they used hoes, because the mountainsides made use of a cultivator plow difficult (ibid.). They had dinner at noon, then "jumped in the river and sat under the trees" (interview by Anderson-Green). After this mid-day rest, they went back to work until time for supper. Ola says that they learned the facts of life in a natural way, realizing in their own family that "it's about time for another baby." They had no radios, no communication with the outside world; they had no fears, day or night, and sometimes slept outside. Ola says that, until she moved away from Ashe County, "I never knew what it was to worry" (interview by Glassie).

Years later, Ola was often interviewed about her Appalachian girlhood, which she loved to discuss: "I've been asked many times to describe my life in the mountains . . . it was alive with the earth . . . you knew every season" (Notes to 1976 Folkways record album *My Epitaph*). Indeed, her people arranged their lives by the season, not by specific dates on the calendar (i.e., they moved to the farm when the cherry trees bloomed). In the same way, they judged time not so much by the clock as by the position of the sun in the sky. They could tell by the signs when the leaves would change and storms would come.

Thus the sense of closeness to nature was always an essential element for Ola, but so was the awareness of community among people, even though families were scattered on farms miles down the road. She says, "There was communication because I think people needed one another and they realized it so much. And I believe one of the reasons was because really and truly we were so close to the earth and the elements and God's creation. I think that's the one thing that made them know" (Notes, *My Epitaph*).

People grew up in a lifestyle that was self-sufficient—based upon supplying their own needs, from food to entertainment—but always within the network of kinship and community. Ola sees all the aspects of her early life—closeness to the earth, farming, the sense of community—linked together in the music of the Appalachian culture. She conveys this by saying, "I think that the music and everything comes through communication with people. The people lived with the earth, they had to make their living. That's why I'm saying that you cannot separate your music from your lifestyle. You cannot separate your lifestyle, your religion, your politics from your music. It's a part of life. And that's what our music was in the mountains. It was a part of our life" (ibid.).

With the seasonal cycle, various agrarian events took place. People gathered at harvest time, bringing out their fiddles and banjos for a "hoe-down." When crops were "laid by" after the last cultivation, then there was time for church homecomings and "all-day singings on the grounds," even a house raising.

Holidays, of course, were special times that highlighted traditional values. Reminiscing about her childhood, Ola recalls the Christmas seasons the family had together: "At Christmas time we didn't go out and go in debt for Christmas gifts. Father brought brown bags for each from the store, with oranges and other fruits; the kids got the tree from the woods and made popcorn and paper chains" (interview by Glassie). All the brown bags and boxes were put under the tree for each child of the family and also for neighborhood children. Ola does not remember believing in Santa Claus, but she did have a sense of the excitement and greatness of the event. They had good, even elaborate Christmas dinners served at a plank table, covered by an oilcloth and bordered by benches. Sometimes chicken and dumplings were served. The children had to come to the table quietly. Ola says that, even today, she likes the smell of old houses, scrubbed wood floors. All the memories of the Appalachian days have great significance for her.

Was I Poor?

Ola's family never was really poor, but, like most families of that region and era in an almost cashless society, hers depended upon subsistence farming. Cratis D. Williams has pointed out that such families lived comfortably according to the standards of the time (Williams, "Who Are the Southern Mountaineers?" 48). Her father managed to provide a satisfactory middle-class lifestyle for a family of thirteen children until the Great Depression.

All the families Ola Belle knew of in her childhood owned land; "no renting I ever heard about" (interview by Anderson-Green). Her Campbell grandparents lived in Grassy Creek, close to Ola's home on New River, and she often was in their house, which was furnished well. It included the pump organ that she played and one of the few telephones in the area—the girls liked to call friends and sing over the phone. On the other side of New River, in Grayson County, Virginia, her Grandfather Osborne owned 1,300 acres on Mount Rogers, much of which was used, according to Ola, for grazing sheep "up on the mountain in the summer." Ola says that, when he died in 1941, Enoch Cicero Osborne's will, in the old tradition of southern hospitality, stated that "the doors of his house would never be closed to anyone who needed a home" (ibid.). A self-sufficient prosperity, as well as a Scripture-based viewpoint, underlay these social attitudes (Hobbs 85).

Despite her family's relative economic stability, Ola Belle had an early experience with an outsider's view of Appalachia. Once she and a friend were taken on a tour as "examples of poor destitute mountain children" by a minister who was trying to raise money for "missionary" work in the mountains (Whisnant, "Notes"). Eventually she became disturbed by these stereotypical views of mountain life.

When the Great Depression of the 1930s came, Arthur Campbell's business in Lansing was hit hard. People could not pay their debts, and eventually he lost the store. He lost even more when people for whom he had cosigned notes went bankrupt. Ola says that she "doesn't feel the depression hit us children," but she thinks it had a great effect on her father, for "there was not a lot men could do."

Although Ola Belle lacked just a few months in her last year of high school, as a result of the Great Depression and her family's move to Maryland, she did not graduate. The previous year, at her older sister's graduation, she had sat in the audience and listened to her school principal, J. B. Hash, speak prophetic words. Hash, born in Piney Creek, North Carolina, in 1892, was a leading figure in Ola's folk group who had a marked influence on generations to come. After his own graduation from Bridle Creek High in Grayson County, Virginia, he went to Peabody Teachers College in Nashville and to the University of North Carolina at Chapel Hill, then returned to the Upper New River Valley, where he spent more than forty years as a teacher, principal, and superintendent, and also as a North Carolina state legislator for Ashe County (Shepherd 563). What he said that day Ola has remembered: "You're going out into a world that you know little about. Never be ashamed of your background, that's your foundation. There were hands that worked hard to put you through" (interview by Glassie). Ola also remembers hearing that sometimes it's not the pleasant things that are most valuable, since people learn from adversity (ibid.).

Heading for Maryland

Faced with the difficult economic situation, people began to go to Maryland for jobs and farm work. The Campbell family joined the stream of outbound migration, leaving the southern mountains for the region encompassing Washington, D.C.; Maryland; Delaware; and Pennsylvania.[1]

The area north of Baltimore was a special focus of migration. In those days, the Glen L. Martin Company and other businesses solicited employees from Appalachia, and Greyhound Bus ran a daily bus from Sparta, North Carolina, to Baltimore (Sturgill family interview by Anderson-Green). Although they were unaware of the historical irony, these New River people were reversing their ancestors' route from the Delaware River Valley to the New River Valley over two hundred years earlier. The southern mountain people who left were motivated by a typically American desire to find a life that was better economically. Like their ancestors, they took their spiritual and musical heritage with them.

Ola Belle's oldest brother went first, got a paying job on a farm, then rented an old farm with a big house. He wrote, telling his mother to come with the others. The father stayed behind with

Ola's uncle when the family moved, but he followed a few months later. A man her father had signed a note for drove the family members up, and they spent the first night in Maryland at his house. Although Ola minimizes the effect on the children, she also says of this event, "The trip up to Maryland was a nightmare . . . the whole thing had changed just that quick."

Symbolizing the situation was an accident she had on arrival. She jumped off the top of the truck as she was used to doing, but previously she had jumped onto dirt roads. This one was pavement! So, she says, "I was hurt for awhile" (interview by Glassie).

In Maryland she got a job housekeeping for $2.50 a week. She says, "It was pretty bleak for me." She was not used to people "taking you only at face value . . . they thought we were different" (ibid.). They said things that hurt her feelings; for example, her employer acted in an arrogant manner and said she "should be glad just to eat, considering the kind of a home you come from." Her mother's advice was to "just nothing them," (ibid.). However, despite such treatment at work, Ola says she gave that employer a flower in a pot when she left that job.

In the notes to *My Epitaph,* a Folkways album issued in 1976, regarding her composition "I've Endured," Ola speaks of having had to cope in the East with discrimination toward those from Appalachia. Even at a young age, she interpreted this experience as an opportunity to interact with others and communicate the values of her lifestyle and tradition. She says, "I've been lucky to have a chance to take a history of our life into places it's never been before . . . If you want a person to understand or learn about a subject such as I have talked about you don't run up and cram it in their mouth. . . . No matter how contrary or how uppity they may seem, you can show them a little love and understanding" (Notes, *My Epitaph* 2). Grounded in Appalachian values that, especially in her family, were based on religious teachings about "turning the other cheek" and respecting others, Ola was able to take a negative experience and turn it into a positive one. Later she made good use of such experiences in song lyrics and talks with young people at colleges.

During those Depression years, Ola says her family moved two or three times in the Maryland-Pennsylvania area, finally securing a big brick house "down in a holler." Rent was cheap, and they took in boarders from "down South." Ola packed lunches for them and did not do any more housekeeping, "because those attitudes hurt her pride too much, not the work itself" (interviews by Glassie and Anderson-Green).

Almost all of Ola's people on both sides of the family moved up to Maryland. Many families began dairy farming there, while others went into construction or industrial jobs. The Campbells eventually opened another general store, Campbell's Corner, in Oxford, Pennsylvania, near the Maryland border.

Making Music

Both at the store and at home, during hours when she was not working, Ola often was making music with her brother, other relatives, and friends. In the Glassie interview, she says that people from all over came to their house in Lancaster County, Pennsylvania, to hear their music; and this encouraged ideas she and Alex had about starting their band. Then the brother and sister began playing up on a pickup truck at Tanersly; they hoed corn by day and played at sales in the evenings. She says she had always wanted music: "Guess I always was a dreamer."

One of her favorite relatives to "pick with" was "Uncle" Joel Sturgill (actually her mother's first cousin), who would come by early on Sunday mornings to talk and play banjo with her. Born in a log house built by his grandfather on Helton Creek in Ashe County, North Carolina, Joel later was a resident in Smyth County, Virginia, where he married Clara Weaver. Eventually they moved to Cecil County, Maryland, where he had a varied career in Elkton. In addition to owning a barber shop, he was a musician and a preacher who presided at marriages of couples who "eloped to Maryland" (Sturgill and Sturgill, *A History of the Sturgill Family* (1983), 141 and 216). Although he never appeared professionally

with Ola Belle, their musical relationship, which was very influential and important to her, lasted over many years.

Frequently, neighbors and friends would drop in at Ola's
house for evenings of music and dancing. She laughs as she recalls
one night: "I remember one time we were having a gathering . . .
everyone was coming . . . we bought a new linoleum rug for the
kitchen—the table was long as mine in there—and at that end was
a fireplace and over there was the stove and we played and they
danced round and round and round that table. And I'll never forget
next morning—we never noticed it at the time—next morning,
there was nothing but black! They wore the whole top off! [laughter]"
(interview by Anderson-Green).

From all of Ola Belle's tales and reminiscences, it is clear
that, although the Blue Ridge people had to give up cherished
home places "down South" due to economic realities, they maintained their relationships and their culture in new places. Throughout the Great Depression and World War II, these people, as well
as other groups in America, experienced not only geographical but
also cultural dislocation, as they gave up their homes in an agricultural folk society and moved to urban or suburban areas with
mixed populations. Through it all, their music and musical events
helped to sustain their spirits.

Soon after Ola began singing and playing with her brother
Alex at carnivals, parks, and other local spots of entertainment in
the tri-state area, a friend introduced her to Arthur ("Shorty")
Woods, formerly of Ashe County, North Carolina, and now in York
Lyn, Delaware. Woods had organized a band—or, actually, restruc-
tured a band begun "down home" by his father and a cousin, John
Miller Sr., who had made and played instruments. This group,
called the "North Carolina Ridge Runners," used to play the Ashe
County–Grayson County circuit (John Miller Jr. interview by
Anderson-Green, Aug. 7, 1994). Now the band resurfaced "up East,"
led by Shorty and including, at times, his sister and some of his
cousins, Lester Miller and John Miller Jr. among them. Ola felt at
home with this group. She sang all the old songs she knew for

Shorty, and he asked Ola Belle to join the new North Carolina Ridge Runners, performing southern mountain music on a circuit throughout the Maryland-Pennsylvania-Delaware area. Ola's mother decided that, at eighteen, Ola was old enough to go, but that Alex was too young (interview by Glassie). Ola gladly accepted.

Transplanted southerners in the area naturally listened to this "hillbilly" music on radio shows, at carnivals, and at music parks, but other locals ("Easterners") did, too. Thus Ola and other such musicians became influential in transmitting traditional old-time, "hillbilly," and "bluegrass" music to a national audience. That influence was to have far-reaching effects later, in the urban folk revival of the 1960s and the dissemination of "country" music worldwide. Of course, at that time, Ola and her friends had no worldwide agenda or vision, just a desire to enjoy making music for an audience and to make some income for their families during the difficult days of the Great Depression.

During her years with the Ridge Runners in the 1930s and 1940s, Ola performed on radio stations in towns such as Wilmington, York, Reading, and Lancaster, and at music parks like Sunset Park near West Grove, Pennsylvania (Whisnant, "Notes"). She first played on the radio at a small Delaware station, WILM, where Woods bought air time for the show. The first song she sang over the air was "Saint Louis Blues," belting it out in true Ola Belle style. She recalls, "The red needle flew over and the engineer jumped ten feet in the air!" Laughingly she adds, "I get paid fairly well for hollering!" (interview by Glassie). That style has its roots in her childhood memories of church in Blevinstown, while her choice of song for the occasion, "Saint Louis Blues," reflects the influence of black music in her Appalachian experience, recalling the days when the Campbells and Spurlins "jammed" together. It is an early indication of her acceptance of racial and socioeconomic diversity within tradition, which existed in Appalachia as well as in other areas of the South (see works by Cohn, Rosenberg, Wolfe, and others on the confluence of musical traditions of different races). Ola's experience with radio performance was successful and seems to have whetted her appetite for the entertainment industry.

Later the Ridge Runners played on a larger station, WDEL, and at Radio Park, one of the major country music parks. By that time, "Western shows"—the Gene Autry type—were popular, so the Ridge Runners dressed in Western style, with Ola wearing a cowgirl hat (interview by Glassie). About this time, at the suggestion of someone in the band, Ola modified her name, changing it slightly from her given name, "Ola Wave," to "Ola Belle." Perhaps her advisor liked the musical and feminine connotations of "belle," with its association to the phrase "southern belle" (interview by Anderson-Green).

The Ridge Runners formed part of a transitional generation that linked the last generation of authentic folk musicians with the first generation of "country-western" professionals. No sharp line existed between the two, just a gradual shift in emphasis, as musicians spent more time performing, before larger audiences, and perhaps receiving more money. Of course, even back in the New River area, groups had played at local gatherings, auctions, sales, and other events, so they had had an identity as performers (Wolfe, "Tracking Lost String Bands," 20; see also Sandberg and Weisman, "Old-time String Bands").

Ola and the Ridge Runners did not modify their musical style or repertoire much. Ola says that they were not polished and had their own sounds (interview by Glassie). According to Pete Seeger, the basic sound of vocal country music "is the resonant rasp of a real country singer which has no vibrato to speak of and often strains the upper registers . . . there should be a matter-of-fact, unmelodramatic, understatement throughout" (352). There is simplicity, above all, and even some irregularity (353). The understatement eventually creates its own emotional impact, like Ola's singing of "Rosewood Casket." Here she projects the "high lonesome" sound without emotional elaboration, while the lyrics, with their simple, straightforward repetition of a request that sister bring the letters, finally convey the great sorrow of the dying person.

In addition to traditional vocal sound and repertoire, the Ridge Runners had the instrumentation typical for that era: two fiddles, two guitars, and a tenor (four-string) banjo, but no bass.

"Inky" Pierson played banjo, while Lester ("Slick") Miller and John Miller Jr., first cousins, were fiddlers who, also being from Lansing in Ashe County, North Carolina, knew the old-time repertoire (see app. D). Later, Deacon Brumfield, who was "not from down where we were," played runs on the dobro. Also "Shorty's sister," Flossie, joined Ola in twin yodeling. In addition, sometimes Hazel Flannery Waltman, of Tennessee, sang.

The Ridge Runner repertoire, as heard on five-inch reels in the collection of the American Folklife Center at the Library of Congress, included:

> Standard traditional favorites, such as "Soldier's Joy."
>
> Tunes such as "Whoa There Mule" and "Bile Them Cabbage Down," which evoked farming life while giving the fiddler fine opportunities to demonstrate his expertise.
>
> Prison songs like "Columbus Stockade Blues."
>
> Songs expressing nostalgia and homesickness, such as "Take Me Back to Carolina."
>
> Hymns, including "Life's Railway to Heaven," with its "climbing the mountain" setting; "When the Roll is Called Up Yonder"; "Will the Circle Be Unbroken"; and "Shake My Mother's Hand," named from the first line, "If you get to heaven before I do, shake my mother's hand for me."[2]

Many of the hymn texts emphasize the kinship bond, not only with mother but also with the whole community of kin. Johnny Miller says that his father, back in North Carolina, always used "Honey in the Rock," an old Baptist gospel tune, as his "wrap-up" number. All these gospel songs fit right into the rest of the performance, having a powerful driving rhythm and almost shouting style in singing, not at all repressed or meditative (interview by Glassie; interview by Anderson-Green; Archive of Folk

Song, Library of Congress, notes on LWO-5847, which includes three tapes given by Ola in 1969 and two tapes of the North Carolina Ridge Runners).

The North Carolina Ridge Runners had a booking agent and secured dates at carnivals, fairs, and sales. Ola says that, when they played the carnivals, someone always asked them into their homes to spend the night, thus continuing the old tradition of southern hospitality even under new circumstances (interview by Anderson-Green). They had great times together that were recalled fondly later.

The group made records at recording sessions in both Maryland and Washington, D.C. Johnny Miller recalls with pride recording at U.S. Recording Studio in Washington, D.C., once in 1947; he was playing dobro then and remembers doing "Orange Blossom Special" with Alex, Ola, and the others. They played varied country music songs, some "western swing," and "western bluegrass," but always fell back upon the basic old-time numbers (Johnny Miller interview by Anderson-Green). The group disbanded around 1948.

New River Boys

From an early age, Ola realized that music gave her life special meaning and continuity. After the war years, when the North Carolina Ridge Runners disbanded, she and her brother, Alex Campbell, home from military service, organized their own band in 1949 and called it "The New River Boys," a name preserving the tie to home. Sometimes it became "New River Boys and Girls."

Alex specialized in playing the guitar, now an instrument of importance which had come into prominence in southern music only around 1900 (Lornell 207). While in the military during World War II, Alex had continued his musical entertaining. Immediately after the war, he had the opportunity to play on stage and radio in Munich, Germany, with Grandpa Jones, of Grand Ole Opry fame. They had a radio show which was produced for the Americans overseas but also attracted the interest of Europeans. Thus Alex had an early experience in broadening the appeal of southern old-time music. Grandpa Jones later reminisced about how that band got started: "In our room in Munich, we always had a crowd of boys because I had carried a guitar with me, and we sang a lot . . . Alex Campbell played guitar; he told me that when he got home he and his sister, Ola Belle Reed, were going to start a band. Now they have a very popular band around Oxford, Pennsylvania; it's the staff band of Sunset Park there" (Louis M. Jones and Wolfe 90). The idea of the New River Boys had been brewing for a long time, then, and finally it came to fruition at the beginning of the 1950s.

In addition to Alex, on open-string guitar, and Ola Belle, on five-string banjo, the New River Boys featured Deacon Brumfield on dobro, Ted Lundy, also from New River, on five-string banjo, John Jackson on fiddle, and Earl Wallace on string bass. They played all the "music parks" along the Maryland-Pennsylvania border, such as Sunset Park and Radio Park. They also played at the Campbell's Corner Store in Oxford, Pennsylvania.

In 1949, Ola married "Bud" Reed, who joined her venture with Alex. Bud played guitar and "a mean mouth organ" and knew many Jimmy Rodgers tunes of the country-western tradition (interview by Anderson-Green). Ola and Bud's wedding in Maryland was performed by Ola's cousin, Rev. Joel Sturgill, with many friends and family in attendance (Marti 18).

The Campbell-Reed musical business ventures at first involved operating Rainbow Park in Lancaster, Pennsylvania, around 1950. However, Ola, Bud, and Alex soon established their own New River Ranch in Rising Sun, Maryland, which opened in 1951 with an act featuring Flatt and Scruggs, already famous on guitar and banjo. Johnny Miller, who was a young man then, proudly recalls that he helped to build New River Ranch. He says he was in the group that "cut all the trees and helped build the stage" (interview by Anderson-Green). The New River Boys did it all themselves. Johnny's brother, Sonny Miller, joined Ola and Alex on-stage, but then Sonny went into the Air Force, so Johnny, on fiddle, took his place in the act. Others who often played with them were Lloyd Adams, guitar; Earl Sexton, dobro; and Frances Mann, bass.

Ola Belle Campbell Reed with the "New River Boys" at American Legion Post, Rising Sun, Maryland, 1959. In back: Ola Belle's brother, Alex Campbell; James Brooks; Jim Cage; Harold Brooks; and Deacon Brumfield. Photograph from Ola Belle Campbell Reed.

Johnny Miller has a vivid memory of one of the first shows, when Hank Williams performed as the main act. Other famous stars came, too. According to Whisnant, "A virtual gallery of the top performers in country music followed during the next six years" ("Notes"). Between the "famous name" acts, Ola, Alex, and the New River Boys did their numbers, and sometimes other locals performed or contests were held.

The members of the New River Boys band varied over time, including Jim Cage and two brothers, James Brooks and Harold Brooks. As word about the music spread, crowds began gathering. Over the years, they expanded. As the "Biographical Notes" in *Everybody's Grandpa* state, Alex and Ola Belle "pioneered the promotion of folk, bluegrass, and country music in Pennsylvania and the Northeast" (Louis Jones and Wolfe 228).

Wider Recognition

Mike Seeger, later well known in the folk music revival, frequently attended in those days, making notes and taping many performances. On a particular day, for instance, he recorded that Ola and Alex performed "John Hardy" and "Good Old Mountain Dew" in one set, and in another "Pretty Polly," "Bringing in the Georgia Mail," and "Bile 'Em Cabbage Down" (Mike Seeger, Dub Tape no. 11, Side B, from MS 24A5-B32, late summer 1955 or early summer 1956, Archive of Folk Culture, Library of Congress).

Mike had the background to recognize the folk tradition represented in Ola's and Alex's repertoires. According to Rosenberg, Mike had learned about traditional music growing up in Washington, D.C., from his older brother, Pete Seeger, and also from his parents. The elder Seegers were transcribing music for a book being prepared by Alan Lomax and John Lomax (Rosenberg 147). Mike's extensive musical experience at New River Ranch expanded his knowledge of southern traditions and would have the effect of connecting Ola, Bud, and Alex to an audience beyond regional boundaries. It was Mike Seeger who, in 1953, brought Ralph Rinzler, then a college student learning to play mandolin, to New River Ranch to hear Ralph Stanley play. The two young men kept coming back to listen to others, such as Bill Monroe (Rooney 77).

Significant developments in country music were occurring in that era, and some milestones took place at New River Ranch. The special stylized form of music which came to be known as "bluegrass" emerged during this period. Rosenberg states that it was in 1956, "at New River Ranch in Rising Sun, Maryland," where Monroe first termed the style of music he played *bluegrass*. Here "he praised the operator of that country music park as 'a wonderful booster of the bluegrass type of music'" (98). Prior to that, Monroe had called his band the Blue Grass Boys, but now the term *bluegrass* would become a generic one, applied to the musical style. Although Rosenberg does not name the operator of New River Ranch, Monroe and others there knew it was Ola Belle Campbell Reed, Alex Campbell, and Bud Reed who were the "wonderful booster[s]" for their beloved traditional southern music, whether "hillbilly," "country-western," or "bluegrass."

Until now, Ola had not perceived herself primarily as a professional, nor had she intended to allow a career to dominate her life. Just prior to her marriage, she had received an offer to play in Roy Acuff's backup band but had turned it down because she did not want to be always on the road, away from home. She was planning marriage and thus preferred to pursue her own ventures with her brother Alex and, later, with her husband Bud (interview by Anderson-Green). Throughout her life, Ola remained loyal to her basic Appalachian values, balancing individualism with family ties while she developed a very successful and meaningful musical career in her own way.

In addition to performing at New River Ranch, Alex, Ola, and the New River Boys, from 1949 to 1960, broadcast live over WASA (Havre de Grace, Maryland) a radio show named for their store in Oxford, Pennsylvania, "Campbell's Corner." This began as a half-hour show and then expanded to three hours, under the guidance of Jason T. Pate, who also recorded and produced their first record, a 78-rpm disc on the Chesapeake label. Favorite songs included were "Orange Blossom Special" and "Poison Love" (*Reed Family Songbook*). Later, in 1960, the group moved over to station WCOJ (Coatsville, Pennsylvania) and continued to broadcast live from their store.

By the mid-sixties, the New River Boys were being heard nationally over WWVA in Wheeling, West Virginia, and had a major country music audience. Also during that time, after closing New River Ranch due to storm damage, they added a stage and live performances at Campbell's Corner. A journalist described the scene at their store: "The most extraordinary theater north of the Grand Ole Opry . . . antique movie seats faced a makeshift stage . . . the radio show . . . was beamed out to the world. But inside their audience would be light years removed.

Ola Belle Campbell Reed and brother Alex Campbell at WCOJ, Coatesville, Pennsylvania, date unknown. Photograph from Ola Belle Campbell Reed.

Once Ola Belle's music began everyone but the Amish, who sat with black hats or somber bonnets pointed straight ahead, commenced to whoop and holler like Judgment Day was just around the bend" (Thompson D9).

This enthusiastic audience, like the earlier ones at New River Ranch, contained a mixture of transplanted southerners, local farmers, the Amish, and even some college students. Throughout this period, famous names in country music—Flat and Scruggs, Hank Williams, Jim and Jesse, the Stanley Brothers, the Louvins, Bill Monroe, and many others—performed on their stage. In addition, the audience at Campbell's Corner included people who were leading the folk music revival of the sixties. Mike Seeger, now performing with the New Lost City Ramblers, became a major link between the Washington bluegrass scene and the New York

City folk revival. He often was present with Ralph Rinzler, who eventually managed the Newport Folk Festival and directed the Smithsonian's Festival of American Folklife (Whisnant, "Notes").

Repertoire

Traditional favorites in the Campbell-Reed repertoire performed at Campbell's Corner, as in the earlier days, included "The Soldier and the Lady," "Pretty Polly," "Flop Eared Mule," "John Hardy," "Billy in the Lowground," "Fly Around My Pretty Little Miss," "Rosewood Casket," and many, many other songs familiar to the southern mountain audience. Numbers Ola had done with the Ridge Runners continued to be featured. One that Ola liked to use for yodeling was "The Echoes from the Hills." Those included on a tape she made with her brother, Alex Campbell, John Miller, and Burl Kilby on April 19, 1966, are "Black Jack Davy," "Cumberland Gap," "Single Girl," and "Sally Goodin," among others. Extensive research (see app. D) has documented the British origins of many of these ballads and folksongs brought to Appalachia by the pioneer settlers, the ancestors of Ola Belle and others in her region. For example, there are Child Ballads such as "Barbara Allen" and "Black Jack Davy" (Roberts and Agey). Other songs, however, originated in experiences in that region. Such American ballads include "New River Train" and "John Hardy," the story of an outlaw who was hanged in Welch, West Virginia (Roberts and Agey). In addition to ballads, many songs in the repertoire could be classified as romantic, lyrical, or satirical folksongs. Intermixed with those were songs from the "cowboy-western," Victorian "parlor songs," and other genres. Whatever the classification, most belonged to, or eventually entered into, the tradition beloved and handed down in the folk community and later admired by the revivalists (see app. D and discography).

Ola's powerful style of clawhammer banjo playing evoked admiration from both the traditional country music audiences and the younger generation of the 1960s. The special appeal of that clawhammer style has been explained by a famous folk revivalist, Pete Seeger, who admits that he only "strums":

> I'm convinced now that my banjo book should not have started off with that strum. I should have started off with single strings, because the banjo is at its best playing single notes. Chords are all right, and when I get a crowd singing, I wham across all the strings and just strum a chord. But, if you want to really hear a banjo, you want to hear single strings. That's why I think Earl Scruggs and people who play bluegrass, and people who frail and play clawhammer banjo, are the best banjo pickers in the country. (Gallanter, "Pete Seeger" 31)

Many critics, including Glassie, Rinzler, and Hawes, laud Ola's own style of clawhammer banjo picking, which they feel establishes her as one of the most outstanding musicians of the old-time Appalachian tradition. Although many listeners were partial to the Scruggs finger-picking style in bluegrass, many others, especially in the folk revival audience, preferred to listen to the authentic old-time style, with its pounding impact.

For additional information on Ola's repertoire, see discography and app. D.

Bridge between Generations

Having gained recognition by urban folk revivalists such as Mike Seeger and Ralph Rinzler during the 1960s, Ola Belle and Alex began to receive attention from a wider audience, beyond people with a traditional southern mountain background or even their neighbors in the tri-state area. According to Whisnant, "The folk revival of the mid-sixties inaugurated a new phase in the music of the Reed family, as invitations began to arrive from college campuses and folklife festivals. The Reeds (joined by their second son David after about 1969) have become regular performers at the Smithsonian's Festival of American Folklife, the Maryland and North Carolina state folklife festivals, the National Folk Festival, Mariposa and elsewhere. In 1976 they performed at Kennedy Center" (Whisnant, "Notes").

During this time, the Reeds—Ola, Bud, and David—usually performed as a family, not with a band; they were not wearing country-western outfits but traditional clothing, with Ola sometimes in long dresses of a more old-timey look. As a "Country Music" column noted with a tone of annoyance in 1974, "About fifteen years ago, when 'folk music' began receiving national attention, Ola Belle threw away her Ridge Runner cowboy hat and immersed herself in recalling the past" (Hurst). Apparently some country music fans of the Nashville type wanted an emphasis on current pop culture rather than the country look of the folk culture.

However, as a musician of the bridge generation, Ola always could move authentically back and forth across the spectrum of mountain or country music. Despite some outward changes over the decades to accommodate audience preferences, the core of Ola's music, in repertoire as well as singing and picking style, retained its traditional base. Ola preserved the music that came from the New River Valley to the mid-Atlantic region in the 1920s and 1930s. Thus, in 1972, Ola Belle, Alex, Bud, and David were proud to represent Maryland at the Smithsonian Institution's Festival of American Folklife on the Mall in Washington and to record on Rounder Records. On another occasion, Ola and Alex were invited to a dinner at the Country Music Hall of Fame in Nashville, honoring those who had made outstanding contributions to country music. Understandably, Ola feels at home among musicians of both groups.

During this period of the 1960s and 1970s, Ola and her family toured widely throughout the United States, gaining a wide national audience for traditional music. Some of the tours focused on the South, where audiences could enjoy a "recognition of the familiar," as well as gain a deeper appreciation of their own folk culture. These southern tours were arranged by Ann Romaine, who was active in the civil rights movement in that region. Southern audiences especially were enthusiastic about Ola Belle and her banjo picking.

Audiences in other regions, too, turned out in great numbers to listen to Ola Belle and her family, as well as other performers of traditional southern music. One who helped to bring an
awareness of this music to northern colleges was Jeremy Foster, a
friend and former classmate of Mike Seeger. Foster, like Seeger
and Rinzler, had been attending and taping shows at Sunset Park
and New River Ranch since the mid-1950s (Rosenberg 155). With
his wife, Alice Gerrard, Foster "coalesced a local college bluegrass
scene," which included students from Antioch and Oberlin colleges
(ibid.). Later Ola Belle and the Reed family performed at these and
other elite northern colleges.

Finally, the Campbell-Reeds went even further, broadening their audience to include the whole nation. In one great 1976

Ola Belle Campbell Reed and brother Alex Campbell, date unknown.
Photograph from Ola Belle Campbell Reed.

tour, called "An Old-Time Music Festival," they swept the West Coast from Seattle to San Diego, receiving outstanding reviews, especially at colleges. Ola Belle particularly enjoyed the college appearances. As she says, "I love the young people. That's why I love the folk festivals. I'm hoping that the seeds will be planted in your minds and that you can go on" (Notes, *My Epitaph* 3). Over the years, Ola's philosophy of life, always significant in her music, increasingly was emphasized in her interactions with audiences, especially students. She felt she had an important message to convey: strive for the right while enduring the wrongs and difficulties of life, always using music as a way to endure and to achieve goals.

While Ola Belle attracted college audiences as a folk singer, she appealed especially to the college girls of this era, at the beginning of a new phase of the feminist movement. She was greatly in demand for appearances at women's colleges. As we have seen, Ola never allowed herself to be bound by gender roles in music, even though she was part of a traditional culture; she had a strong personality that exerted itself within the culture. As a journalist once stated, "Ola Belle Reed has a reputation for being forceful and strong-willed" (Soulsman). These qualities characterized her performance style also. *The Folk Music Sourcebook* describes her voice as "not always polished or centered, but full of feeling; she's the kind of singer who carefully chooses just what she'll sing, and then sings with guts" (Shepherd 74). College women of the 1960s could identify with Ola's personality as well as her talent, so they counted her among their role models as a leader.

In fact, members of Zeta Nu Upsilon Sorority of Goldey Beacom College in Wilmington, Delaware, were so impressed that they compiled *The Reed Family Songbook,* containing more than thirty songs performed by Ola's family during the 1960s. The introduction to the songbook expresses their admiration for Ola Belle herself: "In this day of women's lib, there probably is no greater representative of leadership, not for the liberation cause itself, but for Americanism, than Ola Belle Reed. Her story, views of life, both good and bad, can be seen in this collection of songs." As the college girls realized, Ola's powerful, forceful personality was a function of her musical heritage.

Stereotypes of Appalachia

Although Ola Belle appreciated being invited to colleges to speak to young people as well as to play and sing, she also felt some frustration with these new audiences beyond New River Ranch. Her frustration was occasioned not only by students, but also by journalists, writers, teachers, and others who help to shape public opinion. She was (and remains) concerned about the interpretation of her past life in Appalachia and of the entire culture that formed her: "Well, the first thing they always ask is, 'You're from a poor background, aren't you?' I said, 'Well, by today's standards you might have called us paupers, but,' I said, 'there wasn't enough money in this whole world to buy what we had. We didn't know that people needed . . . pushbuttons'" (interview by Anderson-Green). Thus Ola Belle both identifies the major cultural stereotype of Appalachia, "poverty," and leads the unsuspecting listener with the phrase "there wasn't enough money" into a clever counterpoint, "to buy what we had," an implied criticism of our materialistic and technological society, based on "pushbuttons." Ola's narrative technique conveys her message as effectively as her music does; in fact, that is why she composed quite a number of songs emphasizing the positive heritage of Appalachia and performed in the traditional manner.

The view of Appalachia widespread in American popular culture focuses on two stereotypes: the region's supposed poverty and "backwardness," and romantic notions about the "noble highlander" or "pure Anglo-Saxon." These two elements of the myth of the Upland South have been explored by many scholars (Banes 284). The romantic attitude underlies folk music revivals, whether of the 1930s or 1960s. Whisnant presents a thorough analysis of the complexities of this issue, citing Chapman's study of the "Gaelic revival" in Britain as analogous to efforts in the Appalachian region later. Whisnant points out that "the appetite of outsiders for the romantic, picturesque aspects of an alien culture distant enough to be exotic . . . but close enough to be noticed" is a universal aspect of cultural "revival" efforts serving the "psychic needs and social purposes" of those in the mainstream (Whisnant, *All That Is Native* 259). Popular culture thus shifts from the "quaint" and the "idyllic" to the "backwoods-degenerate" in interpreting Appalachia, depending upon a variety of factors that are shaping its outlook at any given time.

This is why Ola Belle, as a young woman, was perplexed by the audience response she received as early as the 1930s in the mid-Atlantic region: "People would come by the hundreds to hear you, but still looked down their noses at you. I couldn't figure out what it was all about" (Whisnant, "Notes"). In her personal life, then, Ola Belle had to deal with the sense of alienation experienced by so many Appalachian people in moving from a rural region into an urban environment (Banes 286; Schwarzweller, Brown, and Mangalam 73–207).[3] As she grappled with this continuing problem, Ola fortunately was guided by the basic principles she had absorbed in her girlhood in Ashe County—those embodied in the lives of her parents, grandparents, and their folk culture as a whole.

It was these basic traditional values that she wanted her old-time music to convey to the broad American audience. She did not hesitate to exert her influence, even in the early days. She tells about performing in a musical comedy, "The Dark of the Moon." It was "a comedy for elite society" that made fun of the country style, exemplified by the mourner's bench and similar customs. She would not perform until the script was changed (interview by Anderson-Green). From these early experiences, Ola developed a sense of mission about the value of her traditional music for the mainstream society, as well as a sensitivity to anything denigrating or stigmatizing in images of Appalachia.

These concerns were intensified by Ola's contacts with members of the counterculture generation of the 1960s folk revival. She shared many of their values, yet with them she often experienced again the typical misunderstandings. Still, music could help bridge a cultural gulf. As Whisnant says, "Her performances . . . have always been a cultural and political statement." He sees significance in the fact that "she stayed closer to the traditional repertoire than just about anybody else" (Whisnant, quoted in Soulsman J7). He points out that one can find in some current country music lyrics that are "racist, sexist, jingoistic, but Ola Belle has never participated in that. She's taken an enlightened and courageous stand for higher human values." Ola herself emphasized her intentions to present her traditional music not only for its aesthetic but also for its philosophical or moral value: "People are crying out for unity and they don't always know how to get it" (Notes, *My Epitaph* 3). Remembering the underlying sense of unity and connection that characterized her agrarian folk community of the Upper New River Valley, Ola Belle sustained a belief that this could be recreated in a contemporary, urban world, if people only had sufficient endurance and faith to make the effort.

Traditional Values

The firm values that Ola was raised to believe in were rooted not only in oral tradition but also in Scripture, which was the basis of the folk tradition. Hospitality was seen as a sacred duty, set forth in Genesis. The dignity and equality of all people were emphasized in her home, also with reference to the Bible. Usually these values were taught not in a didactic manner but in a way that was integrated with daily life. Ola relates that, during the summers, when she and the other children worked with their father in the fields at planting time, he taught them to follow the traditional method of planting, carefully scooping up a small mound of earth and inserting three seeds of corn in each one. She tells that he always said, "One hill [of seed] was as important as another—and that could apply to people" (interview by Anderson-Green).

The Upland South in general placed greater emphasis on equality—"each man as good as another"—than did the rest of the South (Beaver 144). A nineteenth-century writer in nearby Surry County, North Carolina, stated that the absence of cash made the inhabitants of Surry unusually honest and generally uninterested in social status symbols (Taliaferro 19).

In the middle of the twentieth century, Ralph Rinzler emphasized "the importance and persistence of the pastoral ideal, in relationship to the Christian ethic" in Appalachian culture (124). A self-sufficient agricultural lifestyle, integrated with abiding religious belief, was the bedrock of a solid yeoman culture in the New River area. Although not everyone in the region internalized these standards to the extent that Ola's family did, her people— Campbells, Osbornes, Hashes, Inghrams, and others—had been strong culture bearers, especially in the church, since the days of Bishop Asbury's visit.

The gathering place for worship during Ola's childhood summers was a little church called "the Shelter," nestled in a curve of the road by New River. Ola says, "It was a little, brown church, not much to look at, but up over the door it read 'Welcome to the Shelter'" (interview by Anderson-Green). The feeling there was warm, "everybody took part." Singing was a major part of the service, with such hymns as "The Ninety and Nine," "Sweet By and By," and "Wayfaring Pilgrim" emphasizing the importance of each individual. Strong feelings were expressed in church more often than in other places, perhaps, but the feelings were translated into action whenever anyone in the community needed help. "If somebody got sick, everybody'd be here," says Ola. Sometimes her father would stop by a neighbor's place and just "set a bag of meal inside the door and go on." Such actions were reciprocated as the need arose and, even years later in the urban world during the Great Depression, remembered. Ola's sense of the deep importance of fellowship and community, then, came out of her Appalachian culture, in which such "caring and sharing" could and did exist even in areas where homes were widely dispersed and settlements might appear to have no community identity (see Blethen and Wood).

Once, many years later, Ola had returned from her new life in Maryland to visit "down home" and was enjoying a swapping session with her uncle, John Lee Osborne. They were sharing with each other things they had written; he wrote tales, and she wrote songs. She sang for him one she recently had written about "the Shelter." He did not say anything about it but proposed a ride to see relatives. They headed toward the river; when they came around the curve, she saw that "the Shelter" was gone: "When we came around that curve, 'the Shelter' was gone, the trees was gone, there was a half-acre of big brick building . . . shock, I'm telling you—my uncle, he knew this had happened, but he wouldn't tell me when I was singing that song, see; he said it was just like a, uh, vision of some kind" (interview by Anderson-Green). Despite the loss, Ola's music effectively had transcended the current harsh reality with a "vision" of the past signifying fellowship and communion, and offering solace and hope for the future.

The shock of losing "the Shelter" becomes a metaphor for the experience of thousands of mountain people dislocated by the Great Depression and World War II, and pouring into great industrial cities like Baltimore and Chicago. The shock was not only geographical but also cultural, with the transition from a close-knit folk society to a heterogeneous megalopolis. As Ola says, "When I come out of them mountains, so help me God, I didn't know people didn't like each other" (interview by Anderson-Green). Then she began to learn about class and regional animosities. Throughout her interviews, she reiterates the theme of tolerance and respect for all social groups. "It's sad in our country," she says as she discusses the treatment of minority groups, "people are too quick to judge, just because people are different."

Ola emphasizes being nonjudgmental as a basic Christian virtue. When explaining this, she reveals a "skeleton in the closet" of her family history: in the wake of the Great Depression, her father drank too much and went away for days at a time. Her attitude is to try to understand the stress he was under; she feels that no one can fully perceive another person's situation and that to offer aid rather than criticism is the Christian way (interview by Anderson-Green).

Throughout her life, Ola Belle has had particular empathy for the downtrodden. Although she never suffered extreme poverty, she shared the difficult transition to a very different life on the East Coast, she saw people in great need, and through her music she associated with people from all walks of life, beliefs, ethnic groups, and races. Thus her attitudes sometimes have caused her to be perceived as a radical, although many northern liberals might not understand the sources of her views. Whisnant notes this: "Unlike most radicals of northern or urban background, her own radicalism has its source in a grassroots protest tradition which must be understood in a fundamentalist religious context" (Whisnant, "Notes").

Following the Appalachian traditions taught in her family, Ola often opened her home to friends, traveling musicians, and others needing a place to stay, just as her grandfather's will emphasized. A critic notes, "The house is constantly busy with kin, friends and neighbors. Come nightfall, especially during the summer months, Ola Belle and Bud often don't know how many sleeping bags will be scattered throughout the house" (Notes to record album *Ola Belle Reed,* Rounder Records 0021, 1972). The key values she learned in her home place—compassion, tolerance, belief in democracy and equality—are rooted in her religion and expressed in her music. She has passed these values on in her own immediate family, not only in making music with husband Bud and son David, but also through her other son, Ralph, a Pentecostal minister.

Standing way above the cemetery of her ancestors at Haw Orchard in Grayson County, Virginia, surveying the beautiful Blue Ridge scene, Ola composed a song, "High on the Mountain," with this refrain:

> High on the mountain, wind blowing free
> Thinking about the days that used to be;
> High on the mountain, standing all alone
> Wondering where the years of my life have flown.

Ola Belle's life has been spent maintaining the heritage of Appalachian music and community, improving understanding among cultural groups, and appreciating the kinship among all people. Ola knows that, to work toward these goals, people must have the quality of endurance. With all her experiences in mind and perhaps also remembering the Bible verse, "Blessed are they who endure," she wrote a well-known song, "I've Endured." It contains the following verses:

> Born in the mountains
> Fifty years ago
> Trod the hills and valleys
> Through the rain and snow
> Seen the lightning flashing
> Heard the thunder roll
> I've endured, I've endured
> How long must a man endure?

3

Famous in Fiddle Making and Playing: Albert Hash of Whitetop Mountain

On Cabin Creek in the rugged Whitetop Mountain section of Grayson County, Virginia, Albert Hash was born in the early twentieth century, when old-time music was so alive that practically every household had a musician in residence (E. Spencer, liner notes for *Whitetop*). This western section of the county was so cut off from the rest of the area by its terrain that musicians there developed their own subregional distinctions in style of playing. The rugged Whitetop Mountain area stretches across the Grayson-Ashe County line (which also marks the boundary between Virginia and North Carolina), forming a continuous terrain that holds people together culturally, despite political boundaries. "People in the Whitetop section went down to the Jefferson area of North Carolina rather than east toward Galax or even the county seat of Independence" (liner notes for *Old Originals,* vol. 1, Rounder Recrods, 0058). This pattern seems to have existed from the earliest settlement, according to people interviewed over the years. Even today, access in and out of the Rugby–Whitetop–Mount Rogers section is quite restricted in winter; because of the difficulty of transportation during that season, Mount Rogers High School is allowed to remain the smallest high school in the commonwealth and not be consolidated. In this tightly knit society, the music scene flourished and traditional styles were handed on.

The folk scholars who produced two albums of *Old Originals* were very interested in cultural regions and in subregional variations in the music of the western Virginia-Carolina section of the Blue Ridge Mountains. They pointed out that:

> Generally, the entire area . . . may be viewed as a stylistic whole . . . and exhibits musical techniques indicative of a larger Southern instrumental style. Yet, looking more closely, within this larger framework exist smaller subregions and the presence of recognizable local repertories . . . By talking with the oldest musicians and by studying their repertory and at least some of their stylistic traits, we were able to determine each area's "cognitive map"; we were able to learn from whom these young men and women learned their music and where they went to "hang around" and socialize when they were first learning. (*Old Originals,* vol. 1)

The terrain of the western section of Grayson County, Virginia, so cut it off from other areas that musicians there developed their own subregional playing styles. Noting differences between the eastern and western subregions, Albert Hash, a Whitetop native, told Frank Weston that the music of Galax is closer to that of Mount Airy, North Carolina, than to that of his area, although he acknowledged that, in Galax, one sometimes could find someone "who still can sing our music" (Weston 17).

Therefore the Whitetop Mountain section of Grayson County, Virginia, was home to a tightly knit society composed of extended families (including Blevinses, Campbells, Dolingers,

Hashes, Osbornes, and Sturgills). Albert grew up as an integral part of this musical and cultural scene and learned his music from many relatives and neighbors.

Early Life

During his early years, Albert enjoyed many of the advantages of the traditional culture based on a rural way of life. However, his father, Abram Hash, was not a farmer. An educated man who once had been a teacher, Abram worked for Virginia Supply Company, supplying mainly the railroads, and was away from the home much of the time. Apparently he and Albert were never close. In the Weston interview, Albert was asked, "What did you and your parents do to get by?" Albert responded only by referring to himself. The interviewer then specifically asked, "What did your father do?" Albert explained some of his father's background and main occupation, stating, "He stayed in a railroad car about all the time, lived in that railroad car. He was keeping the books for them, that was his job. I wouldn't get to see him only once in a good while" (Weston 15). This situation must have created some emotional distance between Albert and his father and eventually between his parents. However, Albert cared for both his parents and, in the Weston interview, clearly presented himself as "the son of Abraham Lincoln Hash and Della May [Long] Hash" (11). Albert later referred to a stepfather, so apparently his parents finally parted.

Though he and his father may not have been close, Albert was proud of his Hash name. Albert also was proud of the fact that his father's father, Benjamin Hash, was a fiddler in a medicine show in Whitetop, so the musical talent and heritage ran deep (Albert Hash to Anderson-Green, 1970s). When questioned by Weston in 1980, Albert stated that his father, Abram, had been born in Elk Garden, between Whitetop and Mount Rogers, adding, "That's where my people settled, up there, in 17-something" (Weston 14). The Hashes did come to New River in the 1760s, settling first on the river at Bridle Creek (Fields 33) and probably pushing farther back in the mountains towards Whitetop some-what later. Albert was born not far from his father's birthplace, on Cabin Creek, near the foot of Mount Rogers, the highest mountain in Virginia. When Weston asked about the family's origin, Albert stated that they were from Germany, spelling the name "Hasche." He added that they bonded themselves to the English to "work their fare out," arriving in New Jersey (Weston 15).

The story of the "indentured servant" ancestor obviously had been "passed on" through the generations and most likely was accurate in the main point; however, genealogists have debated whether the Hash family was English or German. Records verify that the Hashes arrived in the Delaware River Valley area of Penn-sylvania and New Jersey early in the eighteenth century. Although some early family historians leaned toward the German theory, because the name "Hash" seemed "different," others claimed that it was English. Later genealogists generally have agreed that it was of English origin, a variant of the name "Hatch," arguing that, in the eighteenth century, *c* and *s* were used interchangeably (see issues of *Hash Family Historian Newsletter*). Many families of English ori-gin, especially groups of English Quakers, traveled southward from Philadelphia down the Great Wagon Road into the Upper New River area of Virginia-Carolina during the middle part of the eigh-teenth century (Anderson-Green, "New River," 413–31). Another factor supporting the theory of English origins is that the first three generations of Hashes in Albert's line in New River married into families of British (English or Scots-Irish) background: Osbornes, Andersons, and Stampers.

A poignant final chapter in the father-son relationship was written some years later. One day, Albert was walking through the hills, carrying the second fiddle he ever made, taking it to show to his elderly father. A neighbor, seeing him walking along, came out to tell him that his father was dying. By the time he got there, it was too late to have that last meeting, for his father had passed away (Albert Hash interview by Anderson-Green, ca. 1976). Albert deeply regretted missing this last chance to see his father and show him the fiddle.

Even though instrumental music seized Albert's attention at a young age, especially since the men dominated banjo and fiddle-playing, the singing traditions in his home and church were also a significant influence on him. Singing, of course, was particularly the role of the women, and as Albert's daughter Audrey points out, they were often singing while working, whether sewing, cooking, or cleaning (interview with Anderson-Green). She says Albert's mother knew "all the old ballads and songs" and frequently sang her favorites, "Handsome Molly" and "Darling Cory." The family also sang a lot at their Lutheran church, where Albert's favorite hymn was "The Great Physician" (Audrey Hash Hamm interview by Anderson-Green, Aug. 30, 1994) It is interesting to note that, although Methodists and Baptists predominate in the southern Blue Ridge Mountains, other groups, such as the Lutherans, do exist. Albert's sister, Audrey, says that there were several Lutheran churches around Cabin Creek and Whitetop, and that a Lutheran deaconess helped to deliver and take care of babies. This difference in religious denominations found in the communities around Albert is another characteristic that set the western section of Grayson County apart as an area "unto itself," isolated from the east.

When talking to Weston, Albert brought up, though with some discomfort, the existence of neighboring Hashes who were black: "There's many of the Hashes that are black in Grayson County over around Galax and Woodlawn, in that vicinity" (Weston 14). Albert's curiosity was aroused sufficiently for him to ask a white neighbor, A. G. Hash, about "Piney Rose, down yonder. She was one of the descendants of the slaves, you know, she's Piney Rose Hash. When they freed the slaves they took the name of their master." Albert related A. G.'s story, which was that Piney Rose was a descendant of a slave given to his great-grandmother by her father when she married. Then Albert added, "A pitiful situation, wasn't it?" Albert always was known as a caring and sensitive man.

In general, Albert said little about family history or his early years. He did remark about the Great Depression, "Well, [during the thirties] you did anything you could to pick up an extra dollar.

You could raise a little stuff on the farm but not enough to say anything" (Weston 13). The Whitetop terrain would not support large-scale farming but was more suitable for grazing and timber.

Albert did some carpentry work in his youth and, as he turned twenty, was working in a camp of the Civilian Conservation Corps (CCC), at Baywood near Whitetop. During this time, people noticed Albert playing fiddle, and they wanted to hear more, so they made it part of his job. Albert says, "I got to fiddle a whole lot in there. They put me on the KP and the cooks liked the music. They would stick me over between the big ranges somewhere with the fiddle, and the rest of the boys, they washed the dishes while I played fiddle" (Weston 13). Albert was very content with that arrangement, but he did not expect to be able to continue fiddling as an occupation.

During World War II, Albert became a master machinist while working for the United States Navy in a torpedo factory in Alexandria, Virginia. In this trade he spent thirty years, continuing it in the postwar period (Blanton 90). Early in this period, he married Ethel Spencer, sister of Thornton Spencer. They lived in Arlington, Virginia, throughout the war years, and their first child was born there (Emily and Thornton Spencer letter to Anderson-Green, early 1990s).

Although Albert played in a few fiddlers conventions around Alexandria, he did not play as much as he had "back home" in the mountains. After the war years, Albert and his family moved back to Grayson County, Virginia, to live out their lives in the Appalachian culture. For them, no other choice was as desirable or meaningful (interview by Anderson-Green).

Back in Grayson County, Albert began working as a machinist at Sprague Electric Company in Lansing, North Carolina, near Whitetop, and "gradually began to play less and less . . . and didn't have a fiddle strung up" (Thornton Spencer and Emily Spencer). After fifteen years at Sprague, Albert went to work for Brunswick Powder Works at Sugar Grove, Virginia, for five or more years. When Weston interviewed Albert years later, he noted a tone of regret in Albert's voice when he spoke of the weapons they manufactured.

Weston said he felt that Albert was "a gentle man" who "did not enjoy" that work (Weston 13).

Even so, Albert, always a perfectionist, gave his best effort to his job. In a letter nominating Hash for the Heritage Fellowship of the National Endowment for the Arts (NEA) in 1982, Alice Gerrard stated, "He worked as a machinist[,] during which time he invented several machines for which he was never given credit or financial reward by the companies he worked for and who used them." She does not specify which companies, but this probably occurred in more than one place. In accord with his rural values which placed little emphasis on materialism, Albert never complained, simply doing the work required to support his family. During this period, he was giving much of his time, energy, and concentration to his job, not his music.

Musical Context

Around Whitetop, individual musicians predominated, while dance bands were found less frequently than in other sections. As one commentator put it, "It has been only in the recent past that ensemble music has become a strong part of the traditional music here, largely due to outside influences brought about by radio, records, and paved roads" (*Old Originals,* vol. 2). Prior to that stage, local musical interest focused either on the vocal tradition, which often was unaccompanied and led by women, or on the individual instrumentalist, playing dulcimer, banjo, or fiddle. Of course, sometimes the musician combined singing and playing, particularly dulcimer or banjo. The dulcimer used to be played widely in the Whitetop region (Smith, *Catalogue*). Many in the area can remember their grandmothers playing it and sometimes singing along (Sturgill family interview by Anderson-Green). Although not as many play dulcimer today, it is still in the tradition and usually is featured in competitions at fiddlers conventions.

The most popular instrument—that is, the one played by more people than any other—probably was the banjo. Whitetop had a distinctive, strongly rhythmic style of banjo playing. According to an observer, "It is played in what might be termed a 'loose' style; the rhythm is decidedly different from that found to the east, and it is less well-suited to accompany dance fiddling," although the same tunes as those associated with fiddles are played (*Old Originals,* vol. 2). In solo playing, many irregularities and peculiarities are allowable (ibid.), just as individualistic tendencies may be tolerated or even encouraged in mountain personalities. At any rate, banjo playing was a mainstay of life in Whitetop. Flurry Dowe, a member of Albert Hash's band, says, "A lot of people about sixty around here, a lot of them can play the banjo a little bit, you'd be surprised how many people that age can" (Trivette).

The strongly rhythmic sound continued to dominate in Whitetop. Even though Albert became a fiddler, he was influenced by the banjo players. Albert could remember, at a very early age, hearing his Uncle Emmitt Long (his mother's brother) play claw-hammer banjo. Later, when Albert was playing fiddle, one banjo player he "really enjoyed playing with was Lee Weaver . . . considered the king of the banjo pickers in his day" (Emily Spencer, liner notes for *Whitetop*). Another old-time banjo player whom Albert remembered with great respect was Jont Blevins, who learned from Albert's Uncle Emmitt. Later Jont Blevins taught Flurry Dowe (Trivette 94). About Flurry, Albert said, "He's really got the old-time technique on clawhammer banjo. There's so much of it that's not clawhammer, not played exactly right, not like our end of the music is, from Independence west. He's got the mountain claw-hammer banjo" (Weston 17). There is no doubt that Albert Hash preferred the Whitetop style, "played exactly right" (ibid.).

Albert's preferred instrument, however, was not the banjo but the fiddle. Although he heard and enjoyed banjo music from infancy, the music that truly galvanized him was fiddling. In fact, he was first fascinated by the instrument itself, before he ever heard the sound it made. As he told it, there was no fiddle in his home, only banjos. His father did not play an instrument because he had lost a hand "in action"; and his mother, who did a lot of singing, probably played banjo only when her brother was around. Few in the area owned a fiddle, but one who did was Albert's great-uncle,

George Finley. From time to time, Albert had seen the fiddle at Uncle George's house, hanging on a wall near the ceiling, away from children, because it was a great treasure. This piqued his interest and respect.

Finally the time came when he had a chance to hear it played, during a great thunderstorm that drove the family out of a cornfield they rented from his uncle and were working in that day. As they ran out of the field and onto Uncle George's porch, Albert's uncle "went in the house and brought that fiddle out, and he started playing that thing" (Weston 12). Although Albert was only ten years old, this moment was overwhelming and life-changing for him: "He decided right then and there that he was going to fiddle and had to have a fiddle somehow" (Thornton Spencer and Emily Spencer). The way Albert tells it in the interview, he was so overcome he felt like running into the woods screaming; he thought that it would "run me crazy" (Weston 12). This great moment of first awareness of a passion for music making, a desire that is very specific and intense, has been described in similar terms by other old-time musicians in the area. Fid Sturgill is one who described the inception of a great obsession with fiddling (see chap. 4 below).

From that moment on, Albert was wrestling with the problem of how to get a fiddle. Even at the age of ten, Albert realized that his family could not afford to buy a fiddle and that "it's taking me too long to get to be a man 'til I can work out one" (Weston 12). All day and through the evening, he was thinking about how to make one. Finally inspiration came to him that night, in a dream in which he saw himself actually crafting a fiddle (Cotton 88; Weston 13; Blanton 87). The next day, he was out before breakfast rounding up materials and tools. The use of tools was forbidden to the small children, Albert said, "So I got the tools and hid out behind the granary and I used them . . . sawed and hacked away" (Weston 13). In the Weston interview, Albert goes into great detail about how he made his childish fiddle, including finding wires and tacks, which he used because he did not have any glue. The bow took a lot of work, and he had to pull out part of a horse's tail for "hair to make a fiddle bow." He also walked six miles to earn a quarter to buy a set of fiddle strings.

Finally Albert thought he was ready, "so when I pulled my bow over it, I was so disgusted and disappointed, not a sound it wouldn't make." But just at that critical moment, along came an adult who realized the problem, got some rosin from his home, used it, and tuned Albert's fiddle (Weston 13; Blanton 87–88). While watching this, Albert was ignited with fire from within, awaiting his turn; when the instrument was handed to him, he ran into the kitchen behind the large cookstove and stayed there playing for a long time, until he had mastered several tunes. "I was determined then, it was no way you was going to stop me from learning to fiddle. I just slept with that fiddle. It was everything I had" (Weston 13).

Making a Life in Music

The dream turned into reality for Albert, based on his talents and his perseverance, his "passion for perfection" (Cotton 88). He would be recognized as one of the finest craftsmen in America. Joseph T. Wilson of the National Council for the Traditional Arts, in nominating Albert Hash for the NEA's 1981 National Heritage Fellowship, wrote of his amazing combination of talents: an ability "to be highly precise in metal or wood," along with "well-developed artistic skills" (Wilson to NEA, Nov. 4, 1981).

The development of artistic skills was an ongoing process throughout Albert's life. His first teachers in fiddling were his great-uncle, George Finley, and another old-timer, Corbitt Stamper. Both were well known in the Whitetop area, where fiddlers were few and banjo pickers many. Luckily, both men lived near enough to Albert to teach him. Although it was Uncle George who first ignited Albert's desire to fiddle, Corbitt Stamper also influenced him greatly early in his life.

In the second album of *Old Originals*, Corbitt, then sixty-three years old, was recorded playing a rendition of "Cumberland Gap" on the fiddle, with Thornton Spencer on guitar. The notes state that this tune "has long been known in this [Whitetop] area and remains one of the favorites." Notes also affirm that, when, as a young man, Corbitt "went to town," *town* meant Jefferson or Lansing, North Carolina, or maybe Konnarock or Damascus, Virginia, to the west, "but seldom did it mean any town to the east."

In this same area, Albert grew up and circulated, observing and learning repertoire and techniques of playing banjo and fiddle. Thus Albert's musical style developed through playing with not only Corbitt Stamper but also others in that section. Some fine fiddlers around Whitetop whom Albert heard while young were Black Charlie Miller, John Stringer, and Howard Wyatt (Thornton Spencer and Emily Spencer).

In the Weston interview, Albert speaks of Ola Belle Campbell Reed, who grew up in Lansing and Grassy Creek: "I used to play [music] with Ola Belle and with some of her cousins that lived up on the creek a little ways—Cassie and Ethel Greer. We had us a band together one time, played for a long time" (Weston 17). Likewise, his brother-in-law, Thornton Spencer, says, "You've heard of Ola Belle Reed? She was partially raised right here over the hill. She is a cousin of ours" (ibid.). Indeed, Albert Hash and Ola Belle Campbell were related through the Hash line, confirming that both kinship and geography constituted important influences on musical style.

During the years of his youth, before World War II, Albert also taught himself to play fiddle by listening to records, especially those of a noted local fiddler named G. B. Grayson and also the Skillet-Lickers of Georgia. His parents had a wind-up phonograph, and they obtained records from mail-order houses. Albert says, "You could listen to those records and learn every note, every bow lick, and everything" (Weston 13). For Albert, this musician, Grayson, was his "idol."

When Albert was about twelve, he made his first appearance playing outside the home, at a school program ending the term. Between acts of the play that was being presented, Albert and a friend went out on-stage to play music (fiddle and guitar), and he got his first taste of pleasing an audience. A little later, Albert was often making music in a group with one or two of his brothers—usually Ernest—playing guitar; Gaither Farmer on banjo; and Huck Sturgill doing guitar and vocals (Thornton Spencer and Emily Spencer).

Although Albert intensely enjoyed playing fiddle with his pals and gaining a little experience on the schoolhouse stage, he later admitted that perhaps he and others took his music for granted or even considered it of little importance. He knew that some people thought the fiddle was "the devil's box," so he carried his around in a flour sack (Audrey Hash Hamm interview by Anderson-Green; Whisnant, *All That Is Native and Fine,* 232). However, when the White Top Folk Festival began to draw crowds in the 1930s and Eleanor Roosevelt attended in 1933, local people began to pay more attention to traditional music. According to David Whisnant, the main organizers of the festival theorized that it would encourage local musicians to "return to the superior traditional culture of their forebears." Whisnant concludes his analysis:

> In some few cases, it appears to have had approximately that effect. Fiddler Albert Hash, for example, was an insecure teenage boy in the early thirties. Raised in the isolated backcountry southeast of White Top, he recalls concealing his fiddle in a flour sack because fiddlers were "looked down on." But Hash played at White Top, and nearly fifty years later still recalled with pleasure how "a Colonel Kettlewell from England" took a picture of his homemade fiddle, how fine other players were, and how for the first time he "realized that it was something that was just more serious than I had heard that music was." For the first time, Hash recalled, "I felt justified in what I was doing." (*All That Is Native and Fine,* 232)

Albert's daughter Audrey concurs, to this day recalling that the "Whitetop [festival] helped him change on that" (interview by Anderson-Green).

Accordingly, Albert applied himself to music more intensely. He kept on listening to those records of Grayson and a musician who played with him, Henry Whitter. Those two, Albert fondly says, "was my main musicians." But, Albert continues, "Grayson got killed. After that his buddy Henry Whitter was alone, and I went to see Henry, who lived over at Crumpler, North Carolina . . . and he liked the way I played" (Weston 13). Whitter asked Albert Hash to join him in musical appearances, to go on the road in his Model A Ford for show dates. Back then the roads were just "ruts," and they could not go far—just to Marion, Chilhowie, or Damascus, all in Virginia. "But we'd go and play schools and theaters and what have you," Albert says, "and made a little money at it" (Weston 13; also see Blanton 88–89). They did this until Whitter's health made it impossible for him to travel. After that, Albert had to find some other work to do, but he kept on playing music with his brother and friends.

Although he was away during the World War II era, Albert returned to Whitetop shortly thereafter. Fortunately, he was able to find some machinist jobs in his home area. In time, he began working in his own shop at his home, not only on instruments but also on furniture, wood and steel works, clocks, engines, and various other items. Above all, though, he became famous for his fiddles.

During the late 1940s and early 1950s, Albert was able to resume playing traditional music more actively than he had in Alexandria, because he was now living in the Whitetop area again, where so many old-time musicians were near at hand. Gradually he had a major impact on the traditional music of the Whitetop Mountain area and the Upper New River Valley.

Albert joined in with a Blevins family group to form the original Whitetop Mountain Boys. Frank Blevins and Henry Blevins played guitar; their father, Print Blevins, clawhammer banjo; Dent Blevins, mandolin; and Albert, fiddle. Sometimes Archie Finley also played guitar and sang with them (Thornton Spencer and Emily Spencer 1). During this period, the Whitetop Mountain Boys were a popular band, playing at many gatherings and fiddlers conventions in the area. Their repertoire was "half and half bluegrass and traditional" (Weston 13). However, that band broke up when Print's family moved to northern Virginia to experience urban

American life. After the Blevins family moved away, Albert played regularly with E. C. Ball of nearby Rugby, Virginia, and also with his own brother-in-law, Thornton Spencer, on guitar. Thornton even learned some fiddling from Albert.

As the years passed, machinist work demanded more of Albert's time, while traditional music was losing its audience, even in the local area, as the contemporary Nashville sound grew popular and then the rock and roll era hit. According to Thornton Spencer and Emily Spencer, Albert Hash, in response to this, "chose not to play rather than play what he didn't feel inside" (Spencers interview by Anderson-Green, Aug. 19, 1994; also discussed in Blanton 89). He continued to play occasionally at home, and he kept all the music in his mind and heart, waiting for an audience to seek it out again.

The folk music revival began in the mid-1960s, with interest surging among young people who were turning away from urban mass culture toward folk arts, in which individuals carried on old traditions. Often members of the younger generation would find mentors who could steer them in the right direction; at the same time, this interest would restore the elders' pride in their traditional heritage.

This is what happened when Wayne Henderson sought out Albert Hash in 1964 (Sacks to NEA, Dec. 9, 1982, p. 2). Wayne had been trying to make a guitar, starting with the bottom of a dresser drawer, but he knew very little of how to proceed. His Dad suggested that he visit Albert Hash, the famous instrument maker over in Lansing. Albert recognized Wayne's talent, praised his first efforts, and gave him some encouraging pointers in the craft. The relationship between the two became special, as "Wayne Henderson helped Albert at the same time by restoring his interest in playing music" (Emily Spencer and Thornton Spencer to NEA, May 20, 1982). Not only did Wayne come around frequently, becoming an apprentice to Albert, but also he started a band with his brother and Boyd Spencer, the "Virginia-Carolina Boys," and talked Albert into playing fiddle with them. For eight years, they played together on their own show every Saturday morning on radio station WKSK

in West Jefferson, North Carolina. The core of the band included
Albert on fiddle; Wayne on guitar; Wayne's brother, Max Henderson,
on mandolin; Boyd Stewart on guitar and vocals; and Trudy Bell,
also on guitar and vocals. Throughout these years, in addition to
the WKSK radio show, they had good times playing at community
functions and fiddlers conventions. Albert was thoroughly involved
in music again.

The second album of *Old Originals* features Albert Hash playing "Cripple Creek," described as "one of the most well-known old-
time tunes anywhere" and certainly a local favorite; and "Nancy
Blevins," a tune created by an older cousin of his grandfather. Since
Albert is related to the Blevins family, one wonders if this "Nancy"
tune was named for a relative. Albert learned the tune from his
stepfather's brother, Jim Reedy, who was from the area around
Crumpler, North Carolina, located just below the state line and thus
part of the Whitetop section.

At the time of the recording, Albert was in his late fifties.
The group he was playing with consisted of Paul Spencer on banjo
and Jones Baldwin on guitar. Their band was part of a larger jam
session held regularly at Spencer's Trading Post in the Whitetop
section. The group there included Thornton Spencer, Flurry Dowe,
and Dean Sturgill, a Spencer cousin. Thornton's family owned the
store, but he acknowledged that it was not a money maker and
that, for the family, its main purpose was hosting the jam session.
Albert Hash said, "Oh yeah, that store was the best thing that ever
happened in this country" (Weston 17). Years later, Albert's widow,
Ethel Spencer Hash, also recalled that one of the main reasons her
brother ran the Trading Post at Cabin Creek was to have a place for
the band to meet. Often as many as thirty played together there
(interview by Anderson-Green, Aug. 30, 1994). The old building
was owned by a cousin, but when it started to deteriorate, the
store had to be closed. However, for quite a few years it served its
purpose for the musicians.

After the "Virginia-Carolina Boys" broke up, Albert later
reconstituted the "Whitetop Mountain Band," with his brother-in-law,
Thornton Spencer; Thornton's wife, Emily; Tom Barr; Flurry Dowe;

and Becky Haga. This group got together during the mid-1970s, when Albert was inclined to move away from bluegrass back to a greater emphasis on the earlier traditional music he had heard during his childhood. Finding traditional old-time players was a problem, but in this Albert was fortunate. Flurry Dowe was a "new young picker" who had come into the area from Alabama and studied clawhammer banjo under Jont Blevins (who as a boy had learned from Albert's uncle). Flurry joined with Albert and the Spencers, both of whom play guitar. Albert had taught Thornton fiddling. Tom Barr, of Galax, Virginia, played bass in the band and also apprenticed to Albert to learn fiddle making. Becky Haga, also from the area, was vocalist and played rhythm guitar. They went on to win many awards at places like the Galax Fiddlers Convention.

Taking part in the ongoing fiddlers conventions was one way Albert shared his talent, craftsmanship, and feeling for music. He attended many fiddlers conventions in Galax and other areas. As Joseph T. Wilson points out, he must have known the playing style associated with the Galax area [called "Round Peak," which includes Mount Airy]. Wilson, however, says that Albert "holds closely to the local stuff and does not musically venture down the east slope of the mountains" (Wilson to NEA, 1981). He thus perpetuated in the Whitetop area a very old-time style of fiddling which was highly rhythmic, with the drones receiving more emphasis than they got farther east ("Albert Hash"; Jabbour 28–32; chap. 4 of this book).

As the Whitetop Mountain Band received wider attention, its members were invited to the Smithsonian's National Folklife Festival, were recorded by the American Folklife Center at the Library of Congress, and eventually performed for the National Folk Festival at Wolf Trap, which was one of Albert's biggest thrills (Cotton 91).

By this stage in life, Albert Hash finally could give most of his attention and effort to his first passions, playing and crafting mountain musical instruments. Often his house was filled with people; students and apprentices began to seek him out as he shared his expertise (Blanton 90). He and his wife offered their hospitality to all, with but one exception. As Cotton puts it, "Ethel smiles and

Fiddler's convention dedicated to Albert Hash after his death. Convention pamphlet, 13th Annual Ashe County Old Time Fiddler's and Bluegrass Convention, Jefferson, North Carolina, August 6, 1983.

comments that all are welcome and only one rule prevails—no one spends the night" (88). Apparently many could find friends to stay with while they flocked to Albert's shop by day, filling it with enthusiasm, camaraderie, and creativity.

Maker of Fine Fiddles

Although Albert never advertised, his reputation as a skilled craftsman of instruments spread far and wide. Wilson also states that "his gentility and genius had made him famous along the mountain spine from Roanoke to Knoxville" (Wilson to NEA, 1981). Many of the violins he made were sold to classical musicians, who wanted the same qualities as those who played old-time Appalachian music.

Cotton described Albert's place as a "rat's nest of a shop," but also as "a landmark for fiddle lovers from all over the world" (88). Albert worked without any assistant on each instrument he made, but he was seldom alone in the shop, which was in the basement of his home. His daughter, Audrey worked on dulcimers, and one or more apprentices often worked on their own instruments under Albert's guidance, often using his tools.

Although Albert was following a tradition, using techniques that had been handed down by older craftsmen, he had developed some variations within that tradition which made his instruments distinctive (Cotton 89; Blanton 91). First, he often made a fiddle longer than the "Long Stradivarius pattern" and with a slightly larger sound box, which he believed produced a more mellow tone, "with a better ring" (Cotton 89). Further, the "secret" to Albert's pattern was the thickness of the fiddle back. In his interview, Cotton says, "Albert just grins when asked the size of the area which is left $3/16$ inch, so obviously he believes this secret 'center of acoustics' is the key to his fiddle's design" (Cotton 89). One has to have an "ear" for "hearing the wood," says Albert, who told Cotton, "Once you learn to make the shape of the box, then you begin to develop this sense of acoustics and that is what takes you the rest of your life" (90).

Learning to use the various tools and machines was another extensive part of the apprenticeship. Several different machines were used to cut and graduate the pieces of each instrument. Other Hash innovations included a bass bar much longer than those usually used, "so you can bow your bass strings as hard as you want without having 'em distort" (ibid.). Also he used a special oil varnish to finish his fiddles which he felt is better than ones which will dry faster.

Not only did Albert refine his instrument-making techniques, equip his shop with the best precision tools that could be bought, and study every aspect of the craft, but also he eventually made nearly all the machines, tools, and special equipment that he used in making fiddles (Cotton 89). As Cotton says, "If an unusual tool is needed, Albert usually can make it on the precision lathe which he has in the shop." Combining his decades of experience as a machinist with his innate artistic ability enabled Albert to turn out highly prized instruments sought by musicians all over the nation. Once Albert was told that a Hash instrument was being sold for one thousand dollars in a music shop in Athens, Georgia; he just joked about it (Cotton 89). He did have the inner desire to make his instruments the best, however.

Albert liked to distinguish his fiddles with carving and a white binding around the instrument. Since each instrument was custom made, no two were exactly alike. Howard Sacks of the National Council for Tradition Arts notes that "intricate carving . . . often graces Albert's finer instruments" (Sacks to NEA, 1982). Albert's own favorite fiddle had a peacock on the back and bird's head on the peghead. Someone once requested a unicorn peghead; this was carved from deer horn and made removable when placed in the case (Cotton 90). Of all the woods he could use, Albert's favorite for fiddle carving and acoustics was the spruce. As Cotton said, "It is the fine acoustics of the Appalachian spruce which make Albert hope that some day his fiddles will compare favorably to the finest in the world" (Cotton 90).

Albert received national recognition as a craftsman and musician when he was nominated for the NEA's Heritage Fellowship in 1981. According to Joseph T. Wilson's 1981 nomination letter, he first met Albert in 1954 because of his reputation for building and repairing musical instruments. Wilson then was a member of a teenage string band in the mountains about fifty miles from Hash's home, but Wilson was willing to drive around "many hairpin turns" to have Albert repair his instrument. Wilson describes Albert and his shop in impressive words:

> He was the first master craftsman I met and a source of wonder. His shop was in the back of his house and his handiwork was everywhere in that house. He had made the big, beautiful grandfather clock, hand painting the dial[,] and had welded together a milling machine from junk to cut the apple wood cogs that drove the clock. His skill with metal was as well refined as his skill with wood . . . What amazed me then as now was the combination of talents found in Albert. The talent to be highly precise in metal or wood is not specially rare and there are many tool-makers and excellent machinists. But in Albert these skills are combined with well-developed artistic skills. He can paint, sketch, inlay, and sculpt . . . I've been seeing his instruments in the hands of fine play-ers. The tone is wonderful and they have the volume needed to be heard over banjo and mandolin.

Many apprentices came to study under Albert Hash; eventually certain ones became outstanding craftsmen themselves. One of these is Albert's daughter Audrey, who is "the only documented female instrument maker of the western Virginia Blue Ridge," according to Ferrum College. She has made many fiddles but specializes in dulcimers, having made over fifteen hundred of them. She laughingly points out that, when she was in Lansing High School (the family lived on the North Carolina side of the line for eleven years), "they didn't let girls take shop," so she did not have that advantage. She had watched her father in his shop rather carefully over the years, however. When she was seventeen, right after graduation from high school, she went down into the shop and told her father that she wanted to make a dulcimer. He handed her a few pieces of wood and turned around and went off, leaving Audrey to her own devices. As she tells it, "That turned out to be the ugliest dulcimer you ever saw." However, then Albert was convinced she was serious, so he helped her with more instruments, teaching her that one of the first things you have to have is patience. She says she also learned to make a good instrument but not to price it too high, because people in this area do not have "bunches of money." She says that there is still great interest in the musical tradition and that half the fiddles she makes go to local buyers. Most of the instruments she makes now are dulcimers, and many of those are sold all over the country, especially through craft shows (interview by Anderson-Green).

The scholars of the Blue Ridge Institute at Ferrum College produced a major exhibit of Blue Ridge folk instruments. An extensive catalog, published in connection with the exhibit, groups the craftsmen into "schools" or "traditions" of craftsmanship. A major division in this study is "The Hash Tradition," which Albert Hash began. Included in this group, in addition to Audrey, are many outstanding instrumentalists. Wayne Henderson of Rugby is renowned for his guitar playing, as well as his craftsmanship in creating various instruments, including excellent guitars. Fred Hensley of Galax specializes in mandolins. Walt Messick, originally from Philadelphia and later of Mouth of Wilson, mainly makes dulcimers. Tom Barr of Barr's Fiddle Shop in Galax not only crafts fiddles in the Hash manner, but also makes other instruments. Homer Austin of Hillsville studied under Tom Barr and carries on the tradition. Gerald Anderson of Troutdale studied under Wayne Henderson and makes mandolins and guitars. David Osbourne, grandson of Albert Hash, started at age twelve and now works on his own in Preston, North Carolina (Roderick, *Blue Ridge*). With this impressive group still working, there is no doubt that the Hash tradition in instrument making will carry on for generations.

Teaching Others

In addition to instrument making, Albert eventually began teaching fiddle-playing classes at Wilkes Community College in North Carolina. The first tune he always taught students was "Sally Ann" (National Council for the Traditional Arts, tape and notes submitted to NEA, 1982). This choice is a strong indication that Albert intended to hand on the traditional repertoire of his region. According to Rounder Records, "Wherever it ["Sally Ann"] is played, it is one of the most popular and often recorded dance pieces in the entire region of southwestern Virginia" (Liner notes to *Old Originals,* vol. 2, p. 6).

Later Albert and some of his band members helped to start a string band composed of students at the Mount Rogers High School. Ever since his earliest experience playing at the White Top Folk Festival, which helped convince Albert of the value of his musical heritage, he had wanted not only to participate in the tradition but also to help insure that it was perpetuated. Thus he, his friends, and Audrey especially loved the Mount Rogers School band and spent many hours with its members, attempting to revive youthful interest in the music of their parents' and grandparents' tradition. Some of the student musicians even made instruments with Albert. After her father's death, Audrey continued with the school band for ten more years, finally turning it over to Emily Spencer, under whose direction it is still going strong. Audrey feels that this organization of young musicians is one of her father's greatest contributions.

Indeed, Audrey recalls that her father's earliest desire was to be either a preacher or a teacher. In his early teenage years, he was very deeply influenced by his minister at the Lutheran church, the Reverend Mr. Killinger, and wanted to become a preacher like him. To do so, he would have had to go off to a seminary, as the Lutherans required. However, his mother was sick and did not want him to go away, so he changed his mind and gave up the idea of preaching. Also he later decided that getting up in a pulpit would make him nervous, but teaching did not bother him as much. Even though he did not pursue teaching in his earliest years, through music he did become an outstanding teacher, first with his apprentices and later with school groups. Emphasizing the meaning of this role, Albert told Audrey, "If a person chooses to spend a portion of his life, even an hour or two, with you, you should really be honored" (Audrey Hash Hamm interview by Anderson-Green). Thus Albert would give the teaching process his fullest energy.

Tributes

No doubt everyone in the Whitetop and Upper New River Valley area was thrilled when Albert and his associates in the Whitetop Mountain Band began to receive national awards, for their own music, their heritage, was being honored. The people of the region have paid tribute many times to Albert and his circle of musicians and craftsmen. At the same time, surely they have pledged to themselves that this music will not be lost to time.

Dean Sturgill, of Spencer's Branch, North Carolina, Albert's neighbor and himself a local musician who led the Grayson Highlands Band, wrote a poem to celebrate the musicians of the region. It is called "The Fiddlers, Thirty and Three." Saving the best for last, he wrote of Albert Hash and Thornton Spencer in the final verses:

> Now I have two spots left and I've saved
> them for the best
> Easily I found Albert Hash and Thornton
> Spencer in my fiddlers quest
> On hand-made fiddles made from Whitetop
> maple and seasoned spruce pine
> Albert played so many tunes, I hope
> none are lost to time.
>
> Thornton traveled the fiddling trails and
> for sure left his mark
> He will tell you (as he did me) "sometimes
> I'd rather hear a coon dog bark"
> Thornton's knowledge of fiddlers and fiddling
> is unsurpassed you see
> for that very reason he should be writing
> this instead of me.

On a later occasion, Dean Sturgill devoted a whole poem to Albert, entitled "The Fees Branch Fiddler." Remembering him forty years ago, "young and thin, . . . He would take the fiddle from the wall, pick and tune the strings . . . I can't do much with the thing," he says, with customary understatement. The poem emphasizes the "fiddle of beauty, of spruce and curly maple, handmade," with "an engraved peacock." When Albert played:

> The "Cackling Hen" cackled and the
> red rooster would crow
> When the Fees Branch Fiddler sawed
> the strings with his bow.
> To the "Arkansas Traveler" boys listened
> as the lamplight danced
> And the love, mystery and magic of the
> fiddle and fiddler were enhanced.

As the poem wraps up, the young boys, with milking done, would return: "again to Fees Branch we would dash, / Because the Fees Branch Fiddler was the great ALBERT HASH." In conclusion, the poet writes that it is forty years later and the great fiddler is gone, but he "didn't leave us alone," for, beside "falling waters," the "resounding sounds of . . . the fiddle still ring."

It is appropriate that Dean Sturgill, one of the many musical Sturgills, kin to "Uncle" Dave and Virgil, wrote this tribute to New River musicians, epitomized by the figure of the fiddler and above all by Albert Hash.

Beyond all the praise for Albert Hash's great musical talent in playing the fiddle and his impressive artistic skill as a craftsman, the most significant point that people always comment on is the humane quality that permeated his heart, his personality, his character. He truly could be termed a "southern gentleman," in the best meaning of that phrase. He personified ingrained Appalachian values: love of the land, love of neighbor and kin, love of community— that is, those who share a certain subregion, such as Whitetop.

Among the accolades that were showered upon Albert, perhaps the most revealing were comments written by friends in letters nominating him for the NEA Heritage Fellowship. Albert is "highly respected and loved . . . one of the most generous of people," one "always willing to teach . . . to share . . . to repair" (Gerrard and Cahan to NEA, 1982). He is "freely giving to those around him" and "can tell a good story too" (Sacks to NEA, 1982). He "is loved every-where he goes" (Emily Spencer and Thornton Spencer to NEA, 1982). Joseph Wilson's comment indicates that, although Albert may have seemed quiet or shy in large gatherings, when he opened up about subjects dear to him, he became vivacious: "Albert is a handsome fellow, gentle and modest, but also highly intelligent and downright infectious when he talks about making better instru-ments" (Wilson to NEA, 1981).

Egalitarian Community Leader

Albert's character and intelligence indeed formed the basis for his leadership role in the Upper New River Valley over the years. As a leader, he could rise above narrow or limiting attitudes. About Albert's teaching, Howard Sacks stated, "He has never shown favoritism toward men in his classes." Although coming from the male-dominated old-time and bluegrass musical tradition, Albert nevertheless was just as interested in teaching women as men. "He has been a total egalitarian in this regard," said Sacks. Perhaps the fact that he had two daughters influenced him, but he was more open to their potential than many fathers of his era. Thus Audrey was able to progress and develop as a craftsman; and Joyce, though not participating herself, encouraged her son to have this interest, so that he in turn became an instrument maker.

Albert's egalitarian way of thinking in fact was extended to the whole community. He did not believe that as many differ-ences existed between classes in his area as they perhaps did else-where. He and Thornton Spencer got into a discussion about that during the Weston interview, as the question arose whether just "lower-class" people were interested in traditional ("folk") music. Albert referred to a doctor who played any instrument, asserting, "They were all interested in it, preachers and what have you"

(Weston 18). Further, Thornton added, "In Ashe County and Grayson County, people say there has never been that much gap between the classes, they all more or less had the same interests, not like a lot of places." Even though in some cases religious attitudes about music differed (in an earlier time, some people were "churched" for playing the fiddle) and there were times when one person felt above another socially, such situations seem to have been unusual, according to the informants in this study. Leaders, who were usually leaders in the community as well as in music circles, affirmed that this was true.

Howard Sacks particularly emphasized Albert's role as a leader in his community, going beyond the usual, making an extra effort:

> Finally, I should note Albert's general contribution to the community of which he is a part. This contribution is not limited to his teaching or instrument making. Along with his Whitetop Mountain Band, Albert plays regularly at functions in the community to help raise funds for the local school, and the community always turns out en masse for these events. Clearly, Albert's devotion to the community is great and extends to the very mountain on which he lives. Albert speaks with great pride of the fact that his instruments are made with local woods, often cut down and hauled away by Albert himself. . . As Albert told me at the World's Fair, he doesn't much like to leave home.

As noted, after World War II, Albert left northern Virginia to return to the New River land of his birth. In their later years, Albert and his wife Ethel even bought her "home place" from her parents, the Orrie Spencers, right at the edge of Cabin Creek, near Albert's birthplace. They moved into that house just about the time of daughter Audrey's graduation from high school. Many years later, Ethel still lived there as a widow, with grandchildren and great-grandchildren usually playing around. This attitude of devotion to the "home place," including community, was a basic factor in the lives of most Upper New River people, typical of the Appalachian character, even though a "community" might consist of farm sites scattered throughout a settlement stretching over hills and valleys.

Epitomizing his concern for community, Albert—like Ola, Dave, and other musicians who became recognized by a wide public audience—had concerns about the way others viewed Appalachian culture. He was very disturbed by the ways in which mountain musicians were "staged" or interpreted. For example, when the scholarly producers of Rounder Records came to Grayson County to record *Old Originals,* vol. 2, Albert was deeply offended by their methods. First, he was angry that the "field fellow" was not open and honest about his purpose: "I believe it was Rounder had this field fellow came around, and it was pitiful because he didn't tell us what he was doing, you know, and nobody cared whether they played good or bad or what. We'd have made him a lot better record out of that. We got several tunes on that. I was ashamed of it. Our part of it was pretty good but if he'd told people that it was for an album they'd have played much better, you know" (Weston 14).

In addition, Albert was aware that the Rounder man actually *wanted* a "rough" sound, to fulfill his idea of what Appalachian music should sound like, and therefore did not allow the musicians to prepare and exert themselves to the fullest, as symphony players would do: "He didn't care, you know, they didn't want it to sound good. They thought these mountain fiddlers was supposed to be rough and sound bad and that's the worst mistake they ever made in their life. There's some of those fellows that can really play it, you know, and they do play it and they don't play rough" (ibid.).

Albert Hash had pride in the mountain music, knew what the musicians were capable of doing, and knew the long tradition and heritage that had "handed down" the techniques of playing. Thus he knew how the music should and could sound. He went on to explain something about this heritage: "They play a lot of the old tunes that the colonists had when they come over here. I play some of them, you know. One especially, 'Sourwood Mountain,' that's an English tune long before that, and 'Hangman's Reel,' that's from either England, Scotland, or Ireland" (ibid.).

So, as Albert stated before, he wanted music done "exactly right" and definitely wanted his Appalachian heritage presented "right." However, he also was able to take life in stride, and even when this event really upset him, he could say, "Our part of it was pretty good." Even so, he preferred "excellence."

Underlying Albert's perfectionist attitude was the fact that the music represented every participant in the heritage, all in the "great chain of being." As he put it, "The music is a part of you. It is you, actually, and it's your uncle over here and your brother back there who's gone on" (Cotton 91). He went on to explain: "Everybody who fiddled helped you and they helped each other. You pick up something from everybody, so no one person takes credit for being the sole teacher of any of us that ever played this mountain music." They are all connected in the musical network, the extended kinship—genetic and psychological—that exists throughout their territory, the beloved hill and valley region of the Upper New River Valley.

Pondering a Life

In the funeral service held for Albert Hash at Faith Lutheran Church in Grayson County, on January 30, 1983, the eulogy was given by Pastor Messick, who opened with these words: "Albert's book of life has many chapters. Let's look at some of the more important ones. The theme that runs throughout his life from beginning to end is that Christ is central to his existence. His life was firmly grounded in Christ and this strong foundation provided the springboard for the way he went about his daily life. He lived his religion. He didn't just talk about it . . . we must always remember that everything he was and did flowed naturally from his deep rooted Christian faith" (printed order of service).

Emphasizing this central aspect of her father's life, Audrey recalls again that his favorite hymn was "The Great Physician," with its focus on Christ as healer of mankind. In both worldview and leadership role, Albert Hash exemplified the life of the "Christian pastoral." In that rural way of life, while working in cornfields, harvesting timber, or grazing sheep or cattle, people daily experienced a closeness to nature. Dramatic occurrences in a natural setting, such as Albert's boyhood experience during a thunderstorm, conveyed insights about life.

From awareness of nature to awareness of the God of Creation, from respect for the community to emphasis on the commandment "Love one another," the agrarian society developed values that were personified in Albert Hash. Ralph Rinzler emphasized the connection between that agrarian world and the culture of the 1960s, discussing "the importance and persistence of the pastoral ideal, its relationship to the Christian ethic, and the influence of both . . . on folklore . . . and the folk revival" (Rinzler 124).

Albert helped to convey these agrarian values to the next generation, even beyond his own region, through the influence of his music. He cared about handing on the music as a way to pass on the heritage. He believed that music is not only aesthetically desirable but is the "tie that binds." The ultimate goal is not possessions, but the relationships of people to each other and to God.

Pastor Messick summarized Albert's life under "chapter headings," including "Humility, Generosity, Talent, Respect for Others, and Love of Children." The pastor recounted many revealing anecdotes about Albert, but among all these, one particularly stands out:

> Albert had no problem with an inflated ego. He didn't need fame, power or material wealth . . . This past summer Albert was invited to the World's Fair . . . On this trip to display his fiddles he was outraged that the Fair wanted to mark the price of his instruments up way beyond what he thought they were worth. So he refused to sell them even though he would have made a good profit.

Daughter Audrey has the same attitude, insisting that the cost of fiddles she makes has to be low enough for local people to afford them (interview by Anderson-Green). In conclusion, the pastor said about Albert:

> Our memories of him are packed with images, stories and events for future recalling and enjoyment. And hopefully our lives are different because of our crossing paths with his . . . One of his special dreams was to provide music lessons for others, that part of his story will live forever as his former students will pass on what he taught them.

The pastor, Walt Messick, was so influenced by Albert Hash and the world he lived in that, after retiring from the ministry, he remained in Grayson County, making dulcimers and taking part in Appalachian festivals. Thus, in the Ferrum College exhibit of traditional instruments, he was included in the section on the "Hash Tradition."

Almost two decades have passed since Albert's death, but, at parking lot pickings and jam sessions, musicians still tell anecdotes about him, admire instruments he made, and recall his "fine bowing" and his rendition of "Hangman's Reel." From the earliest days of his childhood, when he dreamed about making a fiddle, Albert had an awareness of his vocation in life, and he devoted himself fully to that vocation.

In his conclusion to *All That Is Native and Fine,* Whisnant states, "For a half-century after White Top [Festival,] Albert Hash still built and played fiddles in the shadow of the mountain, musing at times about the festival days in August" (253). Yes, Albert was a sensitive man, who mused about many things in life. At the same time, however, he actively worked and carried on a meaningful artistic tradition, passing it on to younger outstanding craftsmen and musicians. In his memory, these followers have instituted the annual Hash Festival every June in Alleghany County, at West Jefferson, North Carolina, where the sound of the traditional fiddle is still heard.

Gravesite of Albert Hash at Haw Orchard Cemetery, Virginia, 1997.
Photograph by Rhett Turner. Used by permission.

Now that Albert himself has "passed on," his body lies buried in Haw Orchard Cemetery on his beloved mountain. A distinctive monument features a fiddle above his name. Now he can muse from a different perspective, looking down over crowds of singers and fiddle players at spots like Galax, Elk Creek, and West Jefferson, both during fiddlers conventions and throughout the year, as the music goes on. ❖

4

"Uncle" Dave Sturgill
Virgil Sturgill, and All the Music-Making Sturgills

In the Blue Ridge hills of North Carolina, the headwaters of the New River arise and the mountains three to four thousand feet high are covered with majestic oaks, hickories, maples, laurel, and dogwood. Here the pioneer Sturgills arrived around the 1770s, wagons piled high with supplies, children, and fiddles, ready to settle in and plant their way of life. That way of life, centering so much on musical traditions, has continued on through ten generations and is still found there today. A visitor can best enter into that tradition by visiting "Uncle" Dave Sturgill of Piney Creek, North Carolina, who is the family historian, as well as an outstanding musician on banjo and fiddle. He is also a master craftsman, chosen for inclusion in Wigginton's *Foxfire 3* for his skill in making instruments. In 1990, he received the North Carolina Folklore Society's Brown-Hudson Award, given to residents of North Carolina who are outstanding in traditional arts and crafts.

Family Music Tradition

"Uncle" Dave explains that music making is so intense in the Sturgill family that, for many of them, it is not just something they want to do, but something they "have" to do. Dave and his son John were talking about this one evening, and laughing about the cousin known as "Fid" Sturgill, who lived over in the Chestnut Hill section of Ashe County. Dave said that, when Fid was a boy, assigned by his father to split rails, he'd "chop awhile and fiddle awhile." It all started when the dad got tired of hearing Fid just play fiddle on the porch while chores needed doing and insisted that he go chop wood. So the boy "went to the mountain with an ax in one hand and a fiddle in the other, to chop a while and fiddle a while. He guessed anybody passing the road down there thought he was crazy, hear the fiddle way up on top of the mountain" (Sturgill family interview by Anderson-Green).

To carry this tale by his father farther, John added his own chapter of Fid's story, reiterating the theme:

> I've heard stories about Fid Sturgill, and he made a comment that fiddling when he was a youngster was not something he could or couldn't do—it was something he had to do. And he'd go out with a team of mules to plow and he'd lay his fiddle down at one end of the field and he'd plow a furrow up and back and then fiddle a tune and then plow another furrow up and back again (laughs) and fiddle another tune, so it took him a little longer than the average farmer to get his field plowed! (Ibid.)

As "Uncle" Dave and John laughed over this story, Dave emphasized again how much Fid felt he just "had" to make music, even though "a lot of other people didn't understand." Dave added, "In other words, it was something he had to do, and I know the feeling because that was exactly the way that I felt about music. It never has been with me something I could do or not do—it's something I *had* to do" (ibid.). For "Uncle" Dave, music has been a creative obsession; indeed, he has modeled himself on Fid, his grandfather's cousin.

Dave Sturgill's intense feeling that he "had" to play music is echoed by many old-time musicians, who, in interviews recorded by Richard Blaustein in other locations, even use the same phrase. Probing this further, Blaustein presents an analytical theory concerning "the attachment of a traditional musician to his instrument, repertory, and style." Participation in traditional music, he feels, generates an intimate connection between the artist and his society. According to this theory, participation in traditional musical events is a significant way for a musician to achieve inner peace and a sense of equilibrium. Supporting this concept is the language that fiddlers use in interviews to describe their intense feeling for participating in the music. As one put it, "It's in your soul; it's part of you, and you have to do it." Another says, about his fellow musicians, "They care more about fiddling than they do about eating" (Blaustein 165).

So it has been for many of the Sturgill clan growing up in Ashe and Alleghany Counties, and even later when migrating as far away as Maryland or Montana. The feeling was inculcated in them during childhood in their folk community in the Upper New River region, via experiences and relationships involving more than one generation. For example, when Dave was a youngster, he and other boys would go over to Fid's house. Fid was in his late sixties then and adopted a mentor role with youngsters, teaching them repertoire and technique: "He showed us some of our first tunes." They lived near each other in the hills and visited frequently, with the older man always interested in the young aspiring musicians. He would tell them tales of his youth, when he and his two brothers—Jesse, who played banjo; and Joshua, who played guitar—performed as a group. They did not have an official name and were known merely as the "Sturgills." Dave says, "They played for many Saturday night dances and 'corn shuckings,' and all agreed that in his prime Will ('Fid') was the greatest fiddler who ever lived in this area" (Sturgill family interview by Anderson-Green). Fid never hung up his fiddle; instead he gave it to his son, Roy, who passed it to his son, Ivan.

Fid lived in Ashe County until "way up in his eighties," but by then all his children had moved away, following the migration to eastern Maryland. Finally, Dave says Fid was "getting helpless . . . so they moved him up there. And he lived the rest of his life up there; he was ninety-one or -two when he died in Harford County [Maryland]. And I used to visit him very regular." This may have been the beginning of Dave's custom of driving long distances to visit kin, exchanging music.

Dave also learned about fiddling from Fid's grandson, Ivan, a cousin of his own generation with whom he used to play when they lived across New River from each other. Later Dave continued to visit Ivan in the Baltimore area, where they would fiddle together. In all of this visiting with relatives that Dave enjoys, the music they make together constitutes a significant part of the fun and cements the relationships.

Fid was one of the earliest and most important mentors in the family, but there were others. Dave emphasizes that his mother and her family, the Weavers, had a major musical influence on him, too. "My mother's family were all musical, my mother could play anything . . . she played the organ in the home," and her brothers played various instruments. He remembers his grandmother Bytha playing dulcimer and singing hymns such as "Wayfaring Stranger." Then, when Dave was about eight years old, the family got a radio and started listening to the Grand Ole Opry, "And I can remember the house would be so full of people on Saturday night, they'd walk for three or four miles and come and listen . . . sitting out on the porch . . . And I had to learn some music" (Sturgill family interview by Anderson-Green).

Realizing how keen Dave was to learn, his mother decided to teach him the banjo on one borrowed from a cousin. Dave relates how he learned his first instrument, before his fiddle experience:

> I had the banjo then for about three years and by that time I learned to play pretty well. But when I first started practicing on the banjo, I almost drove everybody crazy in the house. And my dad had just

built a new granary, and it had an upstairs to it which
was unoccupied, so I moved my bed out in the granary, and I stayed out there all summer, until it got so
cold that fall I had to move back to the house, so I
could practice banjo again. By the time I come back
to the house, everyone would listen to me. (Ibid.)

After three years, the cousin wanted his banjo back; and
Dave, now eleven, faced a new dilemma. There was no extra cash
to buy an instrument, so for weeks he wandered around ponder-
ing this and also looking for pieces and parts to make one. Eventually he assembled his own home-made banjo. This was the
beginning of his lifelong work as a craftsman, which resulted in
his founding Skyland Instrument Company in Piney Creek, North
Carolina, and eventually being featured in *Foxfire 3* (Sturgill family interview by Anderson-Green; Wigginton).

Dave's sustained interest and experience in making both
instruments and music are tributes not only to his own talent and
creativity but also to the richly creative folk culture that he grew
up in, with so many relatives and neighbors actively engaged in
similar pursuits. Dave and certain friends formed a musical group
known as the "River Rats." It consisted of Dave playing banjo,
Ivan Sturgill on fiddle, Gene Vaught playing mandolin, and Don
Moore on guitar. Occasionally others played with them, including
Pete Sturgill, brother of Ivan; and Bob Sturgill, Dave's brother,
both on guitar. Dave writes, "Today (1993) I am the only one of
the original group still living" (David A. Sturgill to Anderson-Green,
Jan. 21, 1993).

During Dave's teen years, the youth of the area used to
gather by the mouth of King's Creek, a low-water place on the
South Fork of New River, to play fiddle, guitar, and banjo, and to
dance outdoors, sometimes almost all night. The "River Rats"
played by the campfire on many occasions. Reminiscing about
this, Dave writes:

For the next three or four years our Saturday night
sessions on the river bank became a regular affair

during the summer months and many others near
our age began to attend to listen to the music and to
dance in the sand. My uncle Willie Sturgill who lived
nearby kept a place cleaned off for us and kept a supply of fire wood on hand. He also built benches
between the willow trees and often sat on one of them
himself listening to our music. This was one of the
few places where local parents would let their children go on Saturday nights without a chaperone.
(David A. Sturgill to Anderson-Green, Jan. 21, 1993)

In a sense, however, Uncle Willie was the chaperone, encouraging
the next generation in a sense of community, as well as a love of
old-time music. Although he stayed more in the background than
a mentor like "Fid," Uncle Willie's role was equally important. He
seemed particularly interested in the Sturgill boys' participation.

Dave also remembers fiddling contests held in area school
buildings, overflowing with people cheering on the musicians
(Sturgill family interview by Anderson-Green). In fact, Piney Creek
Schoolhouse is where, at the mere age of twelve, he first was called
"Uncle" in a performance. Dave relates that "one of the all-time
great bluegrass fiddlers" was "Fiddling Art" Wooten of Alleghany
County, who played with Bill Monroe for seven or eight years. He
managed the shows at the local schoolhouse and had seen Dave
play banjo. One night when calling young Dave up on stage to play,
Art nicknamed him "Uncle Dave" because the youngster reminded
him of the famous Uncle Dave Macon. After that, Dave says, the
other kids kept calling him that at performances, and "it just stuck."
Apparently it was a well established mountain tradition to call musicians "uncle." When Dave came back thirty-five years later, people
who knew him as a boy still called him "Uncle" Dave (ibid.).

In addition to Dave's close family circle, including grandparents and cousins like "Fid," he knew and long remembered
other members of the Sturgill clan in the New River area who were
involved in music. Among these were the brothers Russ Sturgill
and Ralph Sturgill, known as the "Dixie Cowboys," who grew up in

the shadow of Whitetop Mountain in Ashe County. They began to perform at local affairs and then played on radio stations in the area, including one in Bristol (ibid.). During the Great Depression, Russ and Ralph moved with their parents and siblings to the Maryland-Pennsylvania area, where they again performed on radio. "The Dixie Cowboys" were heard on WGAL in Lancaster, Pennsylvania, during the 1930s. In the late 1930s, the family moved again, this time to California. While there, the brothers, grown up, went separate ways.

Russ became interested in making instruments and eventually returned to North Carolina, where he married a musician, Nannie Spurgeon. According to Dave, Russ and Nan soon were in demand for performances at many local events, and their talent attracted the attention of a scout searching for gifted Appalachian musicians to participate in a government-sponsored program. In this way they traveled for a decade all over the eastern United States, taking mountain music to schools and libraries. Eventually they returned to Ashe County, where they restricted themselves to local appearances, except for some radio programs in East Tennessee. These Sturgills formed part of the effort during the 1920s and 1930s to carry traditional Appalachian music beyond its region to a national audience that was being shaped almost entirely by commercial popular culture.

During that same era, another Sturgill, "Singing Ike" of Konnarock, Virginia, made a major contribution to the transmission and preservation of traditional music by originating the idea of the White Top Folk Festival (David A. Sturgill and Mack H. Sturgill, eds., *A History of the Sturgill Family,* 206; Whisnant, *All That Is Native* 187). "Uncle" Dave fondly recalls "Singing Ike" (sometimes known as "U.V." for his formal name, "Ulla Vinton"), a Baptist preacher who was also a musician with a gospel-singing group featured on the radio in Knoxville, Tennessee. In his Baptist circles, to combine singing with instrumental music and preaching was not only acceptable, but soul-stirring; his gospel-singing groups performed in many churches of the area. Singing Ike's homeplace at Konnarock was located at the junction of Smyth, Washington, and

Grayson Counties, near the North Carolina border on the edge of Whitetop Mountain, that "center of gravity" for southern mountain music at the time (Whisnant, *All That Is Native* 187).

As Whisnant points out, although Whitetop Mountain was privately owned by the Whitetop Company, a timber business, local people were allowed to use it for picnicking, hiking, and playing music together. Thus, when Ike got the idea of having a fiddlers convention there on the Fourth of July in 1931, he approached a principal of the company, attorney John Blakemore of Abingdon, Virginia, to get permission for the occasion. In turn, Blakemore mentioned the plan to a cousin and his wife, John Buchanan and Annabel Morris Buchanan, long interested in traditional music. The Buchanans eagerly took over organization of the event, designating it a "folk festival" rather than a fiddlers' convention. Annabel had been educated at a music conservatory in Dallas and later, while living in Marion, Virginia, served as president of the Virginia Federation of Music Clubs. She enlisted the help of John Powell, a noted composer from Richmond, Virginia, in promoting the festival (Whisnant, *All That Is Native* 187–90).

Although these organizers, not natives of the region, changed the planned name and date of the musical gathering, they did encourage traditional musicians of the area by advertising the event widely and offering significant prizes for participants, thus drawing a larger crowd than usual. Further, the annual White Top Festival lasted throughout the 1930s. This probably fulfilled Ike Sturgill's original intention and must have been satisfying to him, since many talented locals performed, including Huck Sturgill, who played in Albert Hash's band, well known in that era.

Other Sturgill neighbors and relatives at the first White Top Festival included the Osbornes from Mouth of Wilson. Oscar Osborne wrote a letter to the officials requesting entry: "We Osborne brothers wish to enter . . . We play violin, banjo, guitar, and harmonica" (Whisnant, *All That Is Native* 188). Ola Belle's family came, too; her mother was an Osborne and probably wanted to see her relatives perform. According to Ola's brother Alex, his family attended the White Top Folk Festival in 1933 and, like all the local people present, was greatly impressed that First Lady Eleanor Roosevelt came (see chap. 2 above).

Mrs. Roosevelt's presence drew media attention to the White Top Festival, which in turn stimulated many urban dwellers to reexamine the roots of American traditions, particularly as seen in "remote" and "picturesque" Appalachia. Of course, this attention further complicated the issue of the interpretation of "Appalachian culture." Whisnant thoroughly discusses this aspect of the White Top Festival, including, for example, efforts by Buchanan, Powell, and others to shape the musical presentations by emphasizing ballad singers and limiting the number of string bands (*All That Is Native* 197).

Perhaps more significant was the outsiders' depiction of the social status of the musicians. A newspaper editor described them as "fantastic hillbillies with fiddles under their arms" (ibid.). Even Whisnant refers to the area's residents as "lower-class," compared to Blakemore, the Buchanans, and their allies (*All That Is Native* 210). However, the main social difference was not class, but "town" versus "country." Many musicians from rural areas, such as the Sturgills, Hashes, and Osbornes, belonged to a yeoman or "minor gentry" level of their society (Anderson-Green, "New River"; Williams, "Who Are the Southern Mountaineers?" 48–55). Despite the views of outsiders, they were respected leaders in their own communities.

As a teenager, Dave Sturgill attended the White Top Festival a couple of times, first with his friend Charlie Cox and then alone in 1933, driving his own car, just before he left his mountain home for young adult adventures. Dave enjoyed the White Top experience, with its unusually large gathering of musicians. Later, hearing stories about those days from relatives and friends intensified his interest in performing. Further, as he matured in awareness of his Appalachian heritage, Dave, a "transition era" musician and local historian, became fascinated by the various images of Appalachia appearing in the mass media. As a result, he began doing extensive research on his own family history, while becoming more aware of other pioneer families and settlements in the area.

Family History

Thinking back on his boyhood days in the area of Alleghany and Ashe Counties and on stories he heard of the early settlement there, "Uncle" Dave speaks in an interview about his ancestors who first came into this land, bringing their musical traditions with them. He loves to tell how he learned about his fifth-great-grandfather, James Stodgill (as it was spelled then). Old James was the grandson of John Stodgill, a Scots-Irishman who went into England and then in 1650 to Essex County, Virginia, as an indentured servant. Later his grandson, James, lived and owned land in Orange County, Virginia, near Standardsville, where he died in 1753. Dave discovered the inventory of his estate, which listed, among other property, two intriguing items: "one small old still" and "one old set of bagpipes—don't work." Dave laughs over this every time he tells it, commenting on how much it reveals about Scots-Irish culture (Cauthen 3–4)! He emphasizes how these elements are reflected in the music: song lyrics about whiskey, and fiddle music emphasizing the drones to sound like bagpipes playing. As a craftsman, Dave points out that making bagpipes was too complex a task for frontier life and that the fiddle was easy to transport. To make the point about fiddles simulating the sound of bagpipes, Dave leans over and picks up his fiddle to demonstrate by playing "Mississippi Sawyer" (Sturgill family interview by Anderson-Green; also discussed in personal communication with Dr. John Burrison, folklorist and professor at Georgia State University, who confirmed that there was a history of piping in Scots-Irish culture, using the lowland pipes).

Dave's ancestor, "Old James," left the set of old bagpipes to his son Francis Sturgill, who was born in Orange County, Virginia. A later generation, James Sturgill II and his family, moved down the Great Wagon Road to Montgomery (now Grayson) County around 1770. There his son, Francis Sr., joined the volunteer militia in 1777, shortly after he had married Rebecca Hash in 1776. She was the daughter of a prominent leader in the early settlement. Francis served in the militia under his brother-in-law, Capt. Enoch Osborne, who was married to Rebecca's sister. According to oral tradition,

Osborne's militia unit fought at the Battle of King's Mountain, but, being practical, went the short way down the mountain into North Carolina and did not join the other American units first in Tennessee, so the unit is not officially recorded as participating (Sturgill family interview by Anderson-Green; see Messick).

After the Revolution, Francis and Rebecca Hash Sturgill were living in Grayson County, Virginia, on Potato Creek; but Francis was granted land nearby in Ashe County, North Carolina, in 1798. He acquired more in 1799, and by 1802 they sold their Potato Creek farm and moved into Ashe, into the section known for generations as Sturgill land. Reflecting on this, "Uncle" Dave writes:

> Of particular interest to me is the fact that all of that land at the forks of the river, down New River and up the south fork was at one time owned by the Sturgill family, part by original grants and part by purchase. The Halsey family got all of the land they owned there from the Sturgills in 1812, 1827, and 1834. I have an original deed in which my gg grandfather's brother sold a tract of the land to Marie's [Dave's wife] gg grandfather in 1837. (David A. Sturgill to Anderson-Green, Jan. 21, 1993)

Thus, the interconnection between Dave and Marie's families was established generations back.

This historic Sturgill and Halsey land along New River is now part of a large tract adjoining the twenty-six-mile section of the New River designated a federal "Wild and Scenic River" by the United States Congress in 1976 (Johnson 209). "Uncle" Dave and others from his neighborhood went to Congress and effectively lobbied the politicians in order to get this law passed; later they were invited to the White House for the signing of the bill saving the New River.

This Halsey-Sturgill land is adjacent to a 350-acre tract acquired by the State of North Carolina in 1990 for preservation in a "natural state." The pioneer ancestors, Francis and Rebecca Hash Sturgill, as well as the parents of Francis, are buried near the river in "the old Sturgill Cemetery" in Ashe County, which is now a part of the New River State Park. Dave likes to wander there at times, contemplating the beauty of the land and river and thinking about the pioneers who brought their families, a few possessions, and musical instruments into these mountains and established the solid, traditional culture that has been "handed-on" for so many generations.

Adult Life

Although his roots run deep in the New River Valley and he intensely loved his boyhood years growing up there, Dave ventured off when grown. He was not the first generation to leave. His parents had moved to Montana in their early married years, where his father, a civil engineer, worked for awhile. Dave was born there, but after a few years the family moved back to Alleghany County and stayed. When Dave graduated from high school in 1933, during the Great Depression, opportunities were limited, so he "started rambling" (Sturgill family interview by Anderson-Green). First, in the fall, he rode his bicycle 450 miles in a three-day trip to his Weaver grandparents' home in Glenville (Harford County), Maryland, where they had migrated earlier and settled. There he spent the winter. Then, Dave says, he went all the way to California, hung around San Francisco, and even met Burl Ives one evening at a musical gathering, at which they talked for three hours. Everywhere Dave went, he took his instruments and jammed with others on banjo, fiddle, or guitar. Dave writes:

> As the big Depression was then well under way and as I had no money to continue my education I became a wandering troubadour for the next four summers, hitchhiking all over the USA and playing a banjo or guitar on street corners or in beer joints, singing and telling stories of the Appalachian mountains. I spent the winters in CCC [Civilian Conservation Corps] camps. (letter to Anderson-Green, Jan. 21, 1993)

Dave was developing many of his "Appalachian" talents, in the process becoming a great raconteur. During this time, too, he won a music talent contest in Twin Falls, Idaho, and as part of the prize was offered the chance to do a brief weekly show on the local radio station, KTFI. However, Dave declined the offer, as he wanted to travel more and had no intention of pursuing a professional music career. He has no regret about this missed opportunity.

In the course of his ramblings, Dave went to visit an elderly cousin, Seymour Sturgill, who was the uncle of Virgil Sturgill, later famous in folk music circles. As Dave tells it, Seymour, a fascinating character, was born and raised in Carter County, Kentucky, so far back in the hills that he never went to school until he was grown. However, then he got his high school equivalency certificate, entered the University of Kentucky, and got a bachelor of arts degree at age twenty-five. He became a teacher in Greenup County, Kentucky; later earned a master's degree; and finally served as superintendent of schools for Greenup for many years. After he retired, he was studying astronomy and spending time making music. Dave was intrigued by him and then even more so by his son, Seymour Junior, who came in from his truck-driving job. When he learned that Dave played banjo, Junior admitted that he "played a little," and went and got his guitar. It turned out he had played professionally for twenty years, had had his own western swing band, and had played in nightclubs all over the West. They all had a great evening making music together (Sturgill family interview by Anderson-Green).

After visiting the Seymours, Dave went on farther in Kentucky to Louisa County, looking up some more relatives that he planned to stay with. After arriving at the Frank Sturgill place, as soon as music was mentioned, all the relatives brought out their fiddles. It turned out that Frank had a band with his brothers and played at local events (after running their furniture store during the day). Dave says, "So we set there till about midnight and had a jam session; and then he was telling me all the Sturgills out there that played. So everywhere I've gone I've found members of the family that were musicians" (Sturgill family interview by

Anderson-Green). Throughout the various branches of the clan and the many locations they moved to, the musical connection has been maintained, and Dave feels he has learned something from each of his relatives.

Another Sturgill who was well known in music in Kentucky was Alfred Sturgill of Morehead, Kentucky, who won local awards and lived to be one hundred years old. He attributed his longevity to learning how to relax by picking a banjo! (David A. Sturgill to Anderson-Green, Jan. 21, 1993). Another Kentucky cousin, Darvin Sturgill of Olive Hill, became a professional musician. He and yet another cousin, Tom T. Hall, learned music together as boys and both went to the Grand Ole Opry in Nashville, getting recording contracts. But Darvin decided that life "on the road" was not for him. He did not like living out of a suitcase, so he returned to Olive Hill to open a music and appliance store and also serve as a pastor, performing music in church. Cousin Tom went on to fame in Nashville (Sturgill family interview by Anderson-Green).

Such are the choices musicians must make, a fact that Dave Sturgill became conscious of as a young man traveling the family network and routes across the United States. During all this unstructured period of his life in the 1930s, Dave was continuing his informal musical education and evolving his view of himself as a musician. Eventually, he came back east and, like so many relatives, went to Maryland, where he studied electronics at Bliss Electric School (later Montgomery Junior College). Then he went to work for Bell Telephone Company and eventually transferred within the corporate structure to Western Electric in Montgomery County, Maryland, near Washington, D.C.

In 1942, Dave returned to the mountain home to marry his childhood sweetheart, Marie Halsey of Alleghany County, then a schoolteacher in Wilkes County, North Carolina. He took her to Maryland, where they bought a home in College Park. During those years, while becoming established economically, he played only in jam sessions and made instruments "on the side."

However, Dave was perfecting his craftsmanship by working under the guidance of an older cousin, Herman Weaver, an

outstanding violin maker in the Washington area. Born in Glouces-
ter Court House, Virginia, in 1886, Weaver began making violins
in 1898, then moved to Portsmouth and eventually around the
country to Denver, Chicago, and Cincinnati, developing his skills,
before settling in the Washington, D.C.–Maryland area (Fairfield
182). Weaver first established his instrument-making business,
Weaver's House of Violins, in Baltimore, but later, in 1935, moved
it to downtown Washington, D.C., near 14th and G streets, while
keeping his residence in Wheaton, Maryland. The business, making violins for classical musicians in the Washington Symphony,
as well as for those playing folk or old-time music, now is located
in Bethesda, Maryland, and has been carried on by Herman's son
and grandson.

In the 1940s, Dave, expanding his knowledge from his boyhood days making banjos, watched Herman Weaver's skillful hands
slowly crafting the finest of beautiful violins and became even more
fascinated with this art. Weaver used European woods and followed
Stradivarian lines, although he later developed patterns of his own;
and his instruments sold for high prices even then (Fairfield). In
fact, a North Carolina newspaper proudly called Weaver one of "the
world's top five fiddle makers" (Brown). After Dave introduced himself to Herman as a cousin through his Weaver grandparents (now
also in Maryland but originally from Virginia), he was allowed to
come into the Weaver shop and work on his own violins under
Herman's guidance. Dave always has acknowledged how much he
learned from Herman, again evidence of the value of his kinship
network. Although it would be many years before Dave opened his
own instrument-making business, for him this apprenticeship in
Weaver's House of Violins was a formative and inspiring time.

Dave learned more than craftsmanship during those years;
he learned how to deal with the tensions of life through his craft
and his music. Journalist Bill Moyers wrote an article on Dave
back then, entitled "One Man's Ulcer Cure," in which Dave tells
how he was getting sick, developing an ulcer, until he turned to
making violins as a way to "work off excess nervous energy." Thus

"Uncle" Dave Sturgill playing fiddle at home, Piney Creek, North Carolina, 1996.
Photograph by Rhett Turner. Used by permission.

he cured not only his ulcer, but also his soul. Gradually, music was becoming Dave's major purpose in life.

Another Weaver cousin in Maryland whom Dave contacted through music was Dale Weaver, who had known Dave when they were boys in Piney Creek. Dale now played in a professional musical group that performed in clubs around Harford County, Maryland, in the tri-state area where so many transplanted New River folks settled. This was not far from the Washington area, an easy drive for visiting. Sometimes Dave reminisced with these cousins about his mother's Weaver history, pointing out that, back in the pioneer days, three children of Francis Sturgill married three children of William Weaver! Thus their interconnections had gone on for generations. Mostly, however, they just enjoyed making music together.

Dave has always valued family and clan very highly. Those growing up in the Appalachian culture absorb this attitude, perhaps almost unconsciously, from early childhood (Coles 500–504). As Dave got older, especially during his traveling days, he became quite aware of this value. So when he settled down in Maryland, he and Marie were eager to begin their own branch of the family. Eventually they had five children, three sons and twin daughters. When the Bell System magazine, *The Transmitter*, ran a story on Dave in 1954, several photos were included. The largest one depicts Dave as a "violin craftsman," sitting at his worktable chiseling the back of a fiddle. The other three photos all show Dave in his role as a father. In two, he is instructing his sons to operate telescopes and toy trains, and the third shows him giving the bottle to an infant daughter. The caption under the father-son picture states, "Life for the Sturgill family is an interesting adventure of learning and doing things together." This was the guiding spirit that led Dave and his sons to found their own instrument-making shop many years later.

In that period from the thirties through the fifties and sixties, Dave also performed on-stage or jammed on the field at Sunset Park and at New River Ranch. At these "music parks" of the Maryland-Pennsylvania border, transplanted mountaineers gathered to hear old-time music. During this time, Dave was playing both clawhammer banjo and fiddle. Here Dave could associate with old friends and relatives from the New River Valley, such as Ola Belle Campbell Reed, his distant cousin through the Hash family. The old-time and bluegrass music was the key factor bringing them together, creating the "ties that bind" through changing decades and cultures—agricultural, industrial, and then postmodern.

Here Dave met and interacted, too, with people from other backgrounds who now were attracted to traditional mountain music, and he now encountered their more complex reactions to his Appalachian heritage. Above all, however, Dave valued the contacts with musicians immersed in the old-time Appalachian repertoire and instrument-making traditions.

Virgil Sturgill

Among these important musical contacts in the family network whom Dave met in the Washington area was his fifth cousin, Virgil Sturgill, a musician who became famous in folk music circles in North Carolina in the 1940s. Dave first contacted him by mail around 1940 regarding the history of the Sturgills, having learned of his interest in Appalachian history and music through an uncle. Virgil then was a teacher and a psychometrician in the Swannanoa Division of the United States Veterans Administration, in its hospital at Oteen, North Carolina, near Asheville. Around 1950 he was transferred to Walter Reed Hospital in Washington, D.C. At that time, Dave states,

> We met personally for the first time and became fast friends from then on. He retired from government service about 1960 and took a job teaching in a college in Baltimore. About 1965 he moved back to Asheville where he still owned a home . . . he did some more teaching in a small community college. I saw him for the last time when we visited him in Asheville in 1979. (Sturgill family interview by Anderson-Green)

Both Dave and Virgil were deeply involved in their Appalachian crafts, music, and heritage. Especially as traditional musicians, they shared a core interest which made them fast friends and allowed a further deepening of their repertoires as they exchanged music. In the 1950s, both were living in the Maryland suburbs of Washington, Dave in College Park and Virgil in Laurel, Maryland. Dave tells that Virgil came to visit frequently, traveling back and forth on streetcars because "he never owned an automobile in his life or learned to drive one" (David A. Sturgill to Anderson-Green, Jan. 21, 1993).

Virgil Leon Sturgill was born in 1897 in a log cabin in Carter County, Kentucky, one of four children of James Monroe Sturgill and his wife, Polly Burris. James was born in Floyd County,

Kentucky, but grew up in Carter County, where he became a schoolteacher and met Polly, whose family owned land on Sutton's Branch (David A. Sturgill, *Branch of Sturgill Family* 116). Reminiscing with his cousin Dave, Virgil told him that his father named all his children for towns along the nearby railroad, one of which was "Leon." That was the only name he got until later when, in the Navy in World War I, he was forced to pick another name (three were required). He chose "Virgil," perhaps for its poetic associations or musical sound (David A. Sturgill to Anderson-Green, Jan. 21, 1993; also see Virgil Sturgill File in American Folklife Center, Library of Congress).

Anyway, his parents raised their children in a large household that included the maternal grandparents. Virgil had an extensive repertoire of folk ballads and instrumental tunes which he had learned growing up in this folk culture and continued playing throughout his life. Although his family nearly always sang unaccompanied and Virgil often performed that way later in concerts, he also came especially to love the dulcimer, whether the three-string dulcimer, in which one string carries the melody; or the four-string instrument with two melody strings and two drones. In his notes, Virgil points out that *dulcimer* means "sweet sound," and that a Bible verse, Daniel 10:3, refers to an instrument that is a dulcimer (Virgil Sturgill File, American Folklife Center, Library of Congress, Washington, D.C.). Although critics point out that the Biblical instrument was not the lap dulcimer, in Sturgill's culture this Biblical reference was used as an important means of establishing significance for a listener or reader (thus the type of dulcimer is not the point).

In an interview recorded at the Library of Congress in July 1957, Virgil discusses his boyhood. His melodious voice, preserved on tape, muses on his "tender formative years . . . hearing mother sing songs from the ancestors." He explains that his people were of English and Scottish origin, with a rich store of ballads and tunes they brought with them to America. He speaks of "my cultural inheritance which I prize highly to this day" and says that, in his home, "to sing was as natural as to breathe." They sang unaccompanied; his mother's people did not play instruments, because they were followers of the religious teachings of Alexander Campbell and used only the voice, as nature's instrument (Virgil Sturgill File, American Folklife Center, Library of Congress).

His father played banjo and sang "more raucous" songs, however, so Virgil was introduced to more than one style. He later sang more in the tradition of his mother's people, but he also admired his father's family. He states that his father's parents, though they never went to school, were highly intelligent and could quote whole chapters of the Bible verbatim, based on auditory memory. When Virgil went to the University of Kentucky, he majored in English and, while reading Shakespeare, recognized his grandparents' speech in the plays. At that point, he states, he began to "reappraise my background."

After earning a B.A. degree in English and an M.A. degree in education at the University of Kentucky, Virgil taught for a while in the public schools. Then he left his home state to work in Civil Service positions in Veterans Administration hospitals. However, Virgil's love for his Appalachian musical heritage never waned, and eventually he became an important figure in disseminating folk music to the wider American audience. He never appeared on-stage until age fifty, but then he started taking part in festivals, such as the Asheville Folk Festival, the Virginia Music Festival at the University of Virginia, and the Carolina Folk Festival held annually at Chapel Hill. Dave Sturgill wrote that his cousin Virgil "had a beautiful and rich baritone voice . . . He liked the old songs which told the story of some kind of tragedy, such songs as 'Barbara Allen,' 'Knoxville Girl,' 'The Death of Floyd Collins,' 'Rosewood Casket,' 'Sourwood Mountain' . . . He also knew many of the old Irish and Scottish ballads" (David A. Sturgill to Anderson-Green, Jan. 21, 1993).

Virgil typically would appear on-stage playing his handmade walnut dulcimer and singing a folk ballad of the type Dave recalled, such as "The Murder of Lottie Yates." Much of the time he sang unaccompanied in his family's old-time style. The crowd was fascinated, and he became a favorite. Virgil opened the folk festival at the University of North Carolina (UNC) at Chapel Hill in 1949; and Dan Patterson, UNC folklore professor, remembers him singing "The Wife of Usher's Well" to a spellbound group (Dan Patterson interview by Anderson-Green). Patterson also recalls a fascinating song that Virgil sang, "Jack Monroe" (Laws N7), emphasizing these words:

> My waist is slim or slender,
> My fingers they are small,
> But it would not make me tremble
> To see a cannonball.

When Virgil performed in the Virginia state capital, the *Richmond Virginia Newsletter* stated that he "simply lifted his voice and let it echo through the hall. The effect was . . . sonorous, deeply moving." From there Virgil went to Washington, D.C., where his performance was reported in the *Washington Post*: "All of the chairs in the hall . . . were filled for last night's program by folk singer Virgil Sturgill. . . . All was relished by the audience . . . warmth . . . enthusiasm" (Virgil Sturgill File, Archive of American Folk Songs, Library of Congress). Virgil's music appealed not only to college students and general audiences, but also to sophisticates who attended his performances in such venues as the Phillips Gallery in Washington.

Virgil reached a still broader audience when he was asked to appear on national radio programs. The *Asheville Citizen-Times* announced in March 1951 that Virgil Sturgill "will be heard on three CBS coast-to-coast broadcasts"—the Renfro Valley, Kentucky, programs, "Country Store" and "Barn Dance"; and the Sunday program, "Gatherin'," on which he would play sacred songs on dulcimer. The article also states that "in January he gave the first program of ballads accompanied with dulcimer in the history of television over WFMY in Greensboro, North Carolina." He went on to sing in Washington, New York, and Philadelphia, as well as at many northern colleges. Thus a wide audience beyond the mountain region was being introduced to the music of Appalachia through musicians such as Virgil Sturgill. The reception was enthusiastic.

Virgil was reaching not only a popular audience but also a scholarly one. He participated in the North Carolina Folklore Society, did some recordings for the Library of Congress, and even published four articles, three in *North Carolina Folklore* and one in the *Kentucky Folklore Record*. These concerned ballads in which he had a strong interest: "Lottie Yates," whose murder occurred near his homeplace in Kentucky; the "lost" "Ballad of George Collins," which he proved was not lost at all; and "Willy Weaver" (see bibliography).

The formative years in Carter County, Kentucky, where he "was born and spent the first fifteen years of my life," made a lasting impact on Virgil Sturgill in many ways, as can be seen particularly in his lifelong kinship ties and his love of Appalachian music (Virgil Sturgill, "Murder"). Later, after he left and moved several times during his career with the Veterans Administration, he wrote, "I, too, have been tormented for years by the 'ghosts' of more than one ballad inherited from my youth in the hills of Kentucky." It was this memory of that special time and place, and the music which evoked it, that gave rise to Virgil's lifelong interest in preserving and rediscovering texts and melodies from that tradition:

> Many of these old songs of the long ago are fragmentary, and the passing of the years has not helped in my recalling them either in whole or in part. But even these fragments hold a fascination for both the scholar and the singer of folk-songs, who enjoys nothing better than occasionally "unearthing" one of these rare "finds." (Virgil Sturgill, "Lost Ballad" 31)

In this case, the "find" was the "Ballad of George Collins," which was brought to Virgil's attention through an article in the Asheville newspaper by a writer who remembered the plot but not the text and music. This intrigued Virgil enough to pursue the ballad, and he later tracked it down in Buncombe County, North Carolina, where he found a man who knew the entire ballad, having learned it from members of his family (32). Further, Virgil found variants of the text and title, tracing the ballad back to the British "Lady Alice." He writes:

> The general pattern . . . is identical with most ver-
> sions whether very old or of later vintage. In every
> instance they all stem from the "Lady Alice" versions
> sung by the peasantry of England centuries ago and
> in America from as early as 1806 . . . No less than
> twenty-five versions of the ballad are known to be in
> print. They help to bridge the gap but do not fully
> explain how a noble English lady's story of frustrated
> love should be reenacted in the life of a simple
> mountain girl in far-off America, and how each of
> them followed her man to the grave. (33)

Virgil recognizes the universality of grief for a dead lover, "down through the centuries," and comments on how a young woman would learn this ballad from her mother, who learned it from her mother "back into the old country and across the sea" (33). As he finishes the story of his "hunt" for this ballad, he emphatically states, "Good folk songs don't die."

Not only were old English ballads transported across the sea by musicians who perhaps transformed the central character, a noble lady, into a "simple mountain girl" (a transformation often seen, for example, in the "Jack" tales), but also the traditional ballad form was used by American singers to compose new ballads based on American events. Virgil found a fascinating example of this in his own home county, in "The Murder of Lottie Yates." Virgil states that, after the girl's murder occurred, the ballad was composed by Elijah ('Lige) Adams, "a folk poet and singer of the late 1890s–1900s. Of the background and training of this itinerant minstrel, verse-maker, and folk historian little is known" (26). However, his exis-tence and his musical work were well known to Virgil's neighbors and relatives, and Virgil states that "Lottie Yates," like Adams's better-known "Ashland Tragedy," "was probably issued originally as a broadside" (26). Virgil in 1957 tape-recorded a rendition of "Lottie Yates" that was sung by an eighty-year-old woman in Carter County, and he included the entire text in an article published in *North Car-olina Folklore* in 1958. This same article was reprinted the following year, 1959, in *Kentucky Folklore Record,* followed by a longer variant of "Lottie Yates" that had been collected by Cratis D. Williams for his master's thesis at the University of Kentucky, completed in 1937. The editor comments, "Williams' notes are in general agreement with the account given by Sturgill," with some additions (65). Further, Dan Patterson, the UNC folklorist, included one of the ballads collected by Sturgill, "Willy Weaver," in "A Sheaf of North Carolina Folksongs," also published in *North Carolina Folklore,* in 1956. Clearly, Virgil Sturgill's work was careful and scholarly.

Virgil Sturgill was awarded the North Carolina Folklore Society's Brown-Hudson Award in 1973, the same award that "Uncle" Dave Sturgill later received in 1990. That two cousins from different branches of the same family tree had similar talents and interests reflects not only their genes but also the power of their rich, shared folkloric heritage. For Virgil, as for others in this folk culture, a spiritual element underlay it all. In a 1978 letter, in which the writer states he is then eighty-one years old, Virgil says he hopes to make it to one hundred but "will be ready when the Lord calls me home. I have tried to live a Christian life" (Virgil Sturgill File, American Folklife Center, Library of Congress). After Virgil Sturgill passed away in 1981 and was buried in Asheville, North Carolina, he was sorely missed, but everyone knew that he had made a major contribution to the heritage of folk music.

Going Home: Skyland Instrument Company

Virgil Sturgill was in the Washington area for only a few years, but "Uncle" Dave was in Maryland for three decades, from 1938 to 1968. By the end of the 1960s, however, metropolitan life was taking its toll on him. First he had health problems, then came riots in Washington, D.C. Dave determined to go back to the hills, despite the fact that he had not worked enough years to qualify for full retirement. Some friends were shocked that he would give up so much, but he has never regretted it. He says, "Smartest thing I ever did as far as I'm concerned, because I know now that if I'd stayed there, I'd be dead. I was getting ulcers and high blood pressure. My heart was bothering me, and several other things. And all that's gone now. And nothing would ever get me back into it, I'll tell you. Not again" (Wigginton 179).

So Dave returned to Alleghany County, North Carolina, to take up residence in Piney Creek near the early Sturgill land grant. As he puts it, "My heart [had] never left the hills. This was where I always wanted to be. There were riots in Washington then, and these hills looked so good every time I came down here that I finally came down here and stayed" (Wigginton 168). After Dave and Marie returned, their grown sons determined to leave the city, too. In 1970, Dave opened Skyland Instrument Company; in 1973, he was joined by two sons, John and Dan. There, in their own shop in the New River Valley, they created highly crafted banjos, guitars, fiddles, mandolins, and dulcimers. They were welcomed back by many relatives and neighbors who were delighted to have them bring their musical talents and endeavors back to Alleghany County permanently.

At the Skyland Company, where they worked together for over a decade, the instruments they made ranged from a simple do-it-yourself kit to the most elaborate, detailed, and individually crafted instruments with engravings and inlay. Each of the Sturgills had his own area of operation. Dave was in charge of instrument assembly; Danny specialized in sanding, binding, and hand-rubbing lacquer finish for guitar, mandolin, and fiddle bodies; and Johnny was in charge of carving banjo heels, rims, and necks, designing rims, and pearl cutting (Abrams 14). It is said that John's pearl inlay work is matched by few in the region (see Farrell).

The guitars and other instruments, as done then and even now by Dave in his smaller shop, are fashioned from a variety of woods, using tools Dave designed. Dave states that, "unless other-wise specified by the customer[,] we use high quality spruce tops on all of the instruments we make or restore. Most of this wood is forty years old or older. On bodies and necks we use figured maple, apple, cherry, walnut, mahogany, rosewood and others; most fretboards are ebony or rosewood." Dave has decided that, in traditional "mountain" banjo making, "a six-inch head with a half-inch-thick top and back rings the best" (Wigginton 185). For this he prefers woods like yellow poplar and red oak. Besides guitars and banjos (for both bluegrass and old-time styles), they made mandolins, violins (fiddles), Appalachian dulcimers, hammered dulcimers, autoharps, and other special instruments to order.

The Sturgills are "especially known for their custom thin-body acoustic guitars, in which the body is only half as thick as that of the dreadnought size" (Abrams 14). According to Dave, they pioneered in this "thin-body" style and showed it first at a trade show in Atlanta in 1975. Dave states that they could get the same tone and volume as larger-sized guitars, and women customers preferred this size, as did people switching over from electric guitars (ibid.).

Each Sturgill instrument is individually crafted, not mass-produced. For example, in choosing the bracing for an instrument, if a highly flexible top is desired, they use bracing made of wider-grained wood, with more flexibility; for stiffer tops, the bracing will have closer-grained wood. All bracing is hand-trimmed. Dave says, "In mass production factories, all the braces are run through a shaper and all are exactly alike. This totally disregards the flexibility of both the bracing and the top itself" (ibid.). Dave explains how they measure to find out whether they have the degree of flexibility they want. Further, during his years in Maryland with the telephone company, he used oscilloscopes to make very accurate measurements of frequencies and sound response. He carried this knowledge into his instrument making and purchased expensive precision oscillators and oscilloscopes for his shop. He adds, "This has paid off in producing the kind of sound we are looking for" (Abrams 16).

Dave has always been fascinated by the scientific, as well as the artistic, aspects of instrument making, and he wrote several articles during the 1970s for *Bluegrass Unlimited,* in which he went into great detail concerning technicalities of construction (see bibliography). In one article, "Strings and Things: The Sound of Music," he focuses particularly on the "science of sound." For example, he discusses the factors that affect the "frequency response" of a guitar top. Summarizing that section, he says, "This is where the crafts-manship of the luthier [maker of lutes, violins, and similar instru-ments] produces the results the musician is looking for" (22).

In a 1974 article for that magazine, "Strings and Things: Hand-crafted Musical Instruments," he discusses what defines a "hand-crafted" instrument, pointing out that, although craftsmen may use some electric-powered tools, the individualized approach makes the difference. He states that "the machine will make them all alike[,] disregarding the nature of the wood being worked," while the craftsman doing the same job can consider grain, density, and texture of each piece of wood, making adjustments that "bring out the best in tonal response" (14). Being both luthier and musician is what made this stage of Dave's life so rewarding to him.

Over the years, "Uncle" Dave has made hundreds of instru-ments, but probably banjos have been his favorite. In fact, one observer notes that, up in Piney Creek, "Uncle" Dave is known as "The Banjo Man" and mail has been addressed to him that way (Wall 23). In another article for *Bluegrass Unlimited,* "Banjo Tone," he explains some differences between old-time and bluegrass banjo music. In old-time music, "a different tone is desired in the first place . . . Most old-time banjo players want a deeper, more 'plunky' tone and are not usually too concerned about the volume pro-duced" (21). As for Dave himself, he likes both styles but usually competes in the old-time category, which is his special love.

During the years that Dave had the large Skyland shop, many apprentices came from all over the United States and as far away as Canada to study instrument making under him, as he had under Herman Weaver. He could teach them to make almost any instrument in the old-time and bluegrass tradition. To support themselves while allowing enough time to learn the craft in Dave's shop, they also worked at other jobs, such as harvesting tobacco or substitute teaching. They were not paid, nor did they pay tuition; further, each had to have a character reference (Corrigan). They began by making a dulcimer and a banjo from mail-order kits; then the Sturgills could observe them and see what skills they excelled at. "Next the apprentices start sanding guitars and learning the 152 steps Sturgill says it takes to make the flat-top acoustic guitars bearing the shop's 'S'" (Corrigan). Scattered about the shop were tables covered with piles of lathes, saws, wood scraps, hand tools, assembly jigs, and cut-out pieces of instruments under construction, but work often came to a standstill when visitors arrived, especially musicians like Doc Watson, who lived not too far away. During the summer months, time was (and still is) spent going to festivals and fiddlers conventions to play music and sell instruments.

Although Hurricane Hugo destroyed much of his shop in 1988, causing Dave to retire a second time, he continues to make instruments in a smaller shop in the basement of his home at Piney Creek, while his sons have moved on to other careers. However, they all still gather at fiddlers conventions, where participation in traditional music reminds everyone of the intimate connection between an artist and his or her society (Blaustein 163).

Magnetic Performer

Since returning to Alleghany County, Dave has participated to the fullest in the extensive network of fiddlers conventions in the area, received many awards, been consulted by others involved in establishing conventions, and served as judge at many of the events. Soon after Dave's return to the mountains, he formed the "Skyland String Band," which has performed at many events and also won numerous awards over the years. In the individual clawhammer banjo competition at Galax in 1986, Dave won fifth place. Furthermore, he was one of the organizers of Alleghany County's first fiddlers convention in 1995. It was such a success that the following year, in 1996, it attracted almost twice as many participants.

Most musicians would agree that, in addition to instrumental competition, a significant part of a fiddlers convention is participating in the traditional informal jam sessions held in the camping areas beyond the main stage. Here old-timers and newcomers interact and exchange playing techniques and repertoires. Year after year the same people gather, making the event an annual "homecoming."

In the parking lot on the grounds at Felts Park, Galax, Virginia, or in the park at Ashe County, North Carolina, Dave Sturgill's "RV" (recreational vehicle), which he named "The Banjo Man," is a favorite hangout for many, including his neighbors, kin, former apprentices, and just about anybody who wants to drop in. Each evening of "Galax week," for example, one can walk by Dave's spot and see folks lounging in folding chairs, telling tales and anecdotes, or picking together, with others flatfooting (dancing) on nearby boards, growing more energetic as the evening deepens into night. All this may go on until 2 or 3 A.M. each night.

At these "jam sessions" at Dave's camper, the atmosphere—the closeness of the people, intensified by their feeling for the music; even the choice of music being played—bears a fascinating resemblance to gatherings in Albemarle County, Virginia, some fifty years earlier, as described by Winston Wilkinson in "Virginia Dance Tunes":

> "Uncle Jim," as he was affectionately called, was one of our best fiddlers; the spirit and charm of his playing and the elegance and refinement of his style will never be forgotten by those who were fortunate enough to hear him. These qualities are not capable of being recorded on music-paper, but the imaginative listener will hear perhaps a reflection of them in the tunes he left behind. He not only played the fiddle, the banjo, and the pipe, but sang a great variety of ballads, folksongs, singing-games, play-party games, and folk-hymns as well. My wife and I noted down more than a hundred fiddle-tunes, songs, . . . his repertory of fiddle-tunes contained examples of every type . . . a large number of country-dance tunes, tunes like "Soldier's Joy," "Haste to the Wedding," "Speed the Plough," and "Mississippi Sawyer," tunes which have been familiar to and beloved by all classes of Virginians since the settlement of our colonies. (3)

One almost feels that it is "Uncle" Dave being described, even to the playing of his favorite "Mississippi Sawyer." Wilkinson mentions other tunes, too, that are in Dave's "stock," including "Shady Grove," which Wilkinson identifies as an American variant of an "English Morris-Dance tune, called 'London Pride'" (6); and "Fire on the Mountain," which Dave particularly likes and included on two tapes. Regarding the latter, Wilkinson claims that "'Uncle Jim's rollicking Mixolydian tune, 'Fire on the Mountains,' is almost identical with one of the Norwegian folk-dance tunes which was set by the great Norwegian composer, Edward Grieg" (9). Allusions to classical composers seem almost to have been required of writers of Wilkinson's era, who wanted to prove that at least some folk music was not "uncouth" (2). Regardless of motive, Wilkinson not only participated in the musical gatherings of Albemarle County during the 1930s and 1940s, but accurately recorded the repertoires, the contagious spirit of the gatherings, and the "handing on" of traditional musical experience—all still found today in the Upper New River Valley.

Through the years, Dave has been very aware of the Appalachian musical tradition as a "total" experience to be handed on. Thus, even though he is proud of his expertise on specific instruments, particularly the banjo, he is proudest of having won the "Best Performer" award eight times, at places including nearby Mount Airy, North Carolina; Independence (in Grayson County), Virginia; Bluefield, West Virginia; and others. This award takes all aspects of being an entertainer into account, and the role of entertainer is one that Dave has cultivated since his boyhood days, when people first started calling him "Uncle" Dave in recognition of his talent. From the Piney Creek schoolhouse stage to the New River Ranch in Maryland and back to Alleghany County, Dave always has cherished being a "performer." While some critics may claim that local awards are too "subjective," in fact the significance of such awards is that they reflect the attitudes and relationships of the people organizing the events. Thus they reflect the folk culture as a whole.

As an entertainer in an age of transition, Dave has seen a shift from the custom of playing on the front porch or in the country store for anyone who dropped by, to that of getting up on a stage in front of an audience outside one's neighborhood. Along the way, he, like others, has adopted some ideas or made some changes to enhance his appeal. He told a reporter that he once returned home from a craft show where his instruments had not sold as briskly as he wanted, and made up his mind to change his style to attract more people. He said he told his son, "I'm going to grow me a beard, get me a straw hat, and start playing in competitions and become a character" (Wall 23). He says his beard has really paid off. To a great extent, though, Dave is his own character, which he has been developing throughout his life, one that is true to his Appalachian culture. He has gone on to win not only "Best Performer," but also specialized awards that depend on talent in certain instrumental styles, such as clawhammer banjo playing, for which, as noted, he received fifth place at the Galax convention in 1986. He also has won ribbons for performances on dulcimer, fiddle, guitar, mandolin, and folk singing.

Mentor to Younger Musicians

Dave was the primary mentor to his younger friend Rick Abrams, who moved to Piney Creek, learned some banjo techniques from Dave, and later won first place in clawhammer banjo at Galax in 1987. Rick stated, "When I met him I did know how to play the banjo, but it was 'Uncle' Dave who taught me the special old-time intonation, the history, flavor, and a real respect for what I was playing" (Hawthorne 38). Rick later moved to Sacramento, California, and had a band he called the "Piney Creek Weasels" in honor of the time he spent living in North Carolina. In 1989, Rick wrote a letter nominating Dave for the Brown-Hudson Award of the North Carolina Folklore Society. In it, he stated that "Dave resists categorization," has "rare humor," and tells "mischievous tales of the mountain folk." In addition, Rick pointed to Dave's substantial achievements over the years: "The guitars Dave has made for Doc Watson . . . the 75 ribbons and trophies Dave has won in fiddlers competitions throughout the South" (Rick Abrams, nomination letter, 1989).

Most of all, though, Rick Abrams emphasized the effect of Dave's personality, noting his friendliness and openness to all people through music, which Dave believes unites them. Explaining his own background, Rick said that he was brought up far away from mountain music, in an Orthodox Jewish family in Charleston, South Carolina; but when fate first brought him to Galax, at age twenty-nine, he immediately was captivated by the old-time music and by Dave's hospitality: "He offered a chair—and in ten years that chair is still there, every year at Galax, where we pick into the night and into the days" (letter). The music became extremely special to Rick, who spoke movingly of "the indescribable exhilaration and joy inherent in the rhythmic and modal strains of the mountain music, most notably that of the five-string banjo." Rick named some of his own favorites that he learned from "Uncle" Dave, such as "Mississippi Sawyer," "Grey Cat on a Tennessee Farm," "The Eighth of January," and, of course, "Wild Goose." This last piece Rick made the "title cut" of his album, which includes Dave's "exuberant fiddling." So Rick and others have become part of Dave Sturgill's "extended family," with its annual reunion at Galax and more relaxing but still music-filled days in Piney Creek. To sum it all up, Rick stated, "But mostly what I can tell you is that Dave Sturgill loves his native North Carolina, its mountains, its history, its people, its music . . . and that he selflessly continues to pass it on" (ibid.). For Rick, as well as for thousands of others, there is that "indescribable exhilaration" every time the frailing begins!

Another younger musician to whom "Uncle" Dave has been a special mentor and friend is Dave Rainwater, also from distant California, who recently reached a pinnacle of his musical career by winning the coveted first-place award in fiddle playing at Galax in 1993. Rainwater first began playing old-time music in the Pacific Northwest, learning the repertoire on the guitar and mandolin and attending the Seattle Folklife Festival. He did not play fiddle until he was thirty, but when he did, he loved it. He moved to Sacramento in 1985 and started playing in contests. He says, "To play out west you have to play 'Texas style,'" which he did, winning many awards. However, he writes, "I was more attracted to other older and 'deeper' styles of fiddle playing," some of which he learned while in California. Dave, having been born in Pennsylvania of a family originally from Surry County, North Carolina (next to Alleghany County), was interested in the New River region, its Cherokee people, its pioneers, and its music. Through his friend Rick Abrams, he was introduced to the Galax Fiddlers Convention in Virginia and began attending. Of course, he met "Uncle" Dave. All this greatly affected his life.

The impact of this Appalachian music on Dave Rainwater is best expressed in his own words: "Rick said I should come to Galax. So I came to my first convention in 1987. I was in heaven. I could really sense the presence of real old-time fiddle and banjo. Uncle Dave Sturgill and all the Orchard Grass Band welcomed me. I knew I met some of the greatest people I could ever hope to meet. I was hearing the real heart and soul music of the mountains" (Dave Rainwater to Anderson-Green, 1994).

Although Dave Rainwater names several musicians at Galax who influenced him, including Benton Flippen, Bill Cannaday, and Wiley Mayo, the most meaningful pair continued to be Rick Abrams and "Uncle" Dave. The two "Daves" shared more than others could realize. They both claim descent from the Cherokees, who were the earliest people of the New River region. Above all, though, what unites them is love of the music being passed on for generations.

"Uncle" Dave and Rick were the ones who guided Dave Rainwater in his choice of repertoire for the Galax fiddlers' contest when he won first prize in 1993. As he tells it, each of the two separately urged him to play a certain old-time tune that is performed only rarely: "Granny Will Your Dog Bite?" First, Rick told Dave that he had had a vision in which Dave won at Galax while playing that tune. Then, after they had arrived in Virginia and were sitting with "Uncle" Dave at the campsite, according to Rainwater, "I played some tunes for Dave the night before the contest. Without knowing what Rick had said to me, after hearing me play 'Granny Will Your Dog Bite?' he told me that was the very tune I should play without a doubt." Dave Rainwater then decided to go ahead with it: "I figured the good Lord was involved. Needless to say, I was stunned Sunday morning when they called my name." He concludes by writing, "As long as the Lord enables me, I will always come to Galax." So the traditions are handed on to younger participants under the guidance of old-timers like Dave Sturgill, who have spent a lifetime cultivating both art and craft.

Handing On the Traditions

In his "spare" time, Dave Sturgill finds additional ways to educate others about his heritage. He has spent hours entertaining tourists on the Blue Ridge Parkway and students in area public schools. He has taught courses in instrument making at Wilkes Community College in Wilkesboro, North Carolina, to new generations of aspiring craftsmen. In all these ways, Dave expands his role as performer.

Although Dave has enjoyed interacting with tourists and presenting old-time Appalachian culture to the public, at times he is concerned—even disturbed—by the usual stereotypes concerning Appalachia that he encounters still circulating in American "pop culture." These usually come to his attention through comments that people make during his presentations or during his travels out of the region. As he says in a *Foxfire* interview,

> The picture that's been drawn of these mountains down through here has been wrong—so much of it— through the years. . . . When I was with Bell, I had several assignments up in New York City . . . and they would call me 'Hillbilly.' They'd get a big kick out of it. And I'd say, 'Yeah, but there's one big difference. You can take any boy out of these hills and turn him loose in New York City and he'll get by. But take one of you fellows down in the hills and turn you loose; you'd starve to death. (Wigginton 179)

Thus Dave, like Ola Belle Campbell Reed, cleverly contradicts the usual interpretation. Here he emphasizes the mountaineers' pride in self-sufficiency, an ability to live off the land and to work hard using one's intelligence. Yet the standard popular-culture view of the "hillbilly" is different. Dave adds, "But the picture most of those people had of those mountaineers was pure Little Abner. Now that's where they got it from—the comic strips" (Wigginton 179). The frustration and resentment aroused by these derogatory comic images can run deep, but usually Dave, the mountaineer, can set them aside and continue pursuing a traditional lifestyle that is deeply satisfying on a personal level. In the twentieth century, remaining in Appalachia or returning to homes there is often a very conscious choice.

Certainly Dave's son, John Sturgill, is very aware of his choice in going back to Alleghany County, North Carolina. He was born in the Washington, D.C., area, but, as he says, that was just an accident of history. He always went back to the mountains for summers, and that is what he considered home. There he heard old-time music and developed an interest in the family musical tradition. Eventually he made instruments with his father, but he did not become a musician until later. He says, "All these years of listening to these jam sessions and I wanted to join in so bad. And I've been making musical instruments for ten years before I ever learned to play one." Then one day at a fiddlers convention, John was sitting where a fellow came and set up his washtub bass, and John experienced an instant of recognition. He says, "Well there it is: I've found my instrument. I've stayed with the bass 'cause it was the first thing I ever picked up I could get a tune out of!" (Sturgill family interview by Anderson-Green).

Dave joined in the conversation at that point to emphasize John's musical ability, telling how he "graduated" from the washtub and they built him a custom bass with a "real sound." He entered competitions until, at the famous fiddlers' convention at Union Grove (North Carolina) in 1975, he won the "world championship playing bass that year, against about eighty upright bass players" (ibid.).

Some years later, in 1987, at the Galax, Virginia, fiddlers convention, a reporter from the *New Yorker* discovered Johnny and his clan of musicians, describing them with interest:

> Later, as I wandered among clusters of parked vehicles, taking in more sessions, I encountered a group of five musicians who were practicing for the old-time band contest . . . Their band was called Skyland Strings and was registered from Piney Creek, North Carolina. The leader was a white-haired guitarist called Uncle Dave Sturgill. His son Johnny, a robust, bearded young man in a fur-trimmed cowboy hat, was the group's bass player. But Johnny Sturgill's bass was a curious object. Patterned after a typical tub bass—essentially an upside-down washtub with a pole attached and with a piece of clothesline running from the top of the pole to the tub—his instrument was made mostly of intricately carved wood. "As far as I know, this is the first wooden tub bass there ever was on the circuit," Johnny Sturgill told me with evident pride . . . "I didn't like the sound people were getting out of their metal washtubs, and I do a lot of fancy carving and inlay work . . . so I made this one myself." (White 85)

John, indeed, has "evident pride" in his craftsmanship and music and is proud, too, of his children's interest in the musical traditions. Several of his family do clogging, especially a daughter, Mary Alice Sturgill, who was clogging and winning prizes for this while attending the University of North Carolina at Chapel Hill. Another grandchild of "Uncle" Dave, Dan Jr., has become well known in guitar playing circles in northern Virginia. Dan Jr., living in Alexandria, is a computer programmer who is also a musician, specializing in playing acoustic guitar in the flat-picking style still popular in that area, a bastion of old-time and bluegrass music.

A poignant moment in the Sturgill family history that clearly illuminates the family's values came when Dave's mother, at ninety-five years of age, lay dying a few years ago in the Ashe County Hospital in West Jefferson, North Carolina. All the clan then living near each other in the Ashe-Alleghany area gathered around her bedside in the hospital room on Christmas Eve and sang hymns to the accompaniment of Dave on harmonica. The hospital staff put it on their sound system so it went all over the hospital. While the mother was making her transition, preparing to "pass over," she was comforted by the words of "Will the Circle Be Unbroken?" sung by her own family, as well as by the presence of the wonderful descendants who would "hand on" the heritage. After a few more days, she requested to be removed from life support and taken home, where she passed away in her sleep three days later (David A. Sturgill to Anderson-Green, Jan. 21, 1993).

For Dave and Marie, watching their children and grandchildren become involved in the Appalachian traditions—instrument making; banjo, fiddle, or bass playing; and clogging—as well as painting watercolors, as John had done, is a great satisfaction. To Dave, creativity is one of the most important aspects of human life. While welcoming visitors into his home, he admiringly pointed to the walls covered with paintings done by John and other relatives, and spoke movingly about the way future generations will have, and treasure, the art and music we create, while having little or no awareness of how much money we earned. As Dave sums it up, what people are remembered for is art, not money.

As this chapter clearly demonstrates, many Sturgills (almost too many to count) have been known as old-time, country-western, or bluegrass musicians on a regional scale, but Dave considers each one to be significant. He spoke sorrowfully of a great loss in 1991, when Buford Sturgill, a deputy sheriff in Wilkes County, North Carolina, and his wife, Billie Jo Sturgill, both accomplished country musicians, were killed in an auto accident on their way to try out their possibilities in the Nashville music industry. They had performed on local radio stations in their home area, and people said they "were as good as Nashville could offer." Currently, in the Upper New River region, Dave's cousin, Dean Sturgill, is leader of the "Grayson Highlands String Band." Formerly it was Dave's "Skyland

Strings Band," which continues to perform under the new name at the Grayson Highlands Festival and other events in Grayson, Ashe, and Alleghany Counties. Undoubtedly influenced by "Uncle" Dave, Dean is not only a musician but also, like Dave, a raconteur, a collector of old tales and jokes; Dean even published a book of these recently (*An Old Fiddler's Book of Rhymes*).

Over the years, Dave Sturgill has been mentor, tutor, and family historian, as well as craftsman and musician, and has maintained an awareness of all this musical talent. He has written:

> The Appalachian mountains of North Carolina, Virginia, and eastern Kentucky have produced many musicians since colonial times and many of them have been Sturgills or related to the family. In recent years many people have contributed their time and talent to programs devoted to keeping this form of music alive and growing. The success of these programs is very evident when one attends any of the fiddlers conventions in the area and notes the number of children under twelve who cross the stage. (David A. Sturgill to Anderson-Green, Jan. 21, 1993)

Thus Dave feels content when thinking that the heritage is being "handed-on."

In 1987, Dave Sturgill was nominated for the Folk Heritage Fellowship of the National Endowment for the Arts (NEA). The nominating letter notes that "Dave has been indefatigable in his work as an instrument maker, as a performer in many regional fiddlers conventions . . . as a 'networker' among musicians . . . and as a culture-bearer . . . indeed representative of the best in Southern Appalachian culture and a fine person to know" (Anderson-Green to National Endowment for the Arts, Sept. 18, 1987). Although he is still not as well known on the national folk music scene as Ola Belle Reed, there is no doubt concerning Dave's contribution. In 1990, as previously noted, he was awarded the North Carolina Folklore Society's Brown-Hudson Award, which was presented in a ceremony at Duke University in Durham, North Carolina.

During all this time, Dave Sturgill has been collecting not only versions of tunes, folk tales, and family history, but also (perhaps most of all) admirers and friends. Appalachian folk culture has been the factor sustaining him, as he sums up his life interest in his own words:

> It has been twenty years now since I came back to these mountains and these have been the happiest and most rewarding years of my life. For a time I felt that I had wasted the years of my life I spent with the Telephone Company and the two years I spent in Nashville trying to save a bankrupt guitar manufacturing company. . . . Again it took a while for me to realize that none of those years had been wasted, they had been a school, they had prepared me for my real mission in life which was the preservation of our Appalachian mountain music and the art and craft of making the instruments with which to make the music. In this I do feel that I have had some measure of success and that some people will remember me when I am gone. (Sturgill family interview by Anderson-Green)

"Uncle" Dave, the tradition-bearer, truly has done much to "hand on" the Appalachian culture. Indeed, the phrase "tradition-bearer" encompasses all his varied interests—craftsmanship, performing music, writing articles on music and family history, teaching and networking extensively as a researcher and as a mentor. For all this he will be remembered, as will the many other Sturgill musicians. ❖

Continuity of the Tradition: Wayne Henderson, Gerald Anderson, and the Next Generation of New River Musicians

Albert Hash's love of the old-time tradition in music was a feeling not only for the pleasure of the moment, but also, as we have seen, a commitment based on the realization that this "handed- on" music transmits cultural values, bonds of kinship and community, and indeed an aesthetic awareness that can rise to a spiritual level.

This deeply ingrained conviction is what made Albert so intense and effective in his role as a mentor of younger musicians and craftsmen, both male and female.

What is found today, early in the twenty-first century, of the traditional music and the traditional life that were loved by Albert Hash, Ola Belle Campbell Reed, "Uncle" Dave Sturgill, and many others?[1]

Wayne Henderson

If a person ventures off the interstate highways (either I-81 or I-77) and drives many miles over winding back roads, finally reaching the banks of the New River near the Virginia-Carolina line, then that musical pilgrim will be approaching the music shop of Wayne Henderson and Gerald Anderson. The shop stands not far from the base of Mount Rogers, near Albert Hash's old home on Cabin Creek in the Whitetop Mountain section. The shop's mailing address is "Mouth of Wilson, Virginia" (Wilson Creek is nearby), but the local area is called "Rugby" and officially forms part of Virginia. When asked about Wayne, anyone around usually will direct a visitor's attention first to his old shop, which is merely a long, nondescript, one-story building without much "signage." It is no longer used, but it contains a wealth of memories. However, Wayne and his partner Gerald are very comfortable in the new shop they built recently right next to Wayne's home.

These two craftsmen and musicians are outstanding among many who were apprentices or followers of the great Albert Hash. They are the younger generation still living in, partaking of, and passing on Appalachian culture—not only music but the culture's entirety. Through days and nights, on front porches and river banks, in country stores and churches, the traditional music—call it old-time or bluegrass or country—still goes on. Teenagers are still forming bands like the old "River Rats." Wayne and Gerald, both now middle-aged, form the nucleus of an old-time band that keeps on going, and both are craftsmen in the Hash tradition.

Wayne was raised in Rugby and thus is practically a native Virginian, although he was born across the line in North Carolina because that was the location of the nearest hospital. He was the son of Walter Byrom Henderson and Sylvia Reedy Henderson. In a letter to the National Endowment for the Arts (NEA), Joseph T. Wilson wrote, "Wayne comes from a family of craftspeople, folks with little cash income who live far up a dirt road in one of the most remote areas of the Blue Ridge Mountains" (Wilson to NEA, Sept. 26, 1986). His family has lived in the area for generations, having come to the New World from Scotland. Wayne is proud to note that there is a kilt pattern for the Henderson clan (Wayne Henderson interview by Anderson-Green, Aug. 4, 1994).

Wayne's mother Sylvia was a Reedy, a family well known in this section, and through his grandmothers he connects to the Hall

Gerald Anderson, *left,* and Wayne Henderson, *right,* at their shop in Rugby, Virginia, 1996.
Photograph by Rhett Turner. Used by permission.

and Davis families. He and Gerald have a familial connection: their great-great-grandmothers were the Sexton sisters. One married a Henderson, and the other married a Shelton, whose daughter married an Anderson. As we have noted, such ties probably exist throughout the population. As W. J. Cash pointed out, such close kinship ties were typical in the agricultural South before World War II (Cash 27–29). In the region of the Upper New River, it is still true today that most people are "distant kin" and know it. Although Wayne and Gerald laughingly try to deny it if anyone brings it up, their bond is solidified by the cousin connection.

Wayne's father, Walter Henderson, was a fiddler, and local musicians would gather at his house. When Wayne was five, he learned three chords on the guitar and could play "Little Brown Jug." Then frequently his father would get the fiddle out, "almost any time I wanted to," says Wayne, and they would play together. Eventually they were going to the Galax Fiddlers Convention on an annual basis, although Wayne says it was quite a few years before he "got up the nerve" to play on-stage (interview by Anderson-Green).

Among the musicians who performed with Walter Henderson in a string band was Estil (E. C.) Ball, a neighbor at Rugby who played on radio stations for years and later was recorded by John Lomax and Alan Lomax. He was a person of great influence with young Wayne. According to Wilson, Wayne as a youngster greatly admired the flat-picking style of guitar playing, as done by Doc Watson of North Carolina. However, the advice he got from Estil was: "Never fool with a flat pick, son" (Wilson, "Notes" [for audio-tape "Wayne C. Henderson and Company"]). Wilson continues, "So Wayne learned to execute what sounds like flatpicking while actually fingerpicking. . . . This unusual technique is the secret of Wayne's elegant phrasing, his clean lines, and his amazingly good sense of timing . . . There's an inherent drive in this way of playing. Also timing may be easier to maintain once the basics of the style are learned" (Wilson, "Notes"). Thus Wayne learned to become an expert guitar player in a very old-time way.

When he was older, Wayne says, he admired a nice steel-string Martin guitar in E. C. Ball's store in Rugby, but of course he couldn't afford it (Henderson interview by Anderson-Green). Ball, as a mentor and friend, let Wayne draw patterns around the guitar; then Wayne, who already was used to making such things as sling shots, toys, and wagons, decided to make his own guitar, like the Martin. He took a dresser drawer bottom which had walnut veneer that could bend, and laid it in a branch (creek) overnight to get it wet enough to bend. He was disappointed when it wouldn't bend but left it longer. When he came back, he found that the veneer had come loose. He then proceeded to make a guitar out of it, using black sticky glue; he said it was "a mess but it worked" (ibid.). He was proud of being a craftsman, a tradition that ran deep in his family. He once told a reporter laughingly, "My grandfather was a coffin-maker, and, well, coffins and instruments are both boxes!" (Fant A2).

In a short while, however, his first guitar came unglued and fell apart. Finally he told his dad. Then his father said, "I'll take you over to see Albert Hash at Lansing (twelve to fourteen miles away), and he can show you how to do it" (Henderson interview by Anderson-Green). At that time, Albert was working for Sprague making clocks and not spending much time on instruments, but he was known for his ability in constructing them. Albert told Wayne that the glue was the problem and that he should get some white glue at the hardware store. Albert said, "That will hold it till the cows come home." He also told him how to bend the wood. Wayne, who was fourteen or fifteen at the time, was willing to spend more time and effort on his guitar, so he followed this advice. It took him a year and a half to finish it, but he was intrigued by the process (ibid.).

From then on, Wayne was committed to the craft of making instruments. Further, he knew that Albert would be his mentor and that he could develop a high level of expertise like Albert's. Wayne always worked in his own shop, but for a long time every instrument he made he took to Albert, for his inspection. This was his apprenticeship. During this time, Albert Hash really got back into making fiddles again as a major endeavor. Wayne says that nobody knows exactly how many Albert made, but his favorite was one he made in 1953. Albert's and Wayne's preferred wood for fiddles was maple and red spruce from local sources. According to Wilson, they "were the first luthiers to use the red spruce that grows at the upper elevations (above 4,000 feet) along the Blue Ridge for instrument tops" (Wilson to NEA, 1986). He adds that some were shocked by this, but "a better sound is claimed." However, making the guitar called for something else. Wayne recalls that Albert gave him a catalog to order from, noting that the preference in guitars was Brazilian rosewood for the body and mahogany for the neck (Henderson interview by Anderson-Green). When Wayne made his second instrument, following Albert's advice, a customer came along and wanted to buy it. That set Wayne on his craft career, specializing in guitars (Hauslohner, "Henderson Hand-crafted Guitars" 35).

Although Wayne has been making guitars since he was a teenager and always has had a place to work in at home, around 1972 he opened the old shop he had in Rugby, "The Henderson Guitar Shop." It was in a "dilapidated country store building" behind the rescue squad's home base, a store that was "abandoned in the '60s . . . a ramshackle, shingled structure . . . with a dark interior" (ibid. 34). Although this location did not have an "upscale" appearance, the atmosphere was charged with a feeling of creativity and often with the sound of music. Finally, after several years of going back and forth to Nashville, doing some work there and then making some instruments at home, Wayne had a place in which he could do all his work.

Wayne spends two to three weeks crafting a guitar, which usually sells for between $600 and $1,500. There is a backlog of orders that will take about two years to build, with Wayne working on the "squeaky wheel system of priorities" (ibid. 36). He starts each day by driving his route for the United States Postal Service, but after that, until late at night, his time is devoted to his first love, instrument making. Wilson also points out that "famous players own and prize his instruments, but Wayne does not bandy their names about or advertise in any way. His problem is not one of too few customers, but rather of too many. Once there was a two-year waiting period for a Henderson instrument, but it has lengthened" (Wilson, "Notes"). Instruments made by both Wayne and Gerald were featured in an exhibition organized by the National Council for Traditional Arts in 1994. As it toured nationally, a wider audience became aware of their craftsmanship.

While young Wayne was refining his abilities and techniques as a craftsman, he was also developing confidence as a performer. Eventually he and his brother, Max Henderson, and a friend, Boyd Spencer, started a band and secured a spot on a radio show. They called their group the "Virginia-Carolina Boys" and even talked Albert Hash into playing fiddle with them. As we have seen, for Albert, this opportunity was a major turning point that revived his belief in the existence of an audience for old-time traditional music. All the material submitted nominating Albert for the NEA's National Heritage Fellowship cites Wayne as the main person who encouraged Albert to perform in public again. The "Virginia-Carolina Boys" played on WKSK in West Jefferson every Saturday morning for eight years, and the group also got jobs playing music locally. Everyone around there went to Jefferson to shop and listened to that radio show, so the group had much local exposure.

One of the early inspirations for Wayne Henderson to perform in public was a one-time revival of the famous White Top Festival in 1967; though it was held on the Fourth of July, that weekend turned out to be very cold. Wayne decided to enter the competition, however. He played guitar and won third place. The festival itself was a "flop," according to Wayne, because of the bad weather and also because a bunch of "rowdies" dominated the scene (Henderson interview by Anderson-Green). Still, Wayne felt encouraged, seeing the event as a turning point on his life path in music.

The following year, 1968, after many years of attending with his father, Wayne finally entered the competition at the Galax Fiddlers Convention. He didn't win there the first two times he entered, but finally he did get a third place in guitar. Then, at age twenty-three, he won first place for the first time; since then, he has won first place twelve times. Since boyhood, Wayne always has enjoyed the "Galax scene"—the jamming, the camaraderie (he says there are "less rowdies now"), and of course the wonderful music. However, he never has camped out there, saying he "couldn't sleep in a tent." He stayed in a van a few times but prefers coming from home each day. It is only a forty-five-minute drive from Rugby over to Galax (Henderson interview by Anderson-Green).

When asked about his favorite songs, Wayne says that he likes all the Carter family tunes—usually the first songs musicians in his area learn—especially "Wildwood Flower." Like others, he learned many songs from listening to old Victrola records, remembering with fondness "Keep On the Sunny Side" and "You Are My Flower." Also he remembers and still enjoys his father's favorites, "Arkansas Traveler" and "Ragtime Annie." Wayne's emphasis is on old-time music, but he can enjoy a mix of styles. As Joe Wilson notes about Wayne and his musical buddies, "They play in a variety of styles. A hot piano is as welcome as a banjo or fiddle in the Henderson Company, and while old-time and bluegrass are the usual musics, swing, blues and classic country are equally appreciated. Old ballads and folk songs are much loved, but so are good honky-tonk songs" (Wilson, "Notes"). The Henderson Guitar Shop has become quite the place for local players to drop by for a jam session.

As he thinks about how traditional music evolves while staying within a tradition, Wayne comments particularly on the role of the guitarist. Traditionally, he says, the guitarist's job was to "back up" the fiddler. In the 1960s, however, musicians all were beginning to spend time picking out tunes on the guitar. During these years, Wayne spent more time developing his own style of guitar playing (Henderson interview by Anderson-Green). Although basically he stays with the old-time finger-picking style advocated by his mentor, E. C. Ball, he does allow for some variety in performances. As Wayne's neighbor, Debby Clark, pointed out in an article for the local newspaper, proudly saluting Wayne, the local man is a "genius who is also just a good old boy, but definitely a genius in music" (Clark).

Another guitar-playing style Wayne uses is called "pinch-picking." It is a "modified picking style with a thumb-pick and two finger-picks, like a banjo player" (ibid.). According to Clark, it's a method that is rarely used except in the Rugby area of the Whitetop section. Thus Wayne is versatile and creative within his Appalachian tradition, just as Ola Belle and other great musicians have always been.

For a while Wayne and Gerald, along with friends Butch Barker and Greg Cornett, played in a band called the "Rugby Gully Jumpers," named after a band Wayne's father played in (Hauslohner, "Henderson Hand-crafted Guitars" 36). This younger group performed music traditional to the area, combining bluegrass, old-time, and gospel in a "Doc Watson–type repertoire." Both Wayne and Gerald employed a finger-picking, instead of a flat-picking, style (ibid. 36). They even played at the 1982 World's Fair in Knoxville.

Wayne's current band is called "Wayne Henderson and Friends," consisting of the following: Wayne on guitar, Gerald Anderson on mandolin, Helen White on fiddle, Herb Key on bass, and Tim Lewis on banjo. All live in the area and have been playing together for several years. Herb was born in Wilkes County,

North Carolina, but his grandfather was born in and lived in Alleghany County and played banjo, along with relatives on guitar and fiddle. Helen came from the Pacific Northwest, as have some others who were attracted to the Whitetop area for its music. In 1994, the group performed at Laurel Bloomery, near Mountain City, Tennessee, the nation's oldest fiddlers convention for old-time music only, celebrating its seventy-ninth convention. Wayne won first place on guitar, Gerald won second on guitar, and Helen White won first place on fiddle.

After all his years winning first place at outstanding fiddlers conventions like Galax, Wayne Henderson has gained enough recognition to be invited to major national events and to go on world tours. In 1982, he went on a tour featuring musicians and their hand-crafted instruments, performing in seven nations of Asia. He also toured Africa and Sri Lanka in 1996. Every year he takes part in the Seattle Folk Festival, the Cumberland Folk Festival, and others, and he has performed at the Smithsonian Institution in Washington, D.C., and at Carnegie Hall in New York City.

At the Carnegie Hall concert on December 15, 1990, Wayne performed in a program called "Guitar Wizards," part of a series entitled "Folk Masters: Traditional Music in the Americas." Wayne, accompanied by Randy Greer of Crumpler, North Carolina, on mandolin and guitar, captured the crowd from the opening moment. As a reporter stated, "The duo opened with a version of 'Leather Britches' that could have served as the grand finale . . . Judging by the toe-tapping and smiles that accompanied his music and the wild applause that followed each piece, Henderson could have easily entertained the audience all night" (Fant). At the concert's conclusion, Wayne, Randy, and others joined a famous black blues guitarist, John Jackson of Fairfax, Virginia, for a "merging of musical styles" in the spiritual "We Shall Not Be Moved." This scene recalls Ola Belle Campbell Reed's stories of her family's jamming with a black group, "Little Wonders," on the porch of the country store in Lansing, North Carolina.

In 1994, instruments made by both Wayne Henderson and Gerald Anderson were included in an exhibition organized by the

National Council for Traditional Arts and displayed at museums around the nation, such as the Hunter Museum of Art in Chattanooga, Tennessee. The exhibition program states:

> Nowadays Wayne in turn inspires a generation of younger luthiers. He turns out about twenty instruments a year, mainly guitars, though he is almost as well known for versions of the Lloyd Loar F-5 mandolin he produced in the 1970s and early 1980s. He produces some elaborately decorated instruments, but is most respected for the volume, tone, and resonance of his guitars. He figures that ease of playing is important, too. (Wilson, *Dixie Frets*)

Wayne is also included in the *Directory of Contemporary American Musical Instrument Makers,* which cites his construction of steel-string guitars, mandolins, and banjos (Farrell 60).

In the fall of 1995, Wayne received the ultimate recognition for both his craftsmanship and performances, being invited to the White House to receive the NEA's National Heritage Fellowship, along with other winners from around the nation. Thus Wayne indeed is following in the footsteps of his mentor, Albert Hash, who was nominated for this NEA award shortly before his untimely death. Wayne's achievement is solid evidence that the traditional music culture of the Upper New River area still flourishes.

Despite his multiple awards, Wayne, while appreciative, remains modest, "low key," and does not seek attention like most popular culture stars. In this he is like others in the old-time Appalachian tradition, whose reserve undoubtedly is based upon an awareness that each is part of a "handed-on" tradition, that it isn't just he who is significant, that each is part of the great chain of being.

Wayne is devoted not only to his music and craft, but also to his family, checking each day on his widowed mother, Sylvia, who used to live near the shop and now lives in his new home. Wayne's only child is a young daughter named Jayne; his face shows pride when she comes out to dance the "flatfoot" to guitar and fiddle music. Although divorced, Wayne is an active parent.

Most often Wayne can be found with his close circle of friends—Helen, Gerald, Herb, and others—at jam sessions. A favorite was the one held every Tuesday night at Blanche Ward Nichols's home on the edge of Buck Mountain. Her family, the Wards, were famous in old-time music. These things—music, crafts (i.e., meaningful work), friends, kin, and faith—are parts of the whole that keep Appalachian culture vital.

Gerald Anderson

Gerald Anderson, too, is part of this way of life. A craftsman in instrument making, he entered Wayne's shop over twenty years ago, in the fall of 1976. He and Wayne are not linked in any formal way; each has his own space and his own customers. This old-time business arrangement has worked well for them. Gerald lives nearby in an attractive A-frame house which he himself built a few years ago atop a high hill above his parents' home. From the deck of his home, he can overlook the highway below leading to the village of Troutdale, Virginia, and also see the Blue Ridge Mountains surrounding his spot, long known as Anderson Hill. His extended family lived all over the hill, leading local people to adopt this name for the neighborhood.

When Gerald was a boy, his grandfather lived across the meadow on this hill, and an uncle and great-uncle were across the highway. In fact, Gerald started playing guitar with that great-uncle. His great-aunt, Zenna Anderson Richmond, lived on the same hill as his parents. He has a fond memory of a jam session at Aunt Zenna's a few years ago, with himself on guitar, Uncle Ray on fiddle, and his cousin, Debbie Tillson Clark, on autoharp. Debbie's mother taped the session, so they were able to preserve the sound as well as the memory.

Gerald was born in his parents' house in 1953 and spent his whole childhood there, except for his fifth year, when his father's job took the family to Manassas, Virginia. After that they returned to their beloved place to stay. Gerald's father and an uncle did construction work on roads; his grandfather, Nathan Fields Anderson, was deputy sheriff for the county (Grayson) and also had a woodworking shop, where he mainly made furniture. Gerald observed and learned craft techniques by watching his grandfather at work. Later the grandfather left his tools to Gerald and his brother Stephen Anderson (Gerald Anderson interview by Anderson-Green, Aug. 2, 1994).

Although Gerald's parents did not play instruments, he was surrounded by relatives who did and was influenced especially by his great-uncle Ray, Nathan's brother, who was both a musician and an artist. He played old-time fiddle in a style like that of Albert Hash. In fact, he and Albert, who were about the same age, often played dances together on the local circuit, such as at the nearby Mill Creek schoolhouse and in people's homes. Gerald laughingly says that they had to walk too far to go anywhere else, so they just pushed back the furniture and held their dances in homes or schools. Gerald played some with his uncle, starting out on guitar, still his main instrument; but he "never did much with it" until he went away to college (Gerald Anderson interview by Anderson-Green).

Also, Gerald knew Wayne Henderson, whom he considers his main influence in music, when he was a boy. They went to school together. Wayne is a little older, so he was in high school when Gerald was in elementary school, but both schools were united under the same name, "Virginia-Carolina," and were in the same location, sitting side by side on the state line at Grassy Creek. According to Gerald, the dividing line between states didn't mean much to people around there, who see the area as one continuous community, with family members on both sides of the line. Virginia-Carolina School burned down after Wayne graduated, when Gerald was halfway through the seventh grade, so Gerald transferred to the Flatridge School, located farther over in Grayson County, to finish the year. Then he attended high school in Independence, Virginia, the Grayson County seat. Although he attended fiddlers conventions, Gerald didn't play the guitar much in high school and wasn't in a band, but he took part in other high school activities.

Then, when Gerald was eighteen, he went off to Emory and Henry College in a nearby part of southwestern Virginia. There he began to "get more into music" again. When he was a college student, during the years 1972–76, he says, the music of Doc Watson was really attracting the attention of students; and bands like the Nitty Gritty Dirt Band were becoming very popular (Gerald Anderson interview by Anderson-Green). Of other students who came from different areas, he recalls, "They would notice things about this area that I never noticed . . . the land, the music . . . they got me interested in things I had taken for granted" (ibid.). Thus the fact that he went to a good liberal arts college in his own region gave him an opportunity to grow and blossom in his traditions, deepening his appreciation for Appalachian life, creativity, and culture.

So Gerald was about twenty when he started playing guitar more seriously, and he still saw Wayne Henderson occasionally at fiddlers conventions. Then, by chance, one summer Gerald worked for a while in Abingdon, Virginia, at the State Water Control Board. Wayne's wife at that time was working there, too, and through her his friendship with Wayne was renewed. After Gerald finished college, earning a bachelor of arts degree in anthropology and sociology, he only got a summer job. After that, he started spending time at Wayne's shop at Rugby, near Gerald's home, watching and learning instrument repair techniques. Having some background in crafts, he now became quite fascinated with instrument making.

Above all, though, what attracted him the most was Wayne's music. As he tells it, "I was real excited about learning how to make them [instruments] but probably initially what attracted me was the music itself and Wayne's guitar playing" (Gerald Anderson interview by Anderson-Green). Music now was becoming a major interest in Gerald's life, and he felt fortunate to join up with Wayne, a person so talented in guitar, always Gerald's favorite instrument. Even though he had gotten an early start watching his grandfather's woodworking and his great-uncle Ray's artistic construction of miniature log cabins and villages, as well as hearing Ray's fiddle playing, Gerald insists that "most of what I learned was from Wayne, and he learned from Albert Hash and Doc Watson." So Gerald eventually joined Wayne in a full-time career of making music and instruments (while driving a mail route to help make ends meet).

After a winter of watching, learning, and doing instrument repair, Gerald set out to make his first guitar the next summer, in July 1977. He acknowledges that "Wayne helped me a whole lot." He says the guitar was shaped like a D28 Martin, made out of rosewood with a mahogany neck and spruce top. Gerald completed it and used it for a few years. Then, in 1980, Wayne made him the guitar which he has used ever since, also a D28 of Brazilian rosewood with a top of Appalachian spruce. With this Henderson guitar, Gerald has won many prizes at fiddlers conventions throughout the region.

Both Gerald and Wayne point out that most of the wood used for guitar bodies now is imported rosewood, but sometimes some local walnut is used. Gerald, however, now specializes in making mandolins, mostly using local curly maple and spruce. Gerald loves doing this intense handcrafting and says it can take him about two hundred hours to make one of the best F-style mandolins. One of these recently was displayed in the 1994 traveling exhibit sponsored by the National Council for the Traditional Arts (NCTA).

Dixie Frets, the catalogue for that NCTA show, emphasizes that Gerald and Wayne do individual work: "Every instrument is an individual effort but thoughtfully appraised and judiciously criticized from the other side of the shop. No one admires Anderson's work more than Henderson, and he always shows a visitor Gerald's latest creation before he shows his own." Thus Wayne and Gerald preserve the Appalachian sense of independence while maintaining the best of friendships in the shop.

Since Gerald has shifted his crafting efforts from the guitar to the mandolin, he likes to tell the history of the mandolin, which he says came into prominence during the 1920s. Before the days of Bill

Monroe, according to Gerald, there were old-time mandolin orchestras, and these included mandolins of different sizes. However, when Monroe came along, he popularized the F-style mandolin. Generally it would take Gerald about one hundred hours to make an F-style mandolin, while a plain guitar takes only about fifty hours to make. There is also another style of mandolin, pear-shaped, A-style, not as much in demand. Gerald is a highly experienced mandolin player, and, when playing in Wayne's band, that is the instrument he performs on, since Wayne is on guitar and there is a need for mandolin. Even so, Gerald considers the guitar his instrument of choice (Gerald Anderson interview by Anderson-Green).

Keeping Old-Time Music Alive

While discussing the history of Appalachian music or demonstrating the techniques of instrument making, Gerald and Wayne frequently are interrupted by phone calls or people coming in to look, make requests, or buy instruments. One teenage boy came in with his grandparents, bringing his guitar for repair. He watched Gerald's explanation of what was needed with great attention and left the guitar, knowing it was in good hands. The grandparents seemed very proud that the boy was involved in this transaction. The incident seemed to illustrate Gerald's earlier comment, "Right around here is a hot-bed for musicians" (Gerald Anderson interview by Anderson-Green). Further, it is obvious that both Wayne and Gerald now are playing Albert Hash's role: inspiring the next generation, encouraging an ongoing local interest in old-time and bluegrass music.

When asked what repertoire people here want played at their dances and shows, Gerald says, "Older tunes, traditional fiddle tunes, and older gospel tunes" (Gerald Anderson interview by Anderson-Green). The standard old-time repertoire still around includes titles such as "Billy in the Lowground," "Cherokee Shuffle," "Sally Goodin," and "Soldier's Joy." Also Gerald mentions "Liberty," one of the first tunes he learned on guitar, and two others which he did as solo instrumentals on a tape: "Leather Britches" and "Forked

Deer." He also likes, and included on the same tape, "I'll Get Over You," which was recorded by Crystal Gale, but which Gerald learned from its writer, Richard Lee, in Nashville. Overall, Gerald says, the preference here is still for old-time and bluegrass music.

In 1994, a typical summer for Gerald and Wayne included playing at some fiddlers conventions, particularly Galax; festivals such as Rocky Gap in Maryland; and the Blue Ridge Institute Festival and Craft Show at Ferrum College. Interspersed with all that, they played at some local spots, such as the Troutdale Fire House for dances on Saturday nights and the Osborne Store near Rugby, location of a live remote radio show on some Wednesday nights. On those Wednesday evenings, people came from their homes all around Rugby and Whitetop, bringing chairs to sit outside if the weather was good or, if not, placing the chairs in the aisles of the grocery store in order to sit and listen to the band up front by the counter. As the spirit moved them, people got up to dance the flat-foot or two-step.

Tunes that Gerald likes to play at such events include "Eight More Miles to Louisville," an old Grandpa Jones favorite on the Grand Ole Opry; "My Window Faces South," which he calls Texas swing; and old-time standards, such as "Sally Ann." The shows wrap up with some gospel songs, which Gerald knows well from boyhood days; his family attended—and still does—at the Troutdale Baptist Church. He likes such songs as "He Leadeth Me," "Little White Church," and "Going Home," the latter making a good ending song.

Although Gerald went off to college and worked for a while in Abingdon, Virginia, over in the Valley of Virginia, neither he nor Wayne would ever consider living anywhere else now. They are rooted in their home place, surrounded by an extended network of kin and friends, as well as by the mountains they love. They are satisfied in this "hot-bed for musicians." To support their needs fully, both work for the United States Postal Service as mail carriers; each working day, they zip around the mountain roads stuffing mailboxes. When finished with the routes, by late afternoon, they arrive at the music shop in Rugby to commence working on instruments.

Wayne began his postal career in September 1969 as a substitute carrier and has advanced to senior status in the system. When important performance dates come up in distant locations, such as Wayne's participation in the Seattle Folk Festival or his performance at Carnegie Hall, vacation days can be obtained or substitutes used. Both musicians do excellent work on their postal jobs, and Wayne has been awarded a pin for "devoted service" in twenty-five years in his job (*Galax Gazette,* Oct. 1994). But, like "Uncle" Dave, these two musicians know that what is important is "art, not money," and that music is what they will be remembered for.

Johnny Miller

Among the seniors in this "hot-bed of musicians" who are in constant touch with the younger generation is that old friend and colleague of Ola Belle Campbell Reed, Johnny Miller. Like "Uncle" Dave, he came back from Maryland to live in his native area, settling at Volney, Virginia, near Mouth of Wilson, Rugby, and his hometown of Lansing, North Carolina. As Thornton and Emily Spencer describe him in a newsletter of the Blue Ridge Music Association, he is a "musician's musician" and "will play with musicians on any level, from rank beginners to the most accomplished." In this way, area youngsters are encouraged to pursue the old-time and bluegrass traditions.

The younger ones like to hear Johnny Miller's stories about his early years learning fiddle, banjo, and guitar from his father and others in the "North Carolina Ridge Runners" band. Johnny was only five years old when he started playing guitar. Visitors also want many tales about his life in the tri-state area with the Ridge Runners and with Ola Belle and her brother Alex Campbell at the New River Ranch, in those tumultuous years of the 1930s through the 1950s, when outmigration for jobs took thousands "up East," carrying their music along with them.

Johnny's whole family consisted of musicians, and all of them liked nicknames: his cousin, Lester Miller, was "Slick"; his brother Arthur was "Sonny"; and he was "Skeeter." After the Ridge

Runners disbanded, the younger Millers got into many acts through their connection to Ola and Alex, playing at parks, fairs, carnivals, and festivals throughout Maryland, Delaware, and New Jersey from about 1945 through the 1960s. Johnny says they had to change styles only "a little bit," playing a mix of bluegrass, old-time, and western swing, all of which appealed to audiences who wanted southern music (Johnny Miller interview by Anderson-Green). He says that, while they never stayed anywhere very long, they often played in Wheeling, West Virginia, on the radio and even played backup for Ola and Alex at several recording sessions.

In those days, Johnny also worked as a backup musician for country music stars he met. His first job was playing electric lead guitar with Ernest Tubb in 1948. Later he also played with Ray Price, Webb Pierce, Mac Wiseman, and Loretta Lynn. He even went to Nashville sometimes, where he played for a time with Don Reno and Bill Monroe and Charlie Monroe. Johnny adds that he actually played with Charlie "quite a lot." Johnny Miller's career in the tri-state area lasted well over two decades, during a significant era for old-time and bluegrass music.

Finally, after coming "back home," Johnny fiddled for the "High Country Ramblers" for many years, a group that has included Wayne Henderson, Paul Gentle, Herb Key, Larry Pennington, and Raymond Pennington (Thornton Spencer and Emily Spencer, BRMA newsletter). Johnny also was in a band that played in Abingdon, Virginia, every weekend. He often serves as a judge at local fiddlers conventions. Back at home, he welcomes anyone interested in the music and, in the old-time way, will often open his home to those needing a place to stay. Thus he creates opportunities to "pass on" his musical heritage (Johnny Miller interview by Anderson-Green).

Another significant old-timer in this music world is Enoch Rutherford, born in 1916 and still living in the Grayson County section, west of Independence, Virginia. Enoch has been recognized with many awards as one of the finest old-time clawhammer banjo players, often winning first place at the Elk Creek Fiddlers Convention and at Galax. Younger musicians gathered around him, eager to learn his techniques. He also led "Enoch and the Gold Hill Band," which won eighth place in Galax in the "old-time" band competition in 1994. Although in his later years he is not able to play as well, due to arthritis, he still attends the fiddlers conventions and has been seen in recent years at Elk Creek with his son and grandson, both musicians. Enoch's son Harvey— named for his grandfather, Harvey Anderson, of the Grubbs Chapel area—played guitar for years; and now his son, Allen Paul Rutherford, a teenager, plays both guitar and mandolin with increasing skill. As the three wandered among the jam sessions at Elk Creek, they obviously were enjoying to the fullest the musical atmosphere and the intergenerational fellowship.

Carrying On the Tradition

Among those of the current generation now carrying on the musical tradition is Albert Hash's daughter, Audrey Hash Hamm, who still maintains Albert's music shop in her widowed mother's home by Cabin Creek. Audrey comes to the music not only through her father, but also through her mother's family, the Spencers, who had the "Trading Post" at Cabin Creek, a main gathering place for musicians earlier in the century (see chap. 3). As we have seen, Audrey's specialty is making dulcimers, and she plays dulcimer occasionally for certain events. For over a decade, Audrey worked at the Mount Rogers School, where she and her father established a band for students to play in. Unlike most high schools in the United States, which feature marching bands for football games, this one encourages young people to carry on their Appalachian music in the string band tradition. After her father's death, Audrey continued to work with the students. They sold tapes for trips and scholarships, and one year she went with them to perform at Cypress Gardens in Florida. Audrey eventually turned this effort over to her relatives, Thornton and Emily Spencer, and the program is still running strong. Audrey has curtailed her work somewhat and now only performs once a year, at Ferrum College's Blue Ridge Festival.

The next generation. Thornton Spencer and fiddle with daughter, Martha Spencer, playing banjo at home, 1997. Photograph by Rhett Turner. Used by permission.

Thornton and Emily Spencer teach classes at the Whitetop Fire Hall, as well as at Mount Rogers School. As a young boy, Thornton learned most about music from Albert Hash, his much older brother-in-law. As Thornton tells it, "I was seven or eight when they [Ethel Spencer and Albert Hash] married . . . and nine when they gave me a guitar" (Emily Spencer, Thornton Spencer, and Dean Sturgill interview by Anderson-Green, Aug. 19, 1994). In fact, Thornton practically grew up in their home; he says, "I stayed at his house a whole lot" during his boyhood. Although he learned guitar, of course, he also paid attention to the fiddle. One day, when Albert saw Thornton looking at one, he showed him how to play two tunes, "Chicken Reel" and "Ragtime Annie." At that time, Albert was leaving on a trip to Appomattox to see his brother. He said to young Thornton, "If you learn these tunes by the time I'm back, I'll give you this fiddle" (ibid.). Thornton took him up on that and eventually went far beyond those two tunes!

Thornton also learned some music from his cousin, Dean Sturgill, whose father played "a little" fiddle. Both Dean and Thornton are related through their mothers, who were sisters with the surname of Spencer (Thornton is a Spencer on both sides of his family). As they talked together in an interview, they got into a lengthy and typically "mountain" conversation about cousins, trying to untangle some connections. They agreed that the Spencers settled early in the pioneer days on Grassy Creek near the state line, but it is unclear on which side, as the line was argued over and resurveyed many times. According to local genealogists, the first Spencer to come to New River was probably Isaac, born in East Haddam, Connecticut, in 1770; but it is definite that at least three of his sons homesteaded in the Grassy Creek area. These were Solomon, who married Nellie Hash; Isaac, who married Phebe Anderson; and William, who married Rebecca Graybeal. There possibly was another son, too (Spencer file, Grayson County Historical Society). In their lengthy conversation about family history, Thornton and Dean agreed that they had heard it said that the Spencers came from England, and they jokingly claimed to be kin to Princess Diana (Emily Spencer, Thornton Spencer, and Dean Sturgill interview by Anderson-Green). This was prior to her tragic death.

The pair also talked at length about their cousin Ola Belle Campbell Reed. Thornton's mother was a first cousin of Ola's mother, making him and Ola second cousins. Most of all, they remembered music played in the home of Ola's uncle, Miles Osborne, who lived nearby with his family. Thornton picked guitar with them and likes to recall how Miles would play banjo and "tell tales every night." Dean and Thornton recall when Ola used to come up to the Miles's house and also to her grandfather Osborne's place and play both guitar and banjo. Her grandparents' house was just down the road from Ethel and Albert's home, and often Thornton would be there. He remembers picking guitar when Ola's husband, Bud Reed, was playing harmonica at a really

Thornton Spencer playing electric fiddle at home, near Haw Orchard, Virginia, 1997.
Photograph by Rhett Turner. Used by permission.

fast pace, and how hard he had to play that guitar to keep up! Although they didn't see Ola and Bud as much later on, when their trips from Maryland became less frequent, they maintained a feeling of closeness through stories passed along in the family network (Emily Spencer, Thornton Spencer, and Dean Sturgill interview by Anderson-Green).

When asked about their favorite tunes, Thornton says, "Anything I played was a favorite!" Dean refers to one "that no-one plays anymore, 'Little Brown Hand.'" Albert used to play this a lot, and it was the first tune Dean heard him play. Dean learned more fiddle playing from Albert than from his own father, who knew how to play fiddle but "didn't like what often went with it" (i.e., the party scene). Since Dean's father was a preacher, he kept his own music limited to a little at home. Dean says, "Dad would be off preaching and me and Mom would listen to the Grand Ole Opry." They also liked hearing Ola Belle Reed and Alex Campbell play over station WWVA from Wheeling, West Virginia (Emily Spencer, Thornton Spencer, and Dean Sturgill interview by Anderson-Green).

Thornton recalls that Albert was noted for his smooth fiddling and his craftsmanship. Because "people came from miles around to bring instruments for him to repair," Thornton as a boy got to meet nearly every musician in the area. Dean, too, recalls how the house was full of "people from everywhere, especially on weekends." He emphasizes that Albert was patient and calm despite the crowd, and Thornton adds that Albert would work till 11 P.M. or later on those nights to get the instruments repaired for his fellow musicians. Thornton and Dean agree that most of these musicians were playing guitar or banjo; few could fiddle. They also agree that many, many people in that area played some instrument. Although some were musicians known to play at cake walks or auctions, the majority just played in their homes for their own families. Thornton tells a joke about a man who had a visitor at his cabin. The visitor asked who played the banjo hanging on the wall. The man said, "The old woman does; she can make it talk! But it don't say much." The group breaks up in laughter. Still, they appreciate a community where most people "play a little" (Emily Spencer, Thornton Spencer, and Dean Sturgill interview by Anderson-Green).

For several years, Dean Sturgill had a band called "Grayson Highlands String Band," named for a state park nearby. He took over this group, which was started by Ken Powers as a spin-off from the "Skyland Strings Band" that Ken used to have with Dave Sturgill (see chap. 4). Dean says he is "a little bit" related to Dave but, of course, knows him well through music. Beyond being a musician, Dean is a poet and has written poems about many musicians, particularly Albert Hash (see chap. 3). Thornton and Emily Spencer also have a band, the "Whitetop Mountain Band" (named for Albert's group), which is heard playing every year at fiddlers conventions in the area. They also play regularly at Sparta's dance hall in North Carolina on Friday or Saturday nights.

Dean and Thornton agree that a strong Appalachian musical tradition is continuing today. They note that, although there are some changes in repertoire, "some tunes are powerful from one generation to the next" (Emily Spencer, Thornton Spencer, and Dean Sturgill interview by Anderson-Green). They also point out that, although there are not as many festivals as there used to be in the 1960s and 1970s, the number has stabilized. They think the decrease in the number of festivals has to do with such things as insurance requirements (the 1980s "got tough") and not with diminishing interest on the part of the general population (ibid.). Thousands still attend the festivals and fiddlers conventions, and new bands still enter competitions.

A Younger Generation

Among the newer bands, an outstanding one is the Konnarock Critters, founded by a brother-sister team, Brian Grim of Independence, Virginia, and Debbie Grim of Konnarock, Virginia. Konnarock stands at the rugged western end of Grayson County, on the border between Washington and Smyth Counties. In fact, land in that community is split among all these counties. Brian and Debbie are young, but their music is truly old-time, in the Appalachian tradition. Brian started learning to play the fiddle at age nine "under the tutelage of Albert Hash" (Patterson, tape notes). Even earlier than that, he and his sister were taught to sing by their mother, also a musician, who later gave lessons along with the Hash family. Debbie began her lessons at age seven, studying with Albert's relatives, Thornton Spencer and Emily Spencer, in their classes at the Mount Rogers Fire Hall on Whitetop Mountain (Hauslohner, "Twenty-nine Hours," 40). Debbie started with guitar for a year and then moved on to clawhammer banjo, often playing in accompaniment to her brother's fiddle. Audrey Hash Hamm says that, if it hadn't been for her family's efforts in establishing the classes at the Mount Rogers School and Fire Hall, the old-time music would have died out. Brian and Debbie are certainly evidence that the music is still alive!

The Konnarock Critters band is probably the best group in the "Hash tradition," having won first prize in old-time bands at

Union Grove, North Carolina, three years in a row (1991–94). The group also won first at Galax in 1990 and at the Elk Creek Fiddlers Convention in 1994. In 1997, Debbie Grim won first on clawhammer banjo at Galax. A longtime observer of the region's musical traditions points out that, when Debbie and Brian were just ten and eleven years old, they and their mother started a band playing for a local dance group, the "Whitetoppers." Brian played fiddle, Debbie played banjo, and the mother was on guitar. They also played for other square dances, as Debbie recalls: "We played every Saturday night for two and a half years at the Troutdale Fire Hall . . . the smaller we were, the more money they gave us" (Hauslohner [91] 40). Now that they are grown, they and others in their band play for various fundraisers, festivals, and fiddlers conventions throughout southwestern Virginia, North Carolina, and Tennessee (Patterson notes).

In November 1990 (the year the Kritters won first at Galax), the group received a call from Dollywood, the Dolly Parton theme park in Pigeon Forge, Tennessee, three hours' drive from Konnarock. The Kritters had auditioned there earlier and now received an offer to take part in a special fall festival event (Hauslohner [91] 38). After this debut, they were given a contract for four shows every Saturday during the summer. At this time, the band consisted of Brian and Debbie; Jim Lloyd of Rural Retreat, Virginia, on guitar; Sam Payne of Fries, Virginia, also on guitar; and Terry Semones of Hillsville, Virginia, on bass.

Every Saturday, starting from the Grims' log cabin "high astride Straight Mountain near Konnarock," the group took off for Dollywood to play music all day and evening and then drive back to their home in the Blue Ridge Mountains (Hauslohner [91] 38). Of course, before they ever left home, they spent much time jamming to prepare for these shows, with everyone calling out favorites. On one evening, "after a rousingly successful rendition of 'Hangman's Reel,' they turned to 'Boys, the Buzzards Are Flying' and then 'Shady Grove.'" Hauslohner points out that the Dollywood entertainment staff, although familiar with "bluegrass" music, really had not been very aware of "old-time" repertoire. At least the Dollywood folks were willing to give it a chance (38). Thus the Konnarock Critters constitute a new generation, as Ola Belle and the Sturgills did in the decades of the 1930s and 1940s, introducing old-time music to national audiences at major tourist attractions like music parks and theme parks.

The intergenerational aspect of the Appalachian music scene remains significant. The energy is so great that it flows both ways: the older ones mentor the younger players, and the younger ones reinvigorate the elders. The relationship between Albert Hash and Wayne Henderson is one of the most famous in this tradition, inspiring Albert to resume his major role in music. Now that Albert and others famous in old-time music have passed on, others still remember and in turn become mentors, fiddling and dancing the nights away with younger people there among their elders.

Among the notable young musicians born and raised in this Blue Ridge Mountain country is Greg Hooven, who led the "New Ballard Branch Bogtrotters," an amazingly talented group that won first place in old-time bands at Galax in both 1994 and 1995. In fact, the *Galax (Va.) Gazette* featured Greg on the cover of its music section for August 9, 1995, proclaiming that he had "swept" the Galax Fiddlers Convention in 1994. Not only had his band placed first, but also he had won first place in fiddle and been named "best all-around performer." Charles Wolfe includes Greg in a group identified as a "new generation of young fiddlers" that has "carried the old-time tradition into the 1990s" (Wolfe, "Old-Time Music," 394).

Greg is a young person with an old-time awareness of his region's history and his family's part in it. He quietly tells of his great-great-great-grandfather Bonham, who settled on Razor Ridge in Grayson County, pioneering on three hundred acres. Greg, who speaks movingly about Razor Ridge, clearly loves the land as well as the music. He learned guitar and fiddle partly from a neighbor and partly just picking it up himself. In the August 1995 *Gazette* interview, he says, "You never quit learning more things. There's always some older musicians that if you look hard enough, their heads will pop up." His favorite styles are old-time and blues. Playing along with him in the "Bogtrotters" were the Halls, also from old Grayson County families (see app. B). Greg points out, "One of the things that is unique to this area is that most musicians around here play old-time style, and it's more here than anywhere else in the world per capita" (*Gazette*, Aug. 9, 1995). So he preferred to stay in his home region for some years in his twenties, earning a living by painting houses and filling his life with music—sometimes even playing in his dreams (Hooven interview by Anderson-Green, June 2000). Later, life's economic realities led him to move farther north, into the Valley of Virginia, to Middlebrook near Staunton, although his intention is eventually to return to live on Razor Ridge, as he emphasized in an interview at the Elk Creek Fiddlers Convention in June 2000. Meanwhile, he continues to take part in all the major musical events.

Another musician of the younger generation who has been receiving attention and awards is Casey Hash, who plays guitar and leads the "Wolfe Brothers Band." Casey, born on a United States Air Force base in Georgia, is a descendant of the pioneer Hash family in Grayson County and so is distantly related to Albert Hash. He spent his boyhood summers in Grayson County on the farm of his grandparents, Gurney Hash and Georgia Harrington Hash. Although Casey mainly lived in Roanoke, Virginia, in those days, now he has moved to Grayson permanently, remodeling the old family homeplace which sat vacant for a few years after his grandparents died. He has poured much effort into restoring their large Victorian home in the Elk Creek section of the county.

Casey also has poured much energy into the music scene, with the formation of his band, participating in fiddlers conventions, and producing several tapes and albums. "Wolfe Brothers Band" members include Jerry Correll, a fiddler who was born in Pennsylvania but moved to Grayson and married Donna Kirk, a Grayson native and also a musician. Although the group likes a mix of music, they compete in the old-time category and in 1995 won first place at the Alleghany County fiddlers convention in Sparta, North Carolina; and ninth place at Galax. At Sparta, Jerry Correll won third in old-time fiddle, and Casey won third place in vocals. More recently, Jerry won fourth place in old-time fiddle at Galax in the year 2000.

In a letter, Casey tells of the complex musical experiences he had in childhood on the Elk Creek farm: "Music was always enjoyed here at the farmhouse with the Hashes, but it was the piano that they and my parents tried to push me into since string music was considered slightly 'low-brow' back then" (Casey Hash to Anderson-Green, 1993). Casey's grandmother really did not want him to get involved with string-band music. As noted earlier, some church-going people in the region felt that the fiddle was "the instrument of the devil," because string band music, especially at fiddlers conventions, was associated with drinking. To be sure, some people attending fiddlers conventions had their "good times" in ways other than music making. However, as Dave Sturgill points out in an article for a local paper, such drinking also took place at auctions, political rallies, and other events; it is unclear why those events were not stigmatized as fiddlers conventions were ("Our Mountain Musical Heritage").

Yet such attitudes persisted. In that era of unpaved roads, many in the Elk Creek Valley probably visited the Whitetop Mountain section only rarely. Thus Gurney Hash and Georgia Harrington Hash likely were unaware of musicians such as Albert Hash, a man of great character who devoted many years to the art and craft of music. Although some people in the county tried to ignore string-band music or discourage their children's interest in it, most cared for it so much that the strong traditional music prevailed. Today, throughout the region, people are proud of their musical heritage.

Despite his grandmother's attitude, young Casey Hash became fascinated with string music. Finally, as he tells it, "When I turned eighteen, my father bought me, at my insistence, a pawn shop guitar. Within four months, I taught myself to play and was playing folk music for extra income in the restaurants and clubs around the Roanoke area" (Casey Hash interview by Anderson-Green). He adds, "In 1992, I sold my house in Roanoke, transferred my job, and moved here to Elk Creek with my family. I'm honored to keep the farmhouse in the family and in the Hash name." He has thrown himself fully into the music scene, playing in two bands, one bluegrass and the other old-time, with the old-time band getting more emphasis now. He plays several instruments, including six-string and twelve-string guitar, piano, mandolin, and even accordion (not a typical Grayson instrument). He has made new friends like the Corrells but also goes back to Roanoke to play with old friends and enjoys variety in music. Above all, he is proud of carrying on the traditional music of his region and being part of the fellowship of musicians (Casey Hash interview by Anderson-Green).

In addition to the major fiddlers conventions, certain well-known parties mark special times of the year. Donna and Jerry Correll, who are in the band with Casey Hash, have established a traditional daytime picnic event at their home in Elk Creek on the Saturday of the Elk Creek Fiddlers Convention. Many of the musicians arrive at the Corrells' lovely log home overlooking a small lake to feast together and then share music before heading to the competition.

At a different time of the year, Brian Grim and Debbie Grim hold a party called "Breaking Up Christmas," which takes place at the end of the twelve days of Christmas, on January 6. This type of party became popular during the folk music revival of the 1960s and has continued to be so in Konnarock. Musicians come from everywhere to party all night at the Grims' place.

Perhaps the biggest party of all is the week-long Galax Fiddlers Convention, where people camp out with friends and find their favorite jam sessions going on day and night. People at this famous event are a mix from everywhere, including Canada and Europe. Of course, many come from adjacent areas of the mountains, such as the famous fiddler Richard Bowman, of the Mount Airy section east of Galax. Many newcomers to this music scene arrive every year. Some come as small children, brought by families already in the tradition; while others, like Rick Abrams, were adults before they learned of it. It is notable, however, that the young people of Appalachia remain eager to participate. Every year, Russell Lowe of Jonesborough, Tennessee, a fiddler, comes for the week, bringing his grandson Monroe, a blossoming musician who also plays fiddle. Recently Monroe won first in his age category and was named best all-around performer at Elk Creek.

An aspect of the fiddlers conventions which is puzzling to some newcomers is that there are two categories in the contests, old-time and bluegrass. Actually, the categories overlap; often the same tunes are played, with variations in instrumentation and style, but musicians usually specialize in one style or the other. The development of "bluegrass" has been analyzed thoroughly by others (see bibliography).

Although the focus in this book is old-time music, it should be recognized that the Virginia-Carolina area along New River has produced outstanding current musicians in the bluegrass tradition, too. Especially well known are Tommy Sells and the "Big Country Bluegrass Band" from the Mouth of Wilson community. Tommy Sells, like most residents of Grayson County, is a descendant of an early pioneer in the region, William Sells of Ireland, who settled near rugged Whitetop Mountain. Thus Tommy grew up in the "hotbed of musicians" and when grown formed a band with his wife, Teresa Bowers Sells, and friends. Tommy plays mandolin, which he learned from his father, who also was a well-known musician. Teresa Sells plays guitar and grew up in Elk Creek, where her father, James Bowers, played bluegrass in the 1950s. Other members of "Big Country Bluegrass" include Larry Pennington on banjo, Jeff Michaels on fiddle, and Alan Mastin on bass. They stay busy performing locally and at more distant locations, winning awards at fiddlers conventions (fourth in bluegrass bands at Galax in 1995 and first at Alleghany County in 1996), and producing many tapes and albums of their bluegrass music (see McGee 25, for discography). Recently this group won a talent search sponsored by the Martha White Company, thus gaining the opportunity to play on the Grand Ole Opry show in Nashville.

Another important local group in Grayson County that plays and sings traditional, old-time, and gospel music is "Elmer Russell and the Flatridge Boys." The group is named for their subregion of the county, Flatridge, Virginia, which used to have its own post office, located on a high, flat spot way up the side of a mountain heading toward Razor Ridge. Elmer Russell plays lead guitar and sings in an effective tenor voice, while his cousin, Ron Russell, does bass vocals and plays a variety of old-time instruments, including autoharp and harmonica. In addition, Gary Shepherd, son of a pastor, plays bass; Wayne Osborne plays guitar and does lead vocals; and sometimes Carol Russell Frenza joins in on mandolin or guitar and sings. All of these "Flatridge" musicians were born in the county and grew up in families that were among the pioneer settlers (for example, Russells, Cornetts, and Osbornes). Their music is definitely in the tradition "handed-on" from the early days. However, they never play at fiddlers conventions, because they use some electrified instruments, which are not permitted in those contests. Instead, from spring through fall, they have a very busy schedule on weekends in the tri-state area of southwestern Virginia, North Carolina, and Tennessee, doing shows at outdoor parks, fire halls, and just about wherever people want them. During the week, they are all busy with timber, cattle, tobacco, and other enterprises.

Above all, Elmer's group represents the continuity of the Christian pastoral tradition, as seen, for example, in their tape entitled "Where No One Stands Alone." This tape emphasizes bonds of Christian love among individuals and, of course, between man and God. One old-time hymn on the tape, "Farther Along," acknowledges the words of the Apostle Paul: "Now we see through a glass darkly" (1 Cor.: 13.12). As the song proclaims, "Farther along, we'll know all about it, / farther along we'll understand why." As a follow-up, the next song promises, "I'll Meet You in the Morning," when the beloved ones who have "passed over" will be reunited on that "beautiful shore." Of two gospel tapes recorded by the Flatridge Boys, one each has been dedicated to Johnny Russell and Calvin Cornett, cousins who died as young men in their twenties. Drawing strength from Christian belief, the kinship group has carried on, expressing profound feelings through music. Thus the Appalachian heritage has been, and continues to be, a living legacy.

As they have done for generations, folks in this Virginia-Carolina area gather to make music in small subregional groups.

Elmer Russell with guitar in his shop at Flatridge, Virginia, 1996.
Photograph by Rhett Turner. Used by permission.

Ron Russell with autoharp at Elmer Russell's shop, Flatridge, Virginia, 1996.
Photograph by Rhett Turner. Used by permission.

Choices of jamming companions are dictated by convenience or personal preference. Groups that gather at Mouth of Wilson, Rugby, and Whitetop constitute one area, quite distinct from Flatridge or Troutdale; nor do people of these areas usually get to Independence. However, for years each Tuesday evening, a jam session took place at Blanche Ward Nichols's house just north of Independence, near the edge of Buck Mountain. These sessions drew a large group of musicians, some even coming from over near Galax. As a commentator points out: "Blanche . . . and her husband Ellis hosted a Tuesday night get-together at their home . . . for many, many years[,] giving young musicians such as Brian and Debbie [Grim] a proving ground to get in there and play with sometimes thirty musicians. . . . Blanche continued this get-together after Ellis's passing on September 12, 1991. Regular pickers come not only from Grayson County, but from far and wide, sometimes as much as an hour's drive away" (Bobby Patterson, "Liner notes").

This more diverse group seems to prefer a very old-time repertoire, which is certainly understandable for Blanche, since she is a member of the Ward family of Buck Mountain, famous in Grayson County old-time music (see app. B). Sometimes Wayne Henderson, Helen White, and others from Rugby and "far-off" places even come here to pick. Blanche would play guitar and occasionally swing her arm with a call to the crowd to arouse the spirit or laugh and tell a funny story.

On a typical Tuesday night in August 1994, the tunes spontaneously selected included: "Hangman's Reel," "John Henry," "Sugar in the Gourd," "Black Mountain Rag," "Sail Away Ladies," "Ebenezer," "Down Yonder," "Fly Around My Pretty Little Miss," "Logan County Blues," and others. A significant number of younger "regulars" came to join in, including one tall young man with red hair and a beard, just learning to pick banjo. He also was continuing the Appalachian pattern of going back and forth from a home in the hills to the tri-state area north of Washington, D.C.; he alternates phases of living in Ashe County, North Carolina, near Piney Creek, with living in Lancaster County, Pennsylvania. Quite a few people one meets in the Upper New River area have a similar history of coming and going, so the music flows back and forth geographically as well as in other ways. Blanche is one who helped unite them all in music. She passed away in 2001.

Throughout the twentieth century, each Appalachian generation has had to deal with its own particular set of challenges. As seen in the story of Ola Belle Campbell Reed, those who left their homes in Appalachia for the workplace in the industrial East in the 1920s and 1930s experienced tremendous stress. In this transition, they encountered the shock of losing "the Shelter" of their beloved mountains and way of life, but at the same time they were sustained by the beliefs and values of their culture and by their love of music. They lost much in that time of economic depression, as Ola's storekeeper father did when customers could not pay their debts at the store and people for whom he had cosigned loans defaulted on these (for many such stories, see Charles Perdue and Nancy J. Martin-Perdue, *Talk About Trouble*). Ola's family lost more when the state government took their land on Mount Rogers by right of eminent domain and they were forced to accept a pittance for their hundreds of acres (Ola Belle Reed interview by Anderson-Green; Perdue).[2] Since they had been well established in a yeoman lifestyle, this "did hurt."

Even more painful, however, was becoming aware of class and regional animosities—finding out that others had negative images of Appalachia. This realization only heightened Ola Belle's sensitivity and gave her a sense of mission. She became especially concerned with the downtrodden and opened her home to people needing assistance, following the guidelines set out in her grandfather's will. Further, she exerted her influence in the entertainment world to communicate authentic Appalachian music and culture— for example, by refusing to take part in a comedy that "poked fun at the mourner's bench."

Finally, during the crucial era of the 1960s and 1970s, she became a leader in improving understanding among racial and cultural groups. These efforts were grounded in her biblical training (for example, the parable of the Good Samaritan) and in her Appalachian roots. She remembered the old days in Lansing, North

Carolina, when her family jammed on Friday nights with the black family group, the "Little Wonders." In racial attitudes, many in Appalachia probably were closer to an egalitarian ideal than people in other parts of the South. Ola always recalled her father, planting seeds, telling her that "each seed was important and that applied to people." Her world of the "Christian pastoral" incorporated not only a close bond between man and nature, but also an awareness of the interconnectedness of all living things and all people.

Ola knew that a person could prevail in difficult times by standing on the "solid rock" (as emphasized in the old hymn, "On Christ the solid rock I stand, / all other ground is sinking sand") and always remembering, "Behold, we count them happy which endure" (James 5:11). This latter verse became the basis for her own musical composition, "I've Endured." All of these feelings and beliefs were absorbed and communicated through the traditional music to which Ola, her husband Bud, her brother Alex, and her son David dedicated their lives. This music they passed on to new generations, especially those at colleges, where Ola felt inspired by the young people.

Others, such as the Sturgill family of Piney Creek, left mountain homes, experienced an urban East Coast life, found material advantages not as fulfilling as expected, and were called home by the virtues of the Appalachian culture. A younger generation continues to return. Here the Sturgills found fulfillment in years of crafting some of the best instruments heard in musical circles; further, they found great enjoyment in performing throughout the Upper New River area. Likewise, Virgil Sturgill eventually left Washington and Baltimore to find a home in Asheville, North Carolina, and a new career singing the old-time ballads, especially for university audiences, just as Ola has done.

"Uncle" Dave Sturgill pronounced these years back in Piney Creek the best years of his life, full of the music he loves and the work of crafting instruments to make it. The Upper New River remains a solid yeoman society, landowning but never cash-oriented. Thus, even today, this local culture is less materialistic than that in much of urban or suburban America. Now Dave and Marie Sturgill live on their Piney Creek land, away from "the rat race," surrounded by the families of their grown sons and daughters. They enjoy time spent in their extended kinship circle, as well as in special gatherings with fellow musicians at fiddlers conventions throughout the year.

Albert Hash's legacy represents those who never left and always stayed rooted in the life of the home place. His legacy will endure, for his memory and his music perpetuate the Appalachian values he cherished. Albert, Ola Belle, "Uncle" Dave, and others shared the same values—a love of the mountains, deep bonds of kin and community, a distrust of materialism, a life rooted in the expression of Christian pastoral through music. All these musicians were representative of the best their culture had to offer, and they stood up to be leaders for it and their people. Albert was more concerned about getting his instruments into the hands of aspiring musicians than about getting a high price for his bank account. Thus he clashed with those running the Knoxville World's Fair. Returning home, he continued to do business his way. As his pastor says, Albert did not need fame or fortune; he had other concerns of greater value.

Albert, like Ola Belle and Dave, had experienced the outsider's view of Appalachia. He always remembered the record-industry man who wanted a "rough" sound to fit his own image of country music. This experience intensified Albert's determination to teach his local students to get it "just right"—that is, the Whitetop way.

Throughout the twentieth century, these key musicians of the Whitetop–New River area—Ola Belle Reed, Dave Sturgill, and Albert Hash—not only performed traditional music and, in the cases of Dave and Albert, crafted the instruments, but also functioned very effectively as mentors and leaders. All had grown up in environments that made them aware of leadership and educator roles. Ola could watch her father, a high school principal in Lansing, North Carolina, encourage others. Dave, son of a college-educated engineer and later married to a teacher, enjoyed teaching music and craftsmanship to such protégés as Rick Abrams and Dave Rainwater. Albert Hash, influenced by his father's prominent role in the community and even more by the Christian pastoral

Martha Spencer playing banjo at her home, 1997.
Photograph by Rhett Turner. Used by permission.

ideal, deeply cherished his role as mentor to a younger generation of musicians and craftsmen growing up in the Whitetop section. Another of his greatest pleasures was teaching classes at the Mount Rogers School, along with his daughter Audrey Hamm, brother-in-law Thornton Spencer, and sister-in-law Emily Spencer. They enjoyed seeing many young students become absorbed in the old-time music.

Now, as each season passes in the Upper New River Valley, musicians, dancers, and audiences continue to gather in groups small and large, in a home, country store, or in the summer at enormous fiddlers conventions. They play the traditional reper-toire, with fiddle strokes hauntingly recalling the bagpipe sound, clawhammer banjo ringing through the night, accompanied by strong guitars, mandolins, and bass. People of all ages get up to

Jesse Lovell with guitar at Elk Creek Fiddlers Convention, Elk Creek, Virginia, 1996.
Photograph by Rhett Turner. Used by permission.

"flatfoot," elders as usual dancing alongside their grandchildren. During breaks between numbers, they often reminisce about past gatherings, telling anecdotes about their favorite musicians of the past, who live on through the music. Participating musicians usually would rather play their instruments than eat. They often refer to the company of musicians as "fellowship" and call their meetings at fiddlers conventions a "family reunion."

After the fiddlers conventions are over, those wanting yet more fellowship with musicians and craftsmen always have a standing invitation to venture back into the hills to Rugby, Virginia. Here they may stop for some hours at the Henderson Guitar Shop to swap stories and tunes with everyone gathered around Wayne and Gerald. Anyone is welcome. Another favorite jam session takes place in Sparta, North Carolina, on Monday nights at the Crouse

Stu Shank with fiddle at Elk Creek Fiddlers Convention, Elk Creek, Virginia, 1996.
Photograph by Rhett Turner. Used by permission.

House; visitors are welcome. Those hungry for music also may drive up to Flatridge, to Troutdale, or over to Konnarock to visit with the younger generation in old-time music, including some of the "Konnarock Critters," the "Flatridge Boys," and many others. These visitors can find notices posted at stores about musical gatherings to be held at local fire halls and rescue squad buildings. Then, as the audiences gather and the musicians tune up, the "high lonesome" sound of old-time Appalachian music again will renew spirits, bond generations, and remain alive in memories forever. ❖

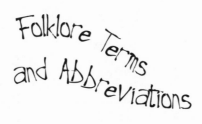

Folklore Terms and Abbreviations

AAFC	Archive of American Folk Culture, Library of Congress
BRMA	Blue Ridge Music Association
Child ballads	Numbered collection of British ballads compiled by F. J. Child in 1882–98
FMSB	*The Folk Music Sourcebook,* edited by Larry Sandberg and Dick Weisman (New York: Knopf, 1976)
Laws labels	Ballads presented in Laws, *American Balladry from British Broadsides*

Appendix A
New River Places
and Music Venues

Places in Four Key Counties

The territory encompassed in the appendices is somewhat broader than that discussed in chapter 1, because today musicians travel farther (even twenty miles or more) for jam sessions and events. Therefore this section includes musicians who live in both Grayson and Carroll counties, Virginia; and in Ashe and Alleghany counties, North Carolina. Among the places mentioned in these counties and the surrounding area are:

Alleghany County, North Carolina: Glade Valley, Piney Creek, Prather's Creek, Twin Oaks, Sparta, and Stratford.

Ashe County, North Carolina: Clifton, Creston, Grassy Creek, Helton, Jefferson, Lansing, Sturgills, Taylorsville, Todd, Warrensville, and West Jefferson.

Carroll County, Virginia: Ballard's Branch, Baywood, Cana, Coleman Ridge, Elk Horn, Fairview, Fancy Gap, Galax, "Happy Hill," Hebron, Hillcrest, Hillsville, Laurel Fork, Monaratt, Piper's Gap, Round Peak, and Woodlawn.

Grayson County, Virginia: Bethel, Big Fox Creek, Brush Creek, Buck Mountain, Cabin Creek, Elk Creek, Flatridge, Fries, Gold Hill, Grant, Grayson Highlands State Park, Green Valley, Grubbs Chapel, Haw Orchard Mountain, Independence, Konnarock, Little Fox Creek, Middle Fox Creek, Mount Rogers, Mouth of Wilson, Razor Ridge, Rugby, Saddle Creek, Stephen's Creek, Troutdale, Volney, and Whitetop.

New River Music Venues

Places in the New River area where jam sessions are held or music is played frequently are listed below.

Alleghany Jubilee (Sparta, North Carolina): Jam session, Tuesday nights. Bands play on Friday and Saturday nights (Thornton and Emily Spencer and Whitetop Mountain Band).

Barr's Fiddle Shop (Main Street, Galax): Jam sessions.

Blue Ridge Music Center on the Blue Ridge Parkway near Fisher's Peak.

Burgess Barn (Laurel Springs, North Carolina): Saturday nights (bands).

Crouse House Community Center (Sparta, North Carolina): Monday nights.

Greenfield Restaurant (near West Jefferson, North Carolina): Friday nights (Red Hill Ramblers).

The Heritage Shoppe/Record Store (Woodlawn, Virginia).

Old Helton School (Helton, Ashe County, North Carolina): Thursday nights.

Rex Theater (Galax, Virginia): Bands play on weekends.

Troutdale Fire House (Troutdale, Virginia): Usually third Saturday night.

VFW Dances (Hillsville, Virginia).

Wayne Henderson's Guitar Shop (Rugby, Virginia): usually Wednesday after work.

Local Annual Fiddlers Conventions

Alleghany Co. (N.C.)—3rd weekend of July

Ashe Co. (N.C.)—1st Saturday of August

Elk Creek (Grayson Co., Va.)—last weekend of June

Fairview (Va.)—last weekend of March

Fries (Va.)—3rd weekend of August

Galax (Va.)—a week-long event from Monday to the Saturday of the 2nd weekend of August

Appendix B

New River Area Musicians

This section lists musicians who were born, grew up, and currently live in the Virginia-Carolina section of the Upper New River covered in this study, as well as a few well-known musicians active in the past. There may be musicians who are not included; however, every effort was made to list those known to be active in the musical circles described. Also included are some people who were born outside the area but brought into these counties to be with grandparents or other family members, in the traditional "going-and-coming" pattern noted in earlier chapters.

Participation as a musician includes playing at various events, including local jam sessions in homes, community centers, fire halls, and stores; competing at local and regional fiddlers conventions; performing in churches; and giving programs for various audiences. As far as was possible, information on the musicians includes date and place of birth, place of residence, kinship network, instrument(s) played, people from whom the performer learned, prizes, and recognition by the community. In most cases the musicians listed below were found playing at fiddlers conventions.

Livingston Acres: Born May 2, 1921, in Green Valley near Fries, Virginia. Plays dobro and guitar. His first band in the 1950s was called the "Virginia Creepers," after the train that ran to Whitetop. His second band was the "Skyline Boys," with David Taylor on guitar and Billy Taylor on fiddle. Often plays with Jesse Lovell and at fiddlers conventions.

Wanda Alley: Born August 22, 1944, in Grayson County. Plays bass in the "Red Hill Ramblers." Learned from Sonny Arnold.

Gerald Anderson: See chapter 5. Born December 12, 1953, in Grayson County.

Sonny Arnold: Born October 12, 1939, in Alleghany County. Plays guitar with the "Red Hill Ramblers." Says that he is "self-taught."

Tommy Arnold: Born c. 1960–65 in Fries, Virginia. Lives in Galax, Virginia. Plays mandolin.

Jimmy Ayres: Born in Carroll County. Plays bass with the "Bluegrass Ramblers."

Oscar Baker: Born May 1, 1923, Grayson County, lives in Galax; plays guitar and sings gospel music on the streets and in nursing homes and jails.

Butch Barker: Born August 3, 1953, in Wilmington, Delaware. His grandparents were in Lansing, North Carolina, where Butch came to live in 1969. Has won many prizes, including first in guitar, Ashe County Fiddlers Convention, 1996; and second in guitar, Alleghany Fiddlers Convention, 1997. Performed with Wayne Henderson in "Rock Bottom Bluegrass," a group he now serves as manager. Learned guitar from Sonny Miller at Sunset Park, Maryland.

Steve ("Stevie") Barr: Born August 4, 1975. Son of Tom Barr and Becky Haga Barr. Played banjo in the "Blue Ridge Traditions" band. Won eighth prize in bluegrass banjo at Galax Fiddlers Convention, 1995 and 1997; first at Fries Fiddlers Convention, 1997; first at Galax, 1999. Now plays in the band "Fast Forward." When Steve was eleven, at Galax, in 1987, he won the prize for youngest best performer and his great-grandfather, George Haga, won the prize for oldest best performer. At thirteen, Steve went on a trip to Italy arranged by Joseph T. Wilson of the National Council for the Traditional Arts.

Tom Barr: Born November 26, 1941, in Hillcrest, Virginia, near Galax. Studied fiddle making with Albert Hash (see chap. 3). Plays bass. Started in bluegrass, then shifted to old-time, playing with Albert in the "Whitetop Mountain Boys." Also played with the "New River Ramblers." Started his own instrument-making shop part-time in the 1970s, went full-time in 1980, and moved it to Main Street in Galax, Virginia, in 1990. Tom married Becky Haga, who is from this area, learned music from grandparents on both sides, and often plays with the Spencers. The Barr family is originally from Ashe County, and Tom is kin to the Sheets and Tompkins families of Alleghany County. He is very interested in family history and has a letter written by his great-great-great-grandfather while in a prisoner-of-war camp in Chase, Ohio, during the Civil War.

Daryl Blevins: Born May 25, 1967, in Sparta, North Carolina, and still lives there. Plays banjo in the band "Alleghany Moon"; also plays guitar with his cousins Tracy and Trevor Nichols. Blevins is an old name in Virginia-Carolina area; the first Blevins arrived in the 1770s and settled near Whitetop.

Jack Blevins: Born November 25, 1929, in Ashe County. Plays banjo in the "Red Hill Ramblers." Learned much from Emily Spencer. Brother of Otis Blevins (see separate entry).

Leon Blevins: Born September 13, 1974, in Whitetop, Virginia. Works at Grayson Highlands State Park. Plays guitar in church. His wife, Crystal Mahaffey, is a musician (see separate entry).

Nave (Michael) Blevins: Born November 27, 1953, in Ashe County, he now lives in Alleghany County. Leads the band "Cranberry Creek." Does vocals and plays rhythm guitar. Makes tapes, does radio shows, etc. He began guitar at age twelve, learning from his parents; an uncle, Donald Osborne; and a cousin, Odell Woodie. His brother, Greg Blevins, also plays.

Otis Blevins: Born January 7, 1925, in Grassy Creek, North Carolina. Plays guitar in "Red Hill Ramblers." His brother, Jack, plays banjo in the band (see separate entry).

Tina Trianosky Blevins: Born September 11, 1980, in Boone, North Carolina, but was brought home to Lansing, North Carolina. Learned banjo from

Dee Dee Price of Whitetop. At age fourteen, she won a prize in old-time banjo at Mount Airy. Won second in old-time banjo at Ashe County Fiddlers Convention, 1996; second at Alleghany Fiddlers Convention, 1999; third at Galax Fiddlers Convention, 1999. She is in band "Appalachian Mountain Girls," with mother Susan Smith Trianosky on guitar. Susan's father, Jerry Smith (see separate entry), played guitar in "Grayson Highlands String Band."

Bobby Ray Bobbitt: Born April 17, 1952, in Pine Mountain area. Lives in Elk Creek, Virginia. Plays guitar and some banjo. Learned guitar from a neighbor, Delbert Bourne.

Eddie Bond: Born August 16, 1971, in Fries, Virginia. Lives in Austinville, Virginia. Plays old-time fiddle (uses his grandfather's fiddle) and banjo; is a member of "Old-Time Traditions" band. Won third in old-time fiddle at Ashe County Fiddlers Convention, 1996; fifth at Alleghany Fiddlers Convention, 1997, and fourth in 1998; seventh in old-time fiddle at Galax Fiddlers Convention, 1998, and second, 1999. Also won sixth in clawhammer banjo at Galax, 1997. Eddie says that his great-great-grandfather, Lee Bond, played clawhammer banjo and that his grandmother, Thelma Hill Widner of Fries, played guitar. Another relative, his grandfather's cousin, Ben Bond, currently plays fiddle and banjo locally. Eddie's wife, Shane Jackson Bond, was born in Carroll County; she plays bass and teaches clogging.

Bond Brothers: Gilmer Bond (born in 1920s), Ben Bond (born February 11, 1924), and Otey Bond (born May 1922), all born in Fries, Virginia. Gilmer plays guitar and sings; Ben plays the fiddle, guitar, and banjo; and Otey plays mandolin, fiddle, and guitar. All were in the band "Virginia Creepers" with Livingston Acres.

Bourne Brothers: Both David Bourne and Billy Wayne Bourne were born c. 1960s, into a family from Elk Creek, Virginia. David, who lives in Fairview, Virginia, plays banjo, dobro, and guitar. Billy Wayne, a resident of Fries, Virginia, plays dobro and guitar.

David Bowers: Born July 13, 1976, in Ashe County. Plays fiddle. Often performed at the "Bean Stalk" in Boone, North Carolina, on Saturday nights, sometimes with Wayne Henderson and Helen White.

Danny Boyd: Born September 26, 1956, in a neighborhood on the boundary between Carroll and Patrick Counties, where the mountainous terrain made a portion of Patrick County part of the Carroll County community. Children there all went to school in Carroll County. Danny lives in Hillsville, Virginia. His father had a band, "Boyd Bluegrass Traditions." Danny plays banjo, as well as guitar, bass, and dobro, in the band "Bluegrass Traditions," which won first place at Fries Fiddlers Convention in 2000. Danny has a son, Jonathan Boyd, born December 31, 1984, who plays bass in the band, carrying on the tradition.

Mikey Brewer: Born October 30, 1949, in Grayson County. Son of Mastin Brewer and Margaret Sexton Brewer. Plays guitar in churches and jams with Wayne Henderson occasionally. Was guitarist for the "Pilgrim Singers."

Jim Brooks: Born April 17, 1932, in Ashe County. Plays mandolin and guitar. He and his brother, Harold Brooks, had the band "Brooks Brothers"; it played at Sunset Park, Maryland, and once or twice at the Grand Ole Opry. Jim played some shows with Bill Monroe in 1951, playing banjo then. Harold played often with Ola Belle Reed. Jim returned to New River and lives near Lansing, North Carolina. Participates in jams at Helton. His daughter is Cindy Brooks Norris (see separate entry).

Frank Brown: Born July 2, 1941, in Ashe County. Later moved to Florida and then returned to Ashe. Plays dulcimer.

Mike Brown: Born January 15, 1955, in Galax, Virginia. Now lives in Woodlawn, Virginia. Is kin to Wayne Henderson; Wayne's father and Mike's grandmother were siblings. Won first in guitar at Galax Fiddlers Convention, 1994, 1995, and 1996.

Mitchell Brown: Born February 3, 1961, in Galax, Virginia. Now lives in Tennessee but comes back for the music scene. Plays bass. Son of Joann Morris Shinault (see separate entry).

Bryan Brothers: James, born April 25, 1953, in Alleghany County, North Carolina. Plays guitar. Learned from Edsel Andrews in Sparta, North Carolina. Is in gospel band at Living Waters Holiness Church. Melvin was born March 14, 1962, in Alleghany County. Melvin plays bass guitar, mostly at home.

Denny Bryant: Born March 17, 1926, in the Hebron section of Galax, Virginia. Plays guitar. Son Donald Bryant (born August 16, 1953) plays bass. Grandson Benjamin Bryant (born September 1983) plays guitar. Denny's nephew, Ricky Bryant (born 1951), plays guitar, too. Elwood Lineberry (see separate entry) is Denny's cousin.

Bobby Bunn: Born September 11, 1955, in Galax, Virginia. Related to Isoms and Catrons there. Plays guitar, which he learned from Jimmy Douglas.

Jennifer Anderson Bunn: Born December 3, 1974, in Radford, Virginia. Lives in Fancy Gap, Virginia. Plays old-time fiddle in band "Jenny Leigh and the Boys." She was raised in Carroll County and is related to the Edmonds family. Her great-grandfather was "Uncle Norm" Edmonds, who played at Galax Fiddlers Convention; his grandson was the famous Jimmy Edmonds (see separate entry).

James Burris: Born October 31, 1961, in Grayson County. Lives in Hillsville, Virginia. Plays fiddle, which he learned from his father, Earl Burris, and his grandfather, Otis Burris of the "Mountain Ramblers." Has won many awards at Galax Fiddlers Convention, including first in fiddle, 1995, 1998, and 1999; first at Fries Fiddlers Convention, 1997. His grandfather, Otis Burris, had placed more times in competition at Galax than anyone else, with twenty-nine wins, sixteen in fiddle and thirteen in dance (*Galax (Va.) Gazette,* August 8, 1996). James is leader of the band "Southern Pride." He is brother of Joey Burris (see separate entry).

Joey Burris: Born April 29, 1963, in Grayson County, near Fries, Virginia. Lives in Hillsville, Virginia. Plays clawhammer banjo. He learned bluegrass style from his father, Earl Burris, and old-time style from Dave Sturgill. Plays in the band "Southern Pride" with brother, James Burris (see separate entry). Won third in old-time banjo at the Alleghany Fiddlers Convention, 1995; second at Galax Fiddlers Convention, 1995, and first, 1999; first at Fries Fiddlers Convention, 1997. Joey's wife is Jin

Burcham Burris, who plays dulcimer and won first at Galax, 1999. She is a niece of Jesse Lovell. The Burris brothers also are related to the Williams (mother) and Lowe families, and paternal grandmother was a Roberts.

Karen Carr: Born March 23, 1956, in Hillsville, Virginia. Related to Rameys and Cockerhams of Low Gap, Surry County, North Carolina. Plays guitar and bass at jams and at church. Learned bass from Bud Russell.

Adam Brant Cassell: Born September 3, 1974, in Grayson County. Plays guitar, self-taught; now learning banjo from Stevie Barr and Kyle Smith. Son of Charles Cassell of Comer's Rock.

Bob Cheek: Born September 14, 1948, in Alleghany County. Plays old-time guitar. Learned from Ed Daniels, who was born in Richmond, Virginia, but moved to Alleghany County.

Jessie Tillson Clark: Born September 1, 1982, in Grayson County. Plays guitar, which she learned from her cousin, Gerald Anderson, and friends. Jessie now is a student at Berea College, Berea, Kentucky, where her music is much appreciated.

Lonnie Cole: Born c. 1920s. Lonnie plays fiddle and lives in Hillsville, Virginia. Son of Calvin Cole of Fancy Gap, Virginia, who played fiddle and banjo.

Carson Cooper: Born January 6, 1943, in Rugby, Virginia. Plays banjo. Founding member of the bluegrass band "Appalachian Trail" and owns music store in Marion, Virginia. Played on tape, "W. C. Henderson and Company." Is cousin to Wayne Henderson and Gerald Anderson; played with Wayne in the first "Rugby Gullyjumpers." Carson was inspired by his uncle Dale Cooper, who played banjo.

Billy Cornette: Born October 22, 1942, in Kentucky, but his family originally came from Grayson County. He moved back and bought a Christmas tree farm. Lives in Hillsville, Virginia. Plays guitar and old-time fiddle. Manages the band "Reed Island Rounders." His wife, Betty Vornbrock (born March 3, 1954, in South Dakota), plays fiddle in the band, as well as some guitar and banjo. His great-great-grandfather, born 1803 in Grayson County, attended Hanks Musical College near his home, then made and played fiddles; also was a Methodist preacher there until he went to Kentucky after the Civil War.

Roger Cornett: Born c. 1945. Lives near Troutdale, Virginia. Plays guitar and some other instruments in jam sessions.

Jerry Correll and Donna Kirk Correll: Jerry was born March 8, 1947, in Pennsylvania. He plays fiddle. His wife, Donna Kirk Correll, was born December 7, 1957, in Jefferson, North Carolina, but was taken home to Grayson County, Virginia. She plays bass. Both Jerry and Donna are in the "Wolfe Brothers Old-time Band" with Casey Hash. Jerry won third place in old-time fiddle at Alleghany Fiddlers Convention, 1995; and third at Galax Fiddlers Convention, 1997. Donna won third in folk song at Galax, 1997. In October 1997, the Virginia Country Music Association presented "Virginia Highlands Appalachian Traditional Music Heritage Awards" to Jerry as fiddler of the year, Donna as vocalist of the year, and the "Wolfe Brothers Old-time Band" as entertainers of the year. Donna is a descendant of the Cox, Phipps, and Hash families in Grayson; she has an 1873 deed to family land. Her Kirk ancestor had land in Elk Creek, Grayson County, Virginia, in 1793.

Brad Cox: Born March 19, 1982, in Grayson County. Son of Harry J. Cox. Learned to play guitar listening to others and using Internet. Harry's uncle, Eugene Lundy (born c. 1930), plays fiddle, has won many competitions, and played in a band.

Everette Cox: Born 1925 in Carroll County. Plays guitar and is learning banjo. His mother played autoharp at Galax Fiddlers Conventions, and his grandfather Landreth made guitars. This family is from an area known as Monaratt, in the Hebron community, Virginia.

Kyle Cox: Born October 1934. Lives in Piper's Gap, Virginia. Plays fiddle.

Harry Cummings: Born July 21, 1930, at Stephen's Creek, near Fries, Virginia. Plays guitar at fiddlers conventions. His father, Virgil Cummings, was in two or three bands in the 1940s and played at schoolhouses and on WBOB radio in Galax, Virginia. Harry's mother, Eula Cummings, is an aunt of Jim Moss, who played guitar. Harry's son, Frank Cummings (born November 29, 1956), also plays guitar. Two grandsons are musicians: Ken Cummings (born in 1979 at Galax) plays mandolin; and Craig Cummings, not in the bluegrass tradition, plays drums.

Ray Dancy: Born December 26, 1927, in Grassy Creek, North Carolina. Plays old-time fiddle. Lived in Maryland for forty-two years but returned to Laurel Springs, North Carolina. While in Maryland, he played with Ola Belle Campbell Reed, Alex Campbell, and Sonny Miller at Sunset Park. All had grown up in Grassy Creek together. Now Ray is in the "Red Hill Ramblers" and plays at the Galax Fiddlers Convention.

Aaron Davis: Born September 27, 1978. Son of Gary Davis of Galax and brother of Brandon Davis (see separate entries). Plays bass in the band "Blue Ridge Traditions," with Brandon Davis on guitar and Stevie Barr on banjo. They play at conventions and festivals from Virginia to Florida and released a tape in 1993.

Beverly Davis: Born October 29, 1943, in Roanoke, Virginia, but was brought home to Galax, Virginia. Plays dobro and banjo. His father, Whitfield Davis, who played fiddle and autoharp, was a doctor and a member of the Moose Lodge; he helped start the Galax Fiddlers Convention. Beverly also learned much from Charles Hawks, Ted Lundy, and Cullen Gaylean. Played in the "Mountain Ramblers."

Brandon Davis: Born February 15, 1977. Brandon was junior guitar champion twice at Fiddlers Grove, North Carolina, at ages twelve and thirteen; and placed third at the Merle Watson Festival, 1993, and second, 1994. Won second in guitar at Galax Fiddlers Convention, 1994. He and brother Aaron Davis (see separate entry) are in the band "Blue Ridge Traditions." Brandon and father Gary Davis (see separate entry) perform at Grayson Highlands State Park.

Gary Davis: Born October 26, 1953, in Galax, Virginia. Father of Aaron Davis and Brandon Davis (see separate entries). Plays guitar, which he learned from Wayne Henderson. Won third in guitar at Galax Fiddlers Convention, 1994—the same year son Brandon won second in guitar. Gary and Brandon perform at Grayson Highlands State Park. The Davis name is on Montgomery (later Grayson) County militia lists in the eighteenth century.

Ronald Davis: Born May 4, 1964, in Galax; plays guitar.

Deana Blevins DeBord: Born November 9, 1964, in Sparta, North Carolina; grew up in Glade Valley; plays guitar; learned from uncle Richard Nichols.

Howard Dillon: Born May 11, 1919, in Carroll County. Plays guitar and banjo.

Will Duncan: Born c. 1935–40, in Alleghany County; lived in Sparta, North Carolina, and now lives in Galax, Virginia. Plays guitar.

Derek Easter: Born March 2, 1975, in Mount Airy but raised in Cana; plays guitar in fiddlers' conventions; his father, Wesley, has a recording studio in Cana and teaches.

Charles L. Eastridge: Born November 11, 1927, in Clifton, North Carolina. Plays guitar, fiddle, and banjo at jam sessions, and also makes fiddles. His father, Carl Eastridge, played guitar.

Jimmy Edmonds: Born November 15, 1958, at Galax, Virginia. Now lives in Myrtle Beach, South Carolina. Son of Frances and Harry Edmonds of Galax. Plays fiddle and other instruments; also makes instruments. Played in the "Carolina Opry." He holds the record for most wins at Galax Fiddlers Convention in bluegrass fiddle (Hiatt data).

Charlie Edwards: Born April 13, 1941, in Aberdeen, Maryland. His parents were from Sparta, North Carolina, so he came back every summer to visit his grandparents (mother's family name was Evans) and learned guitar. Plays in the area.

Jama Lee Edwards: Lives in Baywood, Virginia. Plays bass in "Old-Time Traditions" band. Sister of JoAnne Andrews Redd (see separate entry).

Kenneth Edwards: Born c. early 1920s in the Galax area. Lives on "Happy Hill," near Galax, Virginia. Plays guitar. Was in band "Sunny Mountain Boys." Also did gospel songs and played for square dances for many years at the Veterans of Foreign Wars in Independence, Virginia.

Ronald Edwards: Born November 24, 1952, in Grayson County. Plays guitar, banjo, and fiddle. Learned from his aunts, Pearl Redd and Mary Branscombe.

Ronnie Edwards: Born June 8, 1958, in Alleghany County; now lives in Sparta, North Carolina. Plays guitar. Learned from father, Dean Edwards. Went to live in Nashville, then returned to take part in the music scene at home.

Tom Edwards: Born April 27, 1940, in Alleghany County. Plays guitar. Participates in jam sessions at Crouse House in Sparta, North Carolina.

David Creed Fulton Fant: Born May 4, 1968, in Galax, Virginia. Plays guitar and some banjo with neighbors. His wife, Vanessa Sturgill Fant (daughter of Charles Sturgill), is a teacher of classical music.

Evelyn Farmer: Born September 18, 1918, in Fries, Virginia. Main instrument is autoharp. Evelyn went to work in the Fries cotton mill at age twelve; on Sundays many people came to her family's home to make music all day, and thus she began to play and sing. She only began to perform publicly after retirement and then became famous in her region for her very moving performances. Has placed sixteen times, including three firsts on autoharp at Galax Fiddlers Convention. Has extensive knowledge of folk songs. Her family roots in Grayson go back a long way; the Farmer name is on early militia lists.

Marvin Farmer: Born c. 1955–60. Lives in Hillsville, Virginia. Plays dobro. Is in the "Bluegrass Ramblers" band.

Melvin Felts and Dea Felts: Melvin Felts was born January 16, 1931, in Fancy Gap, Virginia. He plays banjo and fiddle. Learned banjo from his father, T. R. Felts. Dea Felts was born in California. She plays fiddle, guitar, and bass.

Frost Brothers: Carlos Frost was born December 20, 1943, Carroll County, Virginia. He plays fiddle and guitar. Jerry Wayne Frost was born March 12, 1950, in Carroll County. He plays banjo. They play at bluegrass parties and also play gospel music at Round Knob Baptist Church, Fancy Gap, Virginia.

Leon Frost: Born July 21, 1954, in Galax, Virginia. Plays banjo and mandolin. One of the best rhythm makers, using all kinds of rhythm instruments. Performs with the "Courthouse Ramblers" and occasionally with "New Ballard Branch Bogtrotters."

Bradley Gibson: Born 1989. Plays fiddle. Was in junior competition at Galax Fiddlers Convention, 2000. Sister Brittany Gibson plays, too. They live in the Ballard's Branch area, near Galax, Virginia.

Katie Lundy Golding: Born January 30, 1941, in Woodlawn in the Galax area; her father, Charlie Lundy, and brother Ted Lundy were famous in old-time music; Katie plays bass and guitar with the "Blue Ridge Mountain Ramblers," along with Trish Kilby, John Perry, and Lucas Pasley; Katie also acts as a judge at fiddlers' conventions.

Bill Gordon: Born c. 1930s in Galax area. Plays fiddle. Has been governor of Moose Lodge in Galax; did sound systems for the Galax Fiddlers Convention. Daughter Peggy Gordon plays mandolin.

Raymont A. Gordon: Born April 21, 1958, in Nebraska. His mother, Shirley Cox Gordon, was born in Grayson County, and the family moved back to live in Independence, Virginia. Raymont learned guitar and is now in a band, "The Prowlers," which plays a mixture of music, combining both traditional and contemporary, including comic scenes. They play mostly for private parties.

Ronnie Gravley: Born c. 1950 in Fries, Virginia. Plays guitar and bass and also sings; enters fiddlers conventions; his father Alec played guitar and led a gospel group, "Singing Gravleys."

Frank Grayson: Born c. 1930s, now lives in Tennessee but comes back to play. Related to E. B. Grayson, with whom Albert Hash (see chap. 3) played. Plays fiddle at jam in Sturgills, North Carolina.

Randy Greer: Born July 31, 1964, in Pennsylvania, of a New River family; later he moved back and lives in Jefferson, North Carolina. Plays guitar and mandolin, bluegrass style. Featured on tape, "W. C. Henderson and Company." Played with Wayne Henderson at Carnegie Hall. The pioneer Greer family settled on New River land at Wilson Creek around 1788.

Smith Greer: Born c. 1930 on Cabin Creek in the Whitetop area of Grayson County. Plays guitar. Played with Albert Hash, his neighbor (see chap. 3), and also went to Nashville and played with stars.

Brian Grim and Debbie Grim: Brian Grim was born April 18, 1970, in Pottstown, Pennsylvania, of a Whitetop family. His sister, Debbie Grim, was born June 24, 1971. She lives in Konnarock, Virginia; and Brian lives in Independence, Virginia. Brian studied fiddle under Albert Hash (see chap. 3) and now teaches classes himself. Debbie plays clawhammer banjo, having placed fourth at the Galax Fiddlers Convention, 1995, and first, 1997. They play together in the "Konnarock Critters," a band which has won many awards, including eighth at Galax, 1994, and second, 1997. Some say that Brian's fiddling style is the closest to that of Albert Hash (see chaps. 3 and 5).

Charlie Hale: Born 1923 in Grayson County. Lives in Galax, Virginia. Plays fiddle.

Hall Brothers: Dennis Hall, born July 16, 1953; and Dallas Hall, born November 11, 1957. Sons of Oscar Hall, who ran the Galax Fiddlers Convention for years. They play in the "New Ballard Branch Bogtrotters," Dallas on mandolin and Dennis on guitar. The Halls' uncles, Howard Hall and Fred Patton, were both famous for their skill on banjo.

Gene Hall: Born July 25, 1931, in Independence, Virginia. Plays guitar and bass. Learned guitar at age nine from brother-in-law, Wayne Hensdell. He has played with the "Fox Creek Ramblers." Married Anna Lee Delp Hall (born July 13, 1939), who often joins the band, playing spoons. Gene plays backup for bands; he has played with Benton Flippen at Sparta, North Carolina. Both the Hall family (English) and the Delps (German) were pioneers in Grayson County.

Audrey Hash Hamm: Born August 1, 1949, in West Jefferson, North Carolina. Daughter of Albert Hash (see chap. 3). Makes instruments in her late father's shop at the family home on Cabin Creek at Mount Rogers, Virginia. Performs on dulcimer and fiddle. Has taught many students in the Whitetop area. Son is David Albert Osborne (see separate entry).

Hardin Brothers: Brandon Hardin was born July 6, 1981, and Eric Hardin was born October 3, 1984, in Warrensville, North Carolina. Their grandfather is Spencer Pennington, musician (see separate entry). Eric was first in junior banjo at the Alleghany Fiddlers Convention, 1999, and first in bluegrass banjo, 2000. Eric learned from Larry Pennington. Brandon plays guitar and mandolin.

Earl Harless: Born July 2, 1924, in Ashe County; moved to Baltimore in 1951 but comes back to play at fiddlers conventions. Plays bluegrass banjo. Self-taught. His father's family did a lot of singing, and sisters played piano in church. Learned some from a neighbor, "ole man Baker," and listening to Wade Mainer on radio, as well as Mother Maybelle, Flatt and Scruggs, and Bill Monroe.

Harrison Brothers: Born in Elk Horn, Virginia, near Galax. Carroll Harrison was born September 12, 1932. Plays mandolin. Bobby Harrison was born September 17, 1934. Plays guitar. Arlie Harrison, father of Carroll and Bobby, played clawhammer banjo; and their grandfather, Bob Crawford, played fiddle at the first Galax Fiddlers Convention. Bobby's son Ronnie, born July 8, 1964, plays banjo and is minister at Glenmark Baptist Church.

Arnold Hash: Born June 18, 1963, in Grayson County; later lived in Marion. Son of Fred Hash of Elk Creek, Virginia. Plays guitar, banjo, and autoharp.

Casey Hash: See chapter 5. Born March 30, 1957, at a military base in Georgia; raised in Roanoke, Virginia. Although not born in the New River section, Casey spent all childhood summers at the home of his Hash grandparents in Elk Creek. He plays guitar and leads "Wolfe Brothers Old-time Band" of Elk Creek, Virginia. At the Alleghany Fiddlers Convention in 1995, Casey won third place in vocals; another member of the band, Jerry Correll (see separate listing), won third place in old-time fiddle; and "Wolfe Brothers" won first place in old-time bands. "Wolfe Brothers" won ninth place at the Galax Fiddlers Convention, 1995 and 1997. The band performs often and make tapes and CDs. In October 1997, the band received the "Virginia Highlands Appalachian Traditional Music Heritage Award" from the Virginia Country Music Association. Casey now lives in Elk Creek at restored home of his grandparents.

Trudy Belle Hash: Born 1949, York County, South Carolina, but came to New River area, where she had family connections. Maiden name is Belle. Her father was a fiddler who had a band that moved into West Virginia, then to Ashe County, North Carolina, where his half-brother, Manly Shumate, lived and where the family had roots. Trudy plays guitar and sings. She goes to jam sessions at Helton.

Billy Hawks: Born c. 1930s in Galax area. Plays bluegrass fiddle. Won second at the Alleghany Fiddlers Convention, 2000. He holds the most wins on bluegrass banjo at the Galax Fiddlers Convention (Hiatt data).

Rick Hawks: Born Fries, Virginia. Plays mandolin.

Stanley Hawks: Born c. 1953 in Carroll County. Son of Charles Hawks. Plays bass.

Harold Hayes: Born September 10, 1934, in Sparta, North Carolina. Lived in Pennsylvania, then returned. Plays bass and guitar.

Jayne Henderson: Born December 20, 1984. Daughter of Wayne Henderson. Plays dulcimer and other instruments.

Max Henderson: Born June 5, 1938, in Grayson County. Plays mandolin. Brother of Wayne Henderson, whom he encouraged to play (see chap. 5). They learned various instruments from each other.

Wayne Henderson: See chapter 5. Born May 3, 1947, in Ashe County hospital but went home to Grayson County. Brother of Max Henderson and father of Jayne Henderson (see separate entries).

Heath Higgins: Born 1917 near Galax, Virginia. Famous on fiddle.

Robert Higgins: Born September 8, 1931, in Grayson County. Lives near Fairview, Virginia. Plays guitar and autoharp. Entertains at Grayson Highlands State Park. His father played clawhammer banjo.

Ronnie Higgins: Born c. 1965 in Galax, Virginia. Plays guitar in band "Mountain Ramblers" with his father-in-law, James Lindsay.

Rodney Hodges: Born February 1969 in Galax, Virginia. Lives in Fairview, Virginia. Plays mandolin. Plays in two bands, "Fairview Boys" and "New River Bluegrass."

Dennis Holt: Born c. 1945 in Carroll County. Plays bass. Member of the band "Southern Breeze," with Bill Joines, Ronnie Lyons, and Ken Melton (see separate entries).

Greg Hooven: Born March 9, 1969, in Galax, Virginia. Cited as one of the best of a new generation of fiddlers in old-time music (Charles Wolfe, *Encyclopedia of Country Music,* 394). Played with Albert Hash (see chap. 3). Led "New Ballard's Branch Bogtrotters," which won first place in old-time bands at Galax Fiddlers Convention, 1994, 1995, 1996. In 1994 at Galax, Greg also won first place on fiddle and was named best all-around performer, thus "sweeping" Galax that year (*Gazette*). His family goes way back in Grayson County; a great-great-great grandfather was a Bonham with three hundred acres on Razor Ridge.

Abe Horton: Born April 11, 1915, in Laurel Fork, Virginia. Plays clawhammer banjo. Played at many fiddlers conventions.

Rex W. Horton: Born August 24, 1964, in Mount Airy but taken home to Fancy Gap, on the edge of Carroll County and North Carolina; plays bass in the "Nunn Brothers Bluegrass Band," with his father on guitar.

William Mack Houck: Born 1972 in Grayson County. Learned guitar from Wayne Henderson. Also plays bass. Often plays in church.

Penn Isom: Born c. 1925, he lives in Galax, Virginia. Plays guitar. Was a winner at the first Galax Fiddlers Convention. Plays in church.

James Sisters: Jessica James, born July 10, 1990; and Jennifer James, born August 10, 1993. Daughters of Daryl and Rhonda James of Grayson County. Jessica plays guitar and Jennifer old-time fiddle. Both study with Stevie Barr. Their grandfather, Roy James, got them into music.

Allan Johnson: Born in Alleghany County. Plays bass in band "Grass Stain." Band members include Allan's son, Sam Johnson, mandolin; Sam's double first cousin, Matthew Johnson, guitar; Jason Edwards, bass; and Zach Roupe (see separate entry), banjo.

Bobby Johnson: Born December 1, 1958, in Alleghany County. Lives in Sparta, North Carolina. Plays bluegrass banjo. Has won many awards at area fiddlers conventions, including third at Elk Creek Fiddlers Convention, 1999; and second at Axton, Virginia, 1999. His father played old-time banjo.

Johnson Brothers: Dennis Johnson, born February 3, 1958, Grayson County, Virginia. Plays guitar. Hershel Johnson, born July 7, 1963, in Grayson County. Plays banjo and other instruments. Both are "self-taught" but learned in a musical environment. Sons of Noah Johnson and Mary Lou Pugh Johnson of Independence, Virginia. Their mother plays guitar, and her mother played guitar, banjo, and organ; Mary Lou's brother played mandolin, guitar, banjo, and fiddle. Hershel and Dennis had a band, but now they play mostly at jams and usually play gospel music.

Bill Joines: Born July 29, 1953, in Alleghany County. Plays guitar. Was in "Grayson Highlands String Band" with Ken Powers; also other bands, including "Southern Breeze" and "Alleghany Moon." He went to fiddlers conventions with his father, Paul Joines; now he attends with his wife, Sonia Joines, who is master of ceremonies at the Alleghany Fiddlers Convention and a disk jockey at radio station WCOK.

Dennis Joines: Born October 10, 1951, in Sparta, North Carolina. Plays guitar. In various bands, including "Swamp Grass" for five years and "New River Bluegrass." Dennis learned from his father and grandfather. Related to other Joineses who play.

Ernest Joines: Born June 22, 1931, in Alleghany County (Stratford area). Plays mandolin, guitar, bass, and banjo. Owns Alleghany Jubilee (old theater building now used for jams and dances); his wife, Agnes Joines, helped to organize this music venue in Sparta, North Carolina.

Gary Joines: Born July 28, 1949, in Sparta, North Carolina. Plays fiddle. Learned from a cousin, Howard Joines (see Richard Joines entry), and from Art Wooten, Cleve Andrews, and Wayne Williams.

Richard Joines: Born December 26, 1941, in Alleghany County. Plays guitar and mandolin. His father, Howard, played fiddle and taught many in the area. Howard was a brother of Dennis Joines's grandfather (see Dennis Joines entry). Howard's granddaughter, Mary Joines, played clawhammer banjo at Galax Fiddlers Convention, 2000.

Donald Gregory ("Greg") Jones: Born September 4, 1965, in Cana, Virginia. Plays mandolin. Second cousin to Philip Jones (see separate entry).

Dwight Jones: Born c. 1960–65. Plays guitar. Member of committee for Alleghany Fiddlers Convention.

Gary Jones: Born July 5, 1950, in Ashe County hospital, but was taken home to Alleghany County. Plays guitar and banjo. Father, Odell Jones, played guitar and taught him. Gary's mother was a Joines, so he is related to many musicians. Gary's son, Kenneth, born June 30, 1994, is learning guitar.

Philip Jones: Born May 3, 1957, in a hospital in Surry County, North Carolina, but was taken home to Carroll County. Plays bluegrass guitar. Lives in Cana, Virginia, and has office in Hillsville, Virginia. Learned from Wade Jones. Philip played bluegrass music for Hillsville's Fourth of July celebration, 1999, with Ronnie Bowman, Tim Chadwick, and Ronnie Lyons. Philip is teaching his son, Will Jones (born September 24, 1991), guitar. Will is one of triplets; the other two are Mary Alden Jones and Caitlin Jones, who both play piano. Daughter, Laura Leigh Jones, plays mandolin. There is another sister, Ashley Jones. Two of Philip's children took part in the junior competition at Galax Fiddlers Convention, 2000: Laura Leigh won third in mandolin, and Will won fifth in guitar. The family sings a cappella in a style learned in the Primitive Baptist church where Philip's father was a minister.

J. C. Kemp: Born June 25, 1943, in Ashe County. Plays banjo. Self-taught.

Patricia ("Trish") Kilby: Born November 27, 1977, in West Jefferson, North Carolina. Daughter of Charles Kilby and Judy Powers Kilby. Has played with "Fox Creek Ramblers" and with "Farmer's Daughters" band which toured France in "American Music Traditions" program, 1997. Currently manages "Blue Ridge Mountain Ramblers." Won third in clawhammer banjo at Galax Fiddlers Convention, 1995 and 1998; first in old-time banjo at Ashe County, 1996; third at Alleghany Fiddlers Convention, 1999, and first in 2000. Performs at festivals such as "Seedtime in the Cumberland" and at Pine Mountain Settlement School in Kentucky. A descendant of the Hash, Sturgill, Spencer, and Weaver families of the Upper New River. Her paternal grandmother was a Sturgill, and her great-grandmother was a Spencer. Learned banjo from Emily Spencer. Trish is a student at Appalachian State University in Boone, North Carolina.

Steve Kilby: Born November 26, 1954, in North Wilkesboro, North Carolina, with roots in the New River area. Visited his grandmother (a Dowell), who lived near Independence, Virginia. His family was very involved in music. Now lives in Piney Creek, North Carolina. Kilby was first on guitar and best all-around performer at Galax Fiddlers Convention, 1980. More recently, in the year 2000, Steve won first in guitar at Fairview, Virginia; Mount Airy, North Carolina; and Fiddlers Grove, North Carolina. Has produced albums with Heritage (see McGee).

Tony King: Born August 16, 1969, in Galax, Virginia. Plays bass in "New River Bluegrass" band; also plays guitar and mandolin. His mother, of the Pennington family from Ashe County, was born in Fries, Virginia. Tony learned much music from Kyle Smith and Roy Martin.

Roald Kirby and Ellie Kirby: Roald was born October 5, 1951, in Sturgills, North Carolina. Plays banjo. Ellie was born September 22, 1957, in Alabama. Plays fiddle. Roald won tenth prize in clawhammer banjo at Galax Fiddlers Convention, 1997. Their band is "Miss Ellie and the South Fork Ramblers," with Jean Bradford on bass and Terry Gleason on guitar. The Kirbys' daughter, Rosy Fay Kirby (born November 18, 1989, in Grayson County), is learning guitar. Roald and Ellie often play at Grayson Highlands State Park.

LaVerne Osborne Kiser: Born October 12, 1933, on Haw Orchard Mountain, Rugby, Virginia. Played banjo at Blanche Ward Nichols's (see separate entry) "jam" and worked at Grayson Highlands State Park. First cousin, once removed, to Ola Belle Campbell Reed.

Melanie Anderson Koenig: Born 1968. Lives in Tennessee but comes back to visit family in Grayson County. Plays fiddle. Her grandfather Anderson lived across the road from Blanche Ward Nichols, (see separate entry) famous for jams.

Mark Krider: Born c. 1958–60 in Todd, North Carolina (on the border between Ashe County and Watauga County). Plays bluegrass banjo.

Steve Lewis: Born April 17, 1981, in Todd, North Carolina. Plays guitar and banjo. Won second in guitar at Alleghany Fiddlers Convention, 1999; first in bluegrass banjo at Galax Fiddlers Convention, 1996. Also plays bass with the Hardin brothers.

Tim Lewis: Born December 13, 1960, in Chester County, Pennsylvania. Son of Blaine Lewis and Lorraine Cornett Lewis. Soon after his birth, the family moved back to parents' home in Ashe County. He has a silk-screen printing company in West Jefferson, North Carolina. Tim plays bluegrass banjo. Won first at Ashe County Fiddlers Convention, 1996; second at Alleghany Fiddlers Convention, 1997; fourth at Galax Fiddlers Convention, 1997, and second, 1999. Plays on tape "W. C. Henderson and Company."

James Lindsey: Born August 14, 1921, near Hillsville (now lives in Galax, Virginia). Plays mandolin in "Mountain Ramblers" and played at Blanche Ward Nichols's (see separate entry) jam sessions. His band formed in 1953, played on radio, and made albums. His son, Larry Lindsey (born July 1956), plays guitar, as does a nephew, Patrick Lindsey.

Elwood Lineberry: Born May 29, 1924, in Hebron, Virginia, near Galax, Virginia. Plays mandolin. Learned from listening to records. Played at fiddlers conventions.

Tim Lineberry: Born August 25, 1953, in Carroll County. Plays bluegrass banjo. His father, Burgess Lineberry, played guitar and autoharp; and his grandfather, Ernest Lineberry, played clawhammer banjo. His great-uncles played banjo and fiddle. Tim made his own banjo when he started playing in 1976 and the next year joined the band "Bluegrass Ramblers," which he was with until 1981. Now he plays with the "Highlanders." Won second at Galax Fiddlers Convention several times and placed well at many other fiddlers conventions.

J. C. Lovelace: Born April 28, 1937, in Alleghany County. Plays mandolin, guitar, and bass. Started playing on banjo, taught by mother, Lula Billings Lovelace. Won many awards at fiddlers conventions.

Jack Lovelace: Born May 1, 1928, in Ashe County. Plays guitar. Self-taught.

Jesse Lovell: Born April 26,1935, in Fries, Virginia. Plays guitar, banjo, mandolin, and fiddle. Nephew of Evelyn Farmer (see separate entry) and grandson of Glen Smith. His grandfather taught Jesse to play banjo and later passed on his own banjo to his grandson, a memorable moment for both. For decades Jesse has built upon his musical heritage, and he is widely revered in the New River area. Performs in band "Old-Time Traditions" and plays backup in other bands. Has won many prizes at fiddlers conventions, including "Best Performer" on guitar at Elk Creek Fiddlers Convention, 1995; second in vocals at Alleghany Fiddlers Convention, 1998; and "Best Over-all Performer" at Elk Creek Fiddlers Convention, 1999.

Lundy Brothers: Bobby Lundy and Teddy Lundy of Delaware. Related to Ted Lundy of the New River area, who played in band with Ola Belle Campbell Reed. Bobby placed first in bluegrass banjo at Galax Fiddlers Convention, 1997. Teddy placed first in bluegrass fiddle at Galax, 1997.

Ronnie Lyons: Born February 23, 1949, in Carroll County. Lives in Laurel Fork, Virginia. Plays mandolin. Member of band "Southern Breeze," with Dennis Holt, Bill Joines, and Ken Melton (see separate entries).

James MacMillan: Born in Alleghany County. Plays guitar and mandolin. Formerly played in band "Carolina Buddies." Still plays at small gatherings, such as at Troutdale, Virginia.

Thomas MacMillan: Born April 3, 1956, in Galax, Virginia. Plays guitar. Learned from Bill Williams of Alleghany County. Thomas's maternal grandfather was Tom Williams, and his family also was related to the Weavers.

Crystal Mahaffey: Born May 1, 1977, in Boone, North Carolina; grew up in Whitetop, Virginia. Daughter of Michael Mahaffey (see separate entry); connected to Blevins, Cox, and Hash families. Plays fiddle and banjo. Learned some fiddle from her grandfather, James Corbitt Stamper, who taught Albert Hash (see chap. 3). After her grandfather passed on, she studied and played with Thornton Spencer. Crystal plays fiddle with "Fox Creek Ramblers." Married Leon Blevins, also a musician (see separate entry). The Stamper family was among the earliest New River settlers, around 1767.

Michael Mahaffey: Born May 19, 1950, in West Jefferson, North Carolina. Now lives in Whitetop, Virginia. His mother was a Jones. Plays guitar. Learned from Thornton Spencer. Father of Crystal Mahaffey (see separate entry).

Bill Manning: Born c. late 1920s–early 1930s at Woodlawn, Virginia. Plays guitar.

Marshall Brothers: Born in Carroll County, they live in Hillsville, Virginia. Clarence Marshall was born May 19, 1921. Plays guitar, fiddle, and banjo. Jim Marshall, born c. 1930, plays banjo. Jim's wife, Arty Marshall, plays guitar and sings.

Zane Marshall: Born October 13, 1959, in Carroll County. Lives in Fancy Gap, Virginia. Plays guitar. His father and uncle also played guitar. Wife is Sandra Horton Marshall. Sandra helped some young people organize the "American Heritage Dancers," for clogging performances. Their son, Adam (born April 28, 1987), plays mandolin and does clogging.

Alan Mastin: Born January 18, 1956, in Elk Creek, Virginia. Lives in Mouth of Wilson, Virginia. Plays bass with Tommy Sells in "Big Country Bluegrass." Son of Bruce Mastin of Elk Creek, Virginia, who played old-time fiddle. Alan won second in bass at Alleghany Fiddlers Convention, 1996.

Paul Frederick McBride: Born July 8, 1924, in Alleghany County. Was playing banjo at age ten; later also fiddle. Learned from Laud Bowers.

Jim McKinnon: Born November 18, 1938, in Marion, Virginia. Plays mandolin, guitar, bass, and banjo. His family was from the Bethel section of Grayson County, where his roots go back to great-great-grandparents. Jim was always visiting his grandfather there. His father played fiddle and gave him a mandolin on his eleventh birthday. He has twin sons (born July 11, 1986): Kevin McKinnon plays mandolin, and Keith McKinnon plays guitar.

Stephanie McKinnon: Born October 10, 1977, in Marion, Virginia. Roots in Bethel section of Grayson County. Plays banjo. Learned from Debbie Grim and from many relatives who play. Niece of Jim McKinnon (see separate entry).

Fred Medley: Born c. 1957 in Ashe County. Plays guitar. Is teaching his step-son, Donny Yingling (born December 7, 1980, in Baltimore), who was in first grade when they moved to Sparta, North Carolina, and then to Piney Creek, North Carolina. They play and sing in the Church of God Tabernacle in Sparta.

Betty Bledsoe Meikle: Born April 1, 1962, in Wilkesboro, North Carolina. Her parents, William Bledsoe and Marilyn Weaver Bledsoe, were from Ashe County; they have a family farm on New River. Betty plays old-time fiddle and dulcimer and jams every year at Galax.

David Melton: Born April 17, 1956, in Carroll County. Lives on Coleman Ridge near Piper's Gap, Virginia, with wife, Penny Bolt Melton. Plays clawhammer banjo, guitar, and harmonica. Learned banjo from Calvin Cole at the Wildlife Building in the Fries area, which had music on Saturday nights. His grandfather, Brifco Wilson, also played clawhammer banjo. David played in band "Slate Mountain Ramblers" for a while. He likes jam sessions with friends, such as Eddie Bond. He enters fiddlers conventions and has won many prizes, such as sixth in clawhammer banjo at Galax Fiddlers Convention, 54th Convention; and third at Ashe County Fiddlers Convention, 1989.

Kenneth Melton: Born July 8, 1950, in Washington, D.C., but family moved back to Carroll County in 1952. Now lives in Woodlawn, Virginia. Plays bluegrass banjo. Member of band "Southern Breeze" with Dennis Holt, Bill Joines, and Ronnie Lyons (see separate entries). Won first at Alleghany Fiddlers Convention, 1996; sixth at Galax Fiddlers Convention, 1998, and seventh, 1999; first at Elk Creek Fiddlers Convention, 1999; first at Fries Fiddlers Convention, 2000.

Austin Michael: Born 1984 in Lansing, Ashe County; plays banjo at music events; learned from Trish Kilby.

Johnny Miller: See chapter 5. Born August 28, 1929, in Ashe County, North Carolina. Lives in Volney, Virginia, near his birthplace. Plays fiddle. His father, John Miller Sr., was a founding member of the "North Carolina Ridge Runners" and also made instruments. In late 1920s, the family moved to Maryland so that John Sr. could work on the Conowingo Dam.

Johnny says, "We drifted back and forth several times, like they all did."
He learned to play from his father and, along with his cousins and Ola
Belle Reed, became the second generation of the North Carolina Ridge
Runners in Maryland, usually playing fiddle. According to Johnny, they
played at "parks, fairs, carnivals, and festivals in Maryland, Pennsyl-
vania, Delaware, and New Jersey." (Johnny's uncles, Preacher Ambrose
Miller and Calvin Sexton, traveled a similar circuit, preaching out of a
tent.) Later Johnny had a job playing electric lead guitar with Ernest
Tubb. Played with Ola Belle Reed and Alex Campbell at New River Ranch
in Maryland for over twenty years. Backed up famous musicians such as
Webb Pierce, Don Reno, and Charlie Monroe. Later he returned to New
River area, where he played with "High Country Ramblers," which
included Paul Gentle, Wayne Henderson (see chap. 5), Herb Key, Larry
Pennington (see separate entry), and Raymond Pennington. Now plays
in "Flint Hill Bluegrass Boys." Now serves as a judge at fiddlers' conventions. Father of Walter Miller (see separate entry).

Walter Miller: Born January 24, 1966, in Burnsville, North Carolina. Son of
Johnny Miller (see separate entry). The family moved to Delaware and
later back to Grayson County, where Walter graduated from high school
at Independence, Virginia. Walter then moved to Charlotte, North Carolina,
for a musical career but is back and now lives in Volney, Virginia. Walter
plays many instruments, including guitar, bass, mandolin, banjo, piano,
and drums. Also sings and writes songs. Has been in several bands and
now is doing a solo CD.

Harold Mitchell: Born March 22, 1938, at Stephen's Creek, one mile from
Fries, Virginia. Plays guitar. His primary role in music has been as master of ceremonies for years at the Galax Fiddlers Convention and many
other area fiddlers conventions.

Keith Mitchell: Born June 3, 1963, in Marion, Virginia, hospital but was
brought home to Grayson County, where he grew up. Plays guitar and has
made six guitars. Does not enter contests but enjoys playing with others.
Is a cousin to Steve Mitchell (see separate entry).

Steve Mitchell: Born February 1, 1956, in Troutdale, Virginia. Plays guitar and
spoons; also dances. He is a cousin to Keith Mitchell (see separate entry).

Dale Morris: Born November 20, 1950, in Pipers Gap, Virginia; now lives in
Elk Creek, Virginia. Plays guitar, banjo, and bass. Has played with "Wolfe
Brothers Old-time Band" and "New Ballard Branch Bogtrotters." His wife,
Connie Crockett, is from Wythe County. His son, Jesse Morris, plays gui-
tar. Dale learned much from Whit Sizemore. Dale's mother's family, the
Amburns, were musicians who played with Enoch Rutherford.

Newman Brothers: Randy Newman, born c. 1962 in Woodlawn, Virginia; later
moved to Maryland but comes back to play. Plays fiddle, banjo, and guitar. Ronnie Newman, born c. 1966, plays fiddle. J. L. Newman of Carroll
County; moved to Richmond, Virginia. Plays guitar.

Helen Newman: Born October 12, 1948, at Galax, Virginia. Plays autoharp.
Often played at Blanche Ward Nichols's (see separate entry) jams.

Blanche Ward Nichols: See chapter 5. Born June 24, 1915, in Grayson County.
Part of the famous musical Ward family that included Crockett Ward,

Fields Ward, and Wade Ward (see separate entries). Plays old-time guitar. Blanche Ward married Ellis Nichols. For over thirty years, they hosted Tuesday night jam sessions at their home north of Independence, Virginia, near Buck Mountain; Blanche continued the sessions as a widow. These sessions brought together old-timers and newcomers to the musical scene. Ward ancestors settled on Saddle Creek on Buck Mountain, Virginia.

David Nichols: From Sparta, North Carolina. Won first in guitar, Alleghany Fiddlers Convention, 1997.

Richard Nichols: Born May 20, 1940, in Alleghany County. Plays guitar and bass. Member of committee for the Alleghany Fiddlers Convention.

Tracy Nichols: Born February 4, 1965, Alleghany County; plays bass.

Trevor Nichols: Born April 7, 1967, Alleghany County; plays guitar, fiddle, and mandolin.

Tom Norman: Born March 28, 1931, in Surry County, North Carolina, but had grandparents in Grayson County. Lives in Galax, Virginia. Plays old-time banjo. His father played banjo, but he learned from his mother, Sarah Margaret McRoberts Norman. Plays at Fries, Virginia, and played for square dances at Fancy Gap, Virginia, for twenty years. Also played with Whit Sizemore (see separate entry) and "Shady Mountain Ramblers."

Cindy Brooks Norris: Born April 17, 1965. Plays guitar and bass. Serves as master of ceremonies at fiddlers conventions. Her father is Jim Brooks (see separate entry).

Bryan Osborne: Born February 3, 1987, at Creston, North Carolina. Won first in junior bass, Alleghany Fiddlers Convention, 1999.

David Albert Osborne: Born 1964 in Grayson County. Son of Audrey Hash Hamm (see separate entry) and grandson of Albert Hash (see chap. 3). Learned instrument making from both; now has shop in Preston, North Carolina. Also plays guitar and other instruments.

Wayne Osborne: Born April 21, 1948, in Grayson County. His mother was an Anderson. Wayne is a cousin to Ola Belle Campbell Reed. Plays guitar with Elmer Russell (see separate entry) in the "Flatridge Boys." Wayne's ancestor is Capt. Enoch Osborne of the American Revolutionary militia.

Arthur Pasley: Born June 14, 1926, in Grassy Creek, North Carolina. Plays mandolin, fiddle, and guitar. Member of the band "Red Hill Ramblers." Father of Randy Pasley (see separate entry).

Jack Paisley: Born c. 1930 in Alleghany County. Played fiddle with brothers.

Lucas Pasley: Born April 27, 1975, in Tacoma, Washington; his parents were in the military. His father, James Pasley, was born in Glade Valley, North Carolina. His great-uncle, Guy Brooks, was a fiddler in the band "Red Fox Chasers" in the 1920s. Lucas's grandfather and Arthur Pasley's father were cousins. Lucas plays fiddle, banjo, and guitar. He won first in old-time fiddle at the Alleghany Fiddlers Convention, 1999. Lucas is a student at Appalachian State University, Boone, North Carolina.

Randy Pasley: Born July 3, 1965, in Jefferson, North Carolina. Son of Arthur Pasley (see separate entry). Plays all bluegrass instruments except fiddle. Travels to perform. Has band "Alternate Roots." He won second in dobro at Elk Creek Fiddlers Convention, 1998; first at Galax Fiddlers Convention, 1999; "Best All-round Performer" at Galax, 1999; first in dobro at Galax, 2000.

Bobby Patterson: Born April 1, 1942, in Galax, Virginia. Owns Heritage Records store in Woodlawn, Virginia. Plays banjo, guitar, and mandolin. Learned five-string banjo from Charles Hawks and guitar from parents, John Patterson and Ruby Bryant Patterson. Was in various bands: "Virginia Cutups," "Sunny Mountain Boys and Dot," "Highlanders," "Mountain Ramblers" (with James Lindsey), "Camp Creek Boys" (with Kyle Creed). Has played with Tommy Jarrell. Performed at the Smithsonian Institution and Wolf Trap. Bobby's family heritage in music includes his father's father, a fiddler; his mother's father, Virgil Bryant, noted on clawhammer banjo; his paternal grandmother's brother, Uncle Bob Crawford, old-time fiddler. Bobby is also a singer, a member of a gospel trio "Country Friends."

Joy Roupe Patton: Born March 25, 1956, in Alleghany County. Plays fiddle and banjo. Daughter of Fred Roupe (see separate entry).

Larry Pennington: Born August 4, 1946, at Ashe County Hospital. Home is Warrensville, North Carolina. Plays banjo and fiddle. Larry played old-time music with Wayne Henderson and now plays bluegrass banjo with the band "Big Country Bluegrass." Won third at Galax Fiddlers Convention, 1996; second at Alleghany Fiddlers Convention, 1996, and third in 1997. Learned from his father, Hack Pennington, and from Larry Richardson. The Pennington ancestor, a preacher and writer from Kent, England, settled with his family in Ashe County around the 1780s.

Spencer Pennington: Born November 9, 1934, in Warrensville, North Carolina. Plays guitar. Plays music with his grandsons, Brandon Hardin and Eric Hardin (see separate entry).

Kenneth Perkins: Born c. 1965 in Grayson County. Plays mandolin. Learned from Wayne Henderson.

Perry Brothers: Arnold Perry, born September 23, 1939; John Perry, born February 8, 1945; and Buck Perry, born November 4, 1946; all in Independence, Virginia. Their father played some banjo. They had a band, "New River Ramblers," and made records. Arnold played rhythm guitar in the band, John played lead guitar, Buck played banjo, and friend Gilbert Suitt (see separate entry) played bass. They started playing in the 1950s but formed the band in 1969. They also play at fiddlers conventions. John won fifth in guitar at Alleghany Fiddlers Convention, 1998.

Wade Petty: Born January 27, 1938, in Galax, Virginia. Wade grew up in Galax; after he married, he lived farther out, on Fries Road, near Pop Stoneman and his family, and was involved in their revival of old-time music. Wade's uncle by marriage, Clifford Carrico, played banjo and encouraged him in old-time music. Wade plays fiddle, guitar, and bass. He started playing on autoharp, then took up guitar. He began learning to play fiddle by listening to records and from the people around him. His father and brother had played fiddle in local bands in the late 1920s and 1930s. His mother's family, the Caudills, also included fiddlers. Later Wade got into bluegrass music and for some time played bass with Charles Hawks's band. Also played with Tommy Sells's (see separate entry) band "Big Country Bluegrass." Won first in bluegrass fiddle at Fries Fiddlers Convention, 1997. Tied for most wins in fiddle at Galax Fiddlers Convention (Hiatt data). Jams at the Crouse House in Sparta,

North Carolina, on Monday nights and at Claytor Lake Restaurant on Saturday nights. Daughter, Dana Petty Mays (born July 17, 1968), plays guitar. Grandson, Justin Petty (born September 7, 1985), plays guitar and mandolin.

Jean Phipps: Born c. 1925, Anawalt, West Virginia, and was raised there by grandparents with roots in Grayson County, Virginia; later her mother took her back to New River, in Ashe County, North Carolina, and she graduated from Virginia-Carolina High in 1943. Her grandparents were first cousins, and their grandparents were Mr. and Mrs. James Phipps Hash of Grayson County, so traditions run deep. While in the grandparents' home, all the children were raised with music, and they all played guitar, including Jean. She has lived in Mouth of Wilson (Grayson County) since 1980 and plays guitar at jam sessions in West Jefferson, North Carolina, near Greenfield Restaurant.

Josh Pickett: Born in 1983, he lives in Fries, Virginia. Plays bluegrass guitar. Has been playing since age fourteen. Largely self-taught, had a few lessons from Greg Wilson. Plays in band "Fast Forward." Also plays with cousin Robbie Pickett and at fiddlers conventions.

Barbara Edmonds Poole: Born March 13, 1950, in Galax, Virginia. Now lives in Low Gap, Surry County, North Carolina, only a few miles from Alleghany County. Daughter of Harry and Frances Edmonds, and sister of Jimmy Edmonds (see separate entry). Played with Wade Ward's (see separate entry) "Buck Mountain Band" (see McGee 152). Now plays bass fiddle in band "Unique Sounds of the Mountains," with Larry Sigmon on banjo. Still plays in Galax as well as North Carolina.

Archie Powers: Born October 17, 1936, in Ashe County. Plays fiddle. Learned from Albert Hash (see chap. 3).

Ken Powers: Born December 13, 1934, in Whitetop, Virginia. Lives in Independence, Virginia. Learned fiddle from his uncle, Borden Osborne. Played bluegrass on circuit and fronted for Bill Monroe and also the Osborne Brothers. Returning home, he "picked with" Dave Sturgill, who involved him in old-time music. Ken was leader of the "Grayson Highlands String Band" for fourteen years. That band won first in old-time at Galax Fiddlers Convention in 1985. Now Ken serves as a judge at fiddlers conventions. He is distantly related to Ola Belle Reed (his mother was also an Osborne) and to Albert Hash's wife, Ethel Spencer Hash (see chap. 3). His father's family settled in Ashe County.

Mack Powers: Born April 15, 1951, in Lansing, North Carolina. Plays dobro and mandolin. Plays in bluegrass band "Rock Bottom," which won first at Alleghany Fiddlers Convention, 1997. Mack won third in dobro at Alleghany Fiddlers Convention, 1996; first, 1997; and second, 1999 and 2000. He won second at Galax Fiddlers Convention, 1997 and 1999. He is a distant cousin to Ken Powers (see separate entry).

Dee Dee Price: Born September 19, 1945, in Ashe County; grew up in West Virginia and then came back. Lives in Whitetop, Virginia. Teaches banjo, which she learned from Flurry Dowe. Plays in "Old-Time Traditions" band. Dee Dee won fourth in old-time banjo at the Alleghany Fiddlers Convention, 1997, and third in 1998.

Annie Belle Clontz Primm: Born February 27, 1942, Hillsville, Carroll County, and still lives there; her mother was from the Aldermann family; she plays guitar and sings. Ashley Primm (see entry below) is a distant cousin to her husband.

Ashley Primm: Born June 22, 1977, in Galax, Virginia. Lives in Hillsville, Virginia. Plays guitar and bass and sings. Won eighth in folk song at Galax Fiddlers Convention, 1999, and seventh in an earlier year. Manages the band "Fast Forward."

Teresa Profitt: Born 1955, West Jefferson, Ashe County, North Carolina; daughter of Charlie Profitt, banjo player; Teresa plays guitar and sings.

Thurman Pugh: Born March 16, 1935, in Carroll County. Plays bass and fiddle. For forty years, has played with James Lindsey in "Mountain Ramblers." Also sings lead.

Diana Faye Purkey: Born January 12, 1958. Daughter of Bobby Purkey (born 1931) and Trula Faye Parks Purkey; sister of Delbert Glen Purkey (see separate entry). Diana plays mandolin and played with Albert Hash (see chap. 3). She married Keith Gilbert, who plays guitar, bass, and harmonica. Both play in the Purkey family's band.

Delbert Glen Purkey: Born November 23, 1954, in Alleghany County. Son of Bobby Purkey (born 1931) and Trula Faye Parks Purkey. Delbert's father Bobby has roots in Grayson County (Cox family) but grew up in Marion, Virginia. After he and Faye (who was born in Grant, Virginia) married, they moved to northern Virginia, where they lived for forty years. While there, Bobby led the band "Blue Ridge Travelers," for which he played guitar and sang. Other family members were in the band also. It played at festivals and in clubs in Fairfax and Alexandria, Virginia. Then the family moved back to New River. Delbert plays banjo, which he learned from his father. He often plays with the "Flatridge Boys" and Johnny Miller, and he used to play with Albert Hash at Whitetop (see chap. 3). His son Daniel (born August 24, 1982) plays bass. Diana Faye Purkey Gilbert (see separate entry) is Delbert's sister.

JoAnne Andrews Redd: Born April 6, 1938, in Galax, Virginia. Plays autoharp, dulcimer, and clawhammer banjo. Won first in autoharp, Alleghany Fiddlers Convention, 1998; first at Mount Airy many times; fifth at Galax Fiddlers Convention, 1999; and many other awards. Learned much about autoharp from Evelyn Farmer. JoAnne plays autoharp in "Old-Time Traditions" band. Sister of Jama Lee Edwards (see separate entry).

Steven Monroe Redd: Born May 2, 1956, in Carroll County. Plays mandolin. Comes from musical family. His father, Howard Redd (born April 25, 1920), played clawhammer banjo. Howard's father, Troy Bruce Redd (born 1887 in Carroll County), played fiddle; both Howard and Troy played at the first Galax Fiddlers Convention. Steven's maternal grandfather, James Earl Vernon, was a singer whose daughter, Pearl Vernon, played guitar. Steven is a second cousin to JoAnne Andrews Redd (see separate entry).

Charlie Reed: Born December 2, 1942, in Ashe County. Plays guitar. Learned from Randy Greer.

Lisa Reedy: Born July 8, 1959, Marion, Virginia; plays clawhammer banjo. Her grandfather was Jack Reedy of Grassy Creek, Ashe County, North Carolina, who played banjo in various bands and played at the White Top Festival in the 1930s with the "Smyth County Ramblers." He was her inspiration; however, she learned banjo from Emily Spencer and Dee Dee Price. Lisa lives on Pond Mountain in the Whitetop Mountain area.

Reeves Brothers: Homer, born 1912, and Cleo, born 1922, both in Sparta, North Carolina. Both play guitar and live in Alleghany County. Another brother, Del Reeves, is well known in the Nashville music scene.

Lloyd Richardson: Born c. 1965 in Lansing, North Carolina. Lives in Warrensville, North Carolina. Plays bass. Won second in bass at Alleghany Fiddlers Convention, 1997; third in 1999 and 2000. Also plays guitar and is in band "Rock Bottom."

Robbin Richardson: Born March 7, 1973, in Grayson County. Plays guitar. Learned from Wayne Henderson.

Steve Richardson: From Woodlawn, Virginia. Plays dobro. Attends Galax Fiddlers Convention.

Reid Robertson: Born March 18, 1928, in Grayson County. Lives in Elk Creek, Virginia. Plays and makes instruments. Won third in mandolin, Alleghany Fiddlers Convention, 1996, and fourth in 1997; fifth in mandolin at Elk Creek Fiddlers Convention, 1999. Has played in many local bands; now is in "Old-Time Traditions." His father played French harp.

Mark Rose and Lenora Huber Rose: Lenora Huber Rose was born January 3, 1940, in Arlington, Virginia, but returned to live in Grayson County, where her family had originated (her mother was a Cornett, her grandmother a Delp). Among Lenora's ancestors in the New River area was Levi Cornett, a founder of Lebanon Methodist Church in Elk Creek, Virginia. Mark Rose was born in Lexington, Kentucky, but also has roots in the New River area. His great-grandfather, E. R. Rector, a fiddler, was born and lived in Alleghany County. Mark and Lenora met in the New River area and care deeply about it and its music. They lead the "Courthouse Ramblers," an old-time band with a highly varied repertoire, including occasional contemporary comical and musical scenes. Other members of the band include Leon Frost, Bet Mangum, Rob Mangum, Becky Ward, and Edwin Ward. The group performs in theaters and at private parties, as well as playing every year at the Galax Fiddlers Convention. Two notable events the "Courthouse Ramblers" played for were the fifty-fifth wedding anniversary party of David and Peggy Rockefeller at Hudson Pines in New York; and a party for Lady Bird Johnson at Bill Plannill's residence in Roaring Gap, North Carolina.

Osborne Lewis ("J. R.") Ross Jr.: Born October 11, 1941, in Maryland, but grew up in Flatridge, Virginia, where his parents were born and where they returned to raise their family. He is related to Osbornes, Andersons, and Hashes. Plays guitar. Learned from relatives and friends. Sometimes played backup for the "Flatridge Boys," in which his cousin Wayne Osborne (see separate entry) plays.

Dale Roten: Born October 16, 1964, in Warrensville, North Carolina. Lives in West Jefferson, North Carolina. Plays bluegrass banjo, which he learned from J. C. Kemp (see separate entry); and mandolin. Won second in mandolin, Alleghany Fiddlers Convention, 1999. Is a member of the band "Rock Bottom." Brother of John Roten (see separate entry).

John Roten: Born September 17, 1962, in Ashe County. Lives in West Jefferson, North Carolina. Plays mandolin and banjo. Self-taught. Won first in bluegrass banjo at Alleghany Fiddlers Convention, 1999. Brother of Dale Roten (see separate entry).

Mike Roten: Born March 17, 1954, in Ashe County. Lives in West Jefferson, North Carolina. Plays fiddle. Learned from Albert Hash (see chap. 3) and Rita Scott (see separate entry).

Fred Roupe: Born March 13, 1933, on Prather's Creek, North Carolina. Has been playing music for over fifty years. Fred also makes instruments in his shop at home; he has made both fiddles and banjos. Won second in bluegrass banjo, Galax Fiddlers Convention, 1995; and first, Alleghany Fiddlers Convention, 1997. He manages the traditional and progressive bluegrass band, "Swamp Grass," which in 1998 won fourth at both the Alleghany Fiddlers Convention and the Galax Fiddlers Convention. Daughter Joy Roupe Patton (see separate entry) plays fiddle and banjo. Fred lives in Sparta.

Zach Roupe: Born 1981. Lives in Sparta, North Carolina. Plays banjo in band "Grass Stain" with Allan Johnson (see separate entry). Zach is the great-nephew of Fred Roupe (see separate entry). His paternal grandfather is Floyd Roupe, and his maternal grandfather is Floyd Reeves (born May 18, 1925), who plays and also makes fiddles in Twin Oaks, North Carolina.

Bonnie Russell: Galax, Virginia. Won first in dulcimer at Galax Fiddlers Convention, 1996; third in dulcimer, Alleghany Fiddlers Convention, 1997; first at Fries Fiddlers Convention, 1997. Sister of Roy Russell (see separate entry).

Elmer Russell: Born November 12, 1945, in Flatridge, Virginia. Leader of the band "Flatridge Boys." He plays rhythm guitar and does tenor vocals, with cousin Ron Russell on autoharp and harmonica; sister Carol Russell Frenza on mandolin, guitar, and vocals (Carol now lives out-of-state); Gary Shepherd (see separate entry) on bass guitar and bass; Wayne Osborne on guitar and vocals; and Doug Galyean of Baywood, Virginia, on mandolin. This group plays and sings old-time and gospel music. As they use some instrument electrification, they do not play at fiddlers conventions. They play local shows and have made tapes and CDs. The "Flatridge Boys" were nominated for "Amateur Bluegrass Group of the Year" in Nashville in 1997. The earliest Russell in the New River area was James R. Russell, licensed to sell "retail goods" in 1787. Elmer and Ron are also descendants of the Cornetts, who settled Elk Creek (see chap. 5).

Ron Russell: See previous listing.

Roy Russell: Plays guitar and mandolin. Brother of Bonnie Russell (see separate entry).

Enoch Rutherford: Born April 26, 1916, in Grayson County. Lives in the Gold Hill section west of Independence, Virginia. Son of Harvey Rutherford and Maude Phipps Rutherford. Plays clawhammer banjo and fiddle. Has won many awards at Galax Fiddlers Convention and other fiddlers conventions; won fourth in clawhammer banjo at Galax in 1994. Led the "Gold Hill Band." In the eighteenth century, Rutherfords were on the Montgomery (now Grayson) County militia list (see chap. 5).

Sage Brothers: Ted and Andy, born c. 1950s. Ted plays five-string banjo, and Andy plays mandolin; they have a band, "Sagegrass." They play at fiddlers conventions, where they have won some top prizes. The Sage family roots are in Ashe County, North Carolina, but the brothers now live in Washington County, Virginia.

Andy Sawyers: Lives in Fancy Gap, Virginia. Plays guitar.

Donnie Scott: Born c. 1950s, Taylorsville, North Carolina. Won fifth in dobro, Galax Fiddlers Convention, 1995, and seventh in 1997; first at Alleghany Fiddlers Convention, 1996, and second in 1997.

Rita Scott: Born August 14, 1953, in West Jefferson, North Carolina. Lives in Lansing, North Carolina. Plays and teaches fiddle. Was taught by Albert Hash (see chap. 3). Is in old-time band "Dixi Crystals." Daughter Sarah Scott (born December 1, 1980), is also a musician. They play together in band "Appalachian Mountain Girls" with Amy Hauslochner.

Dale Sells: Born July 25, 1972, in a Smyth County hospital, but was taken home to Grayson County. Lives near Volney, Virginia. Plays guitar.

Tommy Sells: Born August 6, 1957, in the Mouth of Wilson section of Grayson County, where he still lives. Descendant of many area pioneers, including Sells (Irish) and Perkins (English). Plays mandolin and guitar. Learned mandolin from his father, a well-known musician. Tommy has won many awards in the bluegrass category, including ninth place in mandolin at Galax Fiddlers Convention, 1995; and first in mandolin at Alleghany Fiddlers Convention, 1996. Tommy heads "Big Country Bluegrass," with his wife Teresa Sells as vocalist. The band won fourth at Galax Fiddlers Convention, 1995; third at Ashe County Fiddlers Convention, 1996; and first at Alleghany Fiddlers Convention, 1996 (see chap. 5).

Michael Sexton: Born August 15, 1978, in Grayson County. Plays guitar, which he learned from Greg Wilson. Also enters clogging competitions, often with his wife, Alana Gravely Sexton.

George Sheets: Born August 18, 1941, in Ashe County. Plays guitar. Member of committee for the Alleghany Fiddlers Convention.

Randy Sheets: Born February 18, 1956, in West Jefferson, North Carolina, and was taken home to Cabin Creek in the Whitetop area of Virginia. Has won many awards, including second in banjo at Bluefield Fiddlers, 1978. Now serves as a judge at Galax and other fiddlers conventions. Related to Perkins (mother). Is an Osborne descendant and is first cousin, once removed, to Ola Belle Reed.

Charles A. Shelor: Born November 19, 1950, in Carroll County. Plays guitar, fiddle, mandolin, and harmonica. Plays with Sammy Shelor.

Gary Shepherd: Born November 23, 1956, in Pennsylvania, but parents were from Rugby, Virginia. Gary returned to Grayson County, where both sets of grandparents lived. Lives in Elk Creek, Virginia. Now plays bass guitar and electric bass with the "Flatridge Boys" (see under "Russell" above). Also plays in gospel group "Southern Echoes." Gary learned music from Donald Absher of Piney Creek, North Carolina. Gary's wife is kin to Elmer Russell through the Cornett family connection.

Joann Morris Shinault: Born January 21, 1942, in Galax, Virginia. Plays bass fiddle. Married to Junior Shinault (born November 30, 1929, in Orange

County, North Carolina), who plays fiddle. Her son, Mitchell Brown (see separate entry), plays bass.

Whit Sizemore: Born April 22, 1934, in Carroll County near Galax, Virginia. Plays fiddle and mandolin; also makes both instruments. Led band "Shady Mountain Ramblers." Learned from the records of G. B. Grayson and from Gordon Shinault; also got help from Dr. Davis of the Galax Moose Lodge. Played some with Bobby Patterson. Whit's son, Mike Sizemore (born August 22, 1958), plays mandolin and some guitar. Mike is in the band "Southern Pride," with the Burris brothers.

Jerry Smith: Born October 16, 1936, in Ashe County. Lives in Jefferson, North Carolina. Formerly wrote newspaper articles and did photography for the *Skyland Post.* Plays guitar. Jerry learned music from Butch Barker and Dean Sturgill. Currently leads "Grayson Highlands String Band." His daughter, son-in-law, and granddaughter are in the band with him. Jerry's grandson, Ryan Smith (born November 22, 1983, in Ashe County), plays bass.

Jessica Elizabeth Smith: Born August 21, 1989, in Petersburg, Virginia, but has roots in Carroll County and comes back every summer. Her great-grand-mother is Evelyn Farmer. Jesse Lovell is her great-uncle; he gave her a guitar. She has been playing several years.

Kyle D. Smith: Born April 28, 1966, in Galax, Virginia. Plays banjo, guitar, dobro, bass, and mandolin. Learned from father, Kyle Smith, and from Wade Petty (see separate entry) and Roy Martin. Kyle D. mostly plays guitar. He is in band "New River Bluegrass," with his father, Rodney Hodges, Dennis Joines, and Tony King (see separate entries). The group plays in the Galax area and in Hickory, North Carolina, at a restaurant. Also plays with "Claude Lucas and the Fairview Boys."

Bill Spencer: Born December 9, 1918, in Ashe County. Lives in West Jefferson, North Carolina. Plays fiddle. Self-taught. Played with the "Brooks Brothers" band and for square dances at West Jefferson.

Thornton Spencer and Emily Spencer: Thornton Spencer was born November 12, 1937, in Whitetop, Virginia. Emily Spencer was born October 4, 1949, and grew up in northern Virginia but came to southwestern Virginia. They live in Whitetop. They make and play many instruments, but Thornton's specialty is playing old-time fiddle and working as a crafts-man on fiddles and other instruments. He learned instrument making from Albert Hash, his brother-in-law (husband of sister Ethel Spencer Hash; see chap. 3). Thornton and Emily give music lessons to many students, teach music at the Whitetop school, and perform at a local dance hall in Sparta, North Carolina. Daughter Martha Spencer (born January 26, 1985) plays dulcimer (see chap. 5).

James Stamper: Born 1915 in Grayson County. Plays fiddle. Taught Albert Hash (see chap. 3).

Roger Stamper: Son of James Stamper. Lives in Mount Airy, North Carolina. Plays guitar and old-time fiddle. Won ninth in old-time fiddle at Galax Fiddlers Convention, 1999.

Dean Sturgill: Born October 14, 1933, in Ashe County, North Carolina. A member of the "Grayson Highlands String Band," he often plays with his first cousin, Thornton Spencer (Dean's mother was a Spencer) and in community jam sessions at Sturgills, North Carolina. He has made many tapes and won many awards (see chap. 5).

Gilbert Suitt: Born August 1, 1954, in Grayson County. Plays guitar and autoharp. Has won many awards; including third in autoharp at the Alleghany Fiddlers Convention, 1995; ninth in autoharp at Galax Fiddlers Convention, 1997; and fifth at Fries Fiddlers Convention, 1997. Lives on Fox Creek and led the "Fox Creek Ramblers," which won eleventh place in old-time bands at Galax in 1994 and tenth in 1995. Members of the band then included Crystal Mahaffey on fiddle, Patricia Kilby on banjo, Gene Hall on guitar (see separate entries), and Anna Lee Delp Hall on spoons. Gilbert is related to Sturgill and Pugh families (grandmother was a Sturgill who married a Pugh).

Glen Sullivan: Born c. 1960 in Ashe County. Plays guitar at jam sessions in Sturgills, North Carolina.

Raymond Sweeny: Born c. 1925; plays banjo at jams in Fries, Virginia.

Freel Taylor: Born March 24, 1941, in Elk Creek, Virginia. Plays bass. Learned some music from Ellis Nichols, husband of Blanche Ward Nichols. Also, in father's family, two uncles played mandolin and guitar, and an aunt played guitar. All encouraged him in music. Freel plays with Elmer Russell in the "Flatridge Boys"; he used to play with Ken Powers. Freel lives in the Bethel area.

Tony Testerman: Born March 13, 1956, in Marion, Virginia, of a Grayson County family. Lives in Jefferson, North Carolina. Works for U.S. Department of Agriculture. Plays bass. Performed on tape, "W. C. Henderson and Company." The Testerman ancestor served in the local militia in 1780s and had land on Little Fox Creek.

Gerelene Trent: Lives in Green Valley, Fries, Virginia. Plays mandolin.

Susan Smith Trianosky: Born August 23, 1959, in Ashe County. Plays guitar. Learned from Butch Barker and Tim Lewis. Susan is the daughter of Jerry Smith of "Grayson Highlands String Band" (see separate entry). She is mother of Tina Trianosky Blevins (see separate entry) and has played with her in "Appalachian Mountain Girls" band.

Ted Trivett: Born November 19, 1946, in Konnarock, Virginia. Plays guitar. Began to play with Thornton Spencer (see separate entry) and Albert Hash (Ted's grandmother was a Hash).

Harold Vass: Born c. 1940 in Carroll County. Lives in Woodlawn. Plays mandolin and guitar. Son is Aaron Vass.

Vaughan Brothers: Philip Vaughan was born on January 19, 1968, in a hospital at Galax, Virginia, but was taken home to Fries, Virginia. Plays bluegrass banjo and guitar. Douglas Vaughan was born July 30, 1962. Lives in Fries, Virginia. Plays fiddle. Son, Garrett (born March 12, 1991), is learning fiddle from Brian Grim. Garrett's mother, Teresa Taylor Vaughan, sings.

Edwin Ward and Becky Deboard Ward: Edwin was born January 2, 1956, in Galax, Virginia; his parents lived in Piper's Gap, Virginia. He plays guitar. Becky Deboard Ward was born May 9, 1964, in Fort Campbell, Kentucky. Her father was in the military, but he was born in Grassy Creek, North Carolina, near New River, and her mother was born in Volney, Virginia, and is a cousin to Wayne Henderson. Becky plays dulcimer. Both Edwin and Becky play in the "Courthouse Ramblers."

John Warren: Born July 2, 1933, in Rugby, Virginia. John plays clawhammer banjo, which he learned from Emily Spencer. His wife, Fay Warren, was born March 4, 1939, in Marietta, Georgia. She plays fiddle, which she learned from Brian Grim and Emily Spencer, as well as guitar. Fay also teaches clogging in Parks and Recreation Department, City of Galax, Virginia. John's family has been in Rugby a long time; he is Thornton Spencer's cousin.

Wayne Peco Watson: Born August 21, 1947, at Brush Creek, Virginia, near Wythe County. Now lives in Fries, Virginia. He won third prize in bluegrass banjo at Galax Fiddlers Convention, 1999. He plays in the "New Ballard Branch Bogtrotters" and jams with friends.

Willey Brothers: James Willey was born November 11, 1959. Joe Willey was born September 13, 1964. Jerel Willey was born July 13, 1968. All were born in Alleghany County, and all play guitar. Their father played guitar, and their grandfather and uncle played banjo.

Bill Williams: Born 1950 in Alleghany County. Plays guitar and dobro.

Dan Williams: Born June 11, 1934, in Alleghany County. Now lives in Galax, Virginia. Plays guitar (sometimes does harmonica with guitar). Learned guitar from sister; mother played dulcimer. Dan played with Whit Sizemore (see separate entry) in "Shady Mountain Ramblers" and later played in "Slate Mountain Ramblers" (see McGee 151).

Greg Wilson: Born July 19, 1954, in Fries, Virginia. Son of Bobby Wilson. Plays guitar. Won second at Alleghany Fiddlers Convention, 1996 and third, 1997; won second at Galax, 1995 and 1997, and eighth in 1998. Also judges at Fries Fiddlers Convention. As a youngster, started band with siblings; they are cousins to Roger Wilson (see separate entry). Brother Gary Wilson plays guitar. Greg's wife is Barbara Redd (born December 15, 1961), who plays bass. Their sons also play: Patrick Wilson (born April 30, 1982), bluegrass fiddle; and Benjamin Wilson (born July 20, 1983), bluegrass fiddle.

Roger Wilson: Born c. 1945–50 in Galax, Virginia. Lives in Fairview, Virginia. Plays banjo. His mother was a Melton. His great-grandfather, Samuel Faultker, played banjo and lived in Cana, Virginia, in the "Round Peak" area of Carroll County that was well known for its musicians. Roger played in "River Rats" band and now sometimes plays with "Wolfe Brothers Old-time Band." Won fifth in old-time banjo at Ashe County Fiddlers Convention, 1996.

Sierra Wilson: Born January 6, 1994, in Ashe County. Plays fiddle. Participated in junior competition at Galax Fiddlers Convention, 2000.

Richard Woodie: Born July 6, 1943, in Ashe County. Lives in Sparta, North Carolina. Has tree farm. Plays banjo, guitar, and bass. Also has made banjos, a craft that he learned from "Uncle" Dave Sturgill. Played with Art Wooten. Member of Alleghany Fiddlers Convention committee.

Ray Wooten: Born in Alleghany County. Plays guitar. Grandson of Art Wooten, who played with Bill Monroe.

Lynn Worth: Born November 5, 1959, in Ashe County. Lives in Alleghany County, North Carolina. Plays bass, banjo, and fiddle. Learned fiddle from Thornton Spencer and Rita Scott. Lynn is a cousin to Betty Bledsoe

Meikle, also a musician; their mothers are sisters (Weaver family). Grandfather played mandolin. Brothers are Thomas Worth and Phil Worth (see separate entries).

Worth Brothers: Thomas, born November 2, 1955, plays guitar and mandolin. Phil, born December 23, 1957, plays banjo. Lynn Worth (see separate entry) is sister.

Herman Wyatt: Born July 25, 1936, in Pennsylvania to parents born in Ashe County, North Carolina, who later moved north for work. Herman's great-grandfather had come to Ashe County from Germany c. 1810–15. Herman's family always kept close contact with relatives in North Carolina, and Herman came back every year to hunt deer; he moved to Troutdale, Virginia, in Grayson County, and now lives there. He plays rhythm guitar and was in the "Grayson Highlands String Band" with Ken Powers. Herman's cousin, Howard Wyatt, played at the White Top Festival in the 1930s.

Well-Known Past Musicians

"Ike" Sturgill: Lived in Konnarock, Virginia. Initiated idea for the White Top Folk Festival; was a musician for gospel-singing groups.

Joel Sturgill: Son of William Sturgill and Emma Weiss Sturgill. Fiddler and banjo player. Spent most of his life in Ashe County until all his family moved, then he joined them in Harford County, Maryland. A cousin and friend of Ola Belle Campbell Reed, he also was the preacher who performed her wedding. He died in Maryland.

Ora (O. V.) Sturgill: Born 1916 in Chilhowie, Virginia. Son of Ocran Sturgill and Susan Blevins Sturgill. Had a gospel-singing group on radio in southwestern Virginia. Later built the Mount Rogers Inn in Mount Rogers, Virginia.

Crockett Ward and Fields Ward: Brothers, from Buck Mountain, Grayson County, Virginia. In the 1920s, had a band that recorded in Winston-Salem, North Carolina, and also in Richmond, Indiana, for the Gennett Record Company. The group successfully auditioned for Okeh Records also. Later they were reissued on Historical Records, Archive of American Folk Song, Library of Congress. In New River area, they were later known as the "Bogtrotters." Fields also recorded for Rounder in the 1970s (Lornell 205).

Wade Ward: Resident of Buck Mountain, Virginia. Kin to Crockett Ward and Fields Ward, and all of them were related to the Sturgills. Wade recorded for Okeh in the 1920s and later for the Library of Congress in 1938 (Lornell 207). However, Wade's main job as a musician was with Parson's Auction Company of Grayson County; he played at auctions for fifty-one years.

Appendix C
Chronologies

Ola Belle Campbell Reed

August 17, 1916: Born at family homeplace at Grassy Creek on the New River in Ashe County, North Carolina.

1933: Leaves Ashe County just prior to graduating from high school. Moves with family to Cecil County, Maryland, and later to Lancaster and Chester Counties, Pennsylvania.

1936: Joins the "North Carolina Ridge Runners" as vocalist and banjo picker; will be with this group until it disbands in 1948. The group performed on radio stations, made albums, and played at "music parks" such as "Sunset Park" in the Maryland-Pennsylvania-Delaware area.

1948: "North Carolina Ridge Runners" disbands.

1948: Ola Belle and brother, Alex Campbell, found the "New River Boys and Girls."

1949: "New River Boys and Girls" begin broadcasting on radio station WASA, Havre de Grace, Maryland. Show is named for the family store, "Campbell's Corner." Later "New River Boys and Girls" broadcast from radio stations WCOJ in Pennsylvania and WWVA in Wheeling, West Virginia.

"New River Boys and Girls" record and perform at music parks. The band will perform through the 1970s.

1949: Ola marries "Bud" Reed.

1950: Ola and Bud Reed begin operating "Rainbow Park" in Lancaster, Pennsylvania.

1951: Ola, Bud, and Alex found "New River Ranch," at Rising Sun, Maryland. It will operate until 1958.

1958: "New River Ranch" severely damaged by storm. Stage and live performances at the store, "Campbell's Corner," are added.

1960s: Recordings on Starday (see discography).

During the "urban folk revival," performances at various colleges and festivals, often on tours throughout the United States. Performances at colleges include: Bethany College, University of Delaware, East Tennessee State University, Indiana University, Lehigh University, University of Maryland, Ohio State University, Peabody Conservatory of Music, University of Pennsylvania, Pennsylvania State University, Rutgers University, and Yale University.

1969, 1972, and 1976: Performs at Festival of American Folklife, Smithsonian Institution, Washington, D.C.

1970s and 1980s: Ola Belle Reed, sometimes "with family," records on Folkways and Rounder record labels (see discography).

1975: Performs at Philadelphia Folk Festival.

1975: Performs at University of Chicago Folk Festival.

1975 and 1976: Performs at Maryland Folklife Festival.

1975 and 1976: North Carolina Folklife Festival.

1976: Performs at Kennedy Center, Washington, D.C.

1978: Honorary Doctorate, University of Maryland.

1982: Performs at World's Fair, Knoxville, Tennessee.

1986: National Heritage Fellowship, National Endowment for the Arts.

Honors and grants from Maryland State Arts Council.

Albert Hash

June 27, 1917: Born on Cabin Creek, Mount Rogers, Grayson County, Virginia, very close to North Carolina border in the Whitetop area.

Learns fiddle at an early age from his great-uncle George Finley and from Corbitt Stamper.

Plays in schoolhouse performances in Mount Rogers–Whitetop area.

Plays professionally with Henry Whitter (after death of Whitter's partner, G. B. Grayson) for one and a half years.

Forms band with Albert on fiddle; his brother, Ernest Hash, guitar; Gaither Farmer, banjo; Huck Sturgill, guitar and vocals.

1933 and successive years: Performs at the White Top Folk Festival; receives recognition for talent.

Around 1934–35: Graduates from Mount Rogers High School.

Works in Civilian Conservation Corps, where he also performs on fiddle.

Early 1940s: Moves to Alexandria, Virginia, during World War II. Works in torpedo factory, where he becomes a machinist.

January 17, 1944: Marries Ethel Spencer of Grayson County. They live in northern Virginia and begin family there.

Plays in a few fiddlers conventions.

After World War II: Returns to Grayson County. Will continue to work as a machinist for over thirty years, with companies such as Sprague Electric in Lansing, North Carolina; and Brunswick Powder Works in Sugar Grove, Virginia.

1940s: Forms "Whitetop Mountain Band," with Albert on fiddle; Frank Blevins, guitar; Henry Blevins, guitar; their father, Print Blevins, banjo; Dent Blevins, mandolin. Will play until the Blevins family moves to northern Virginia.

1940s and 1950s: Becomes well known as a craftsman. Begins his own shop in home for instrument making. Later will teach apprentices, such as daughter, Audrey Hash Hamm; and Wayne Henderson. Will continue as craftsman and teacher throughout life.

1950s: Plays off and on with several musicians.

1960s: Forms band "Virginia-Carolina Boys," with Wayne Henderson on guitar; Wayne's brother, Max Henderson, mandolin; Boyd Stewart, guitar and vocals; Trudy Bell, guitar and vocals; and Albert Hash, fiddle.

Late 1960s and 1970s: For eight years, plays with "Virginia-Carolina Boys" on radio station WKSK, West Jefferson, North Carolina.

1975: Forms a new "Whitetop Mountain Band" with Flurry Dowe, banjo; Albert's brother-in-law Thornton Spencer, guitar; Emily Spencer, vocals; Tom Barr, bass; and Becky Haga Barr, guitar and vocalist. Various other musicians sometimes will play with them.

Makes records on Heritage and Mountain record labels and also on Rounder Records (see discography).

Teaches fiddle classes at Wilkes Community College, North Carolina, and helps form string band at Mount Rogers High School.

1977: Plays at the 39th National Folk Festival, Washington, D.C.

1978: Plays at the National Folk Festival, Wolf Trap Farm in Virginia, near Washington, D.C.

1981: Nominated for National Heritage Fellowship, National Endowment for the Arts.

1982: Performs at World's Fair, Knoxville, Tennessee.

January 28, 1983: Dies in Jefferson, North Carolina. Buried at Haw Orchard Cemetery, Grayson County, Virginia. Funeral at Faith Lutheran Church, January 30, 1983; Pastor Messick gives eulogy.

David Andrew ("Uncle" Dave) Sturgill

January 21, 1917: Born in Chateau County, Montana, to parents from Alleghany County, North Carolina. Father is a civil engineer, graduate of North Carolina A&M University.

1921: Moves with family back to Alleghany County, North Carolina.

1925: Learns banjo at age eight.

1929: Made first banjo at age twelve.

By 1929: Forms band, "River Rats," while a preteen. Plays at schools, civic functions, and local dances, usually in someone's home.

October 13, 1933: Leaves Alleghany County after high school graduation; rides bike to grandparents' farm in Glenville, Harford County, Maryland. Next five years travels the United States, playing banjo, collecting folk songs, working in Civilian Conservation Corps, etc. Finally returns to Maryland.

1938: Enters Bliss Electric School, Montgomery County, Maryland; secures diploma.

1939: Obtains job with Bell Telephone Company. Later transfers to Western Electric.

1942: Marries Marie Halsey of Alleghany County, North Carolina, in Bristol, Tennessee. They buy home in College Park, Maryland. Eventually they have three sons and two daughters.

1940s: While still working at Bell, studies musical-instrument making under a distant cousin, Herman Weaver of Weaver's House of Violins, Washington, D.C., then Maryland.

Performs at fiddling conventions and music parks in Maryland, including New River Ranch owned by another distant cousin, Ola Belle Campbell Reed.

1960: Publication of David A. Sturgill and Mack H. Sturgill, eds., *A History of the Sturgill Family* (Marion, Va.: Carolina Printing Co).

October 1968: Leaves Washington, D.C.–Maryland and Western Electric to return, with wife and grown children, to Alleghany County, North Carolina. Settles the family at Piney Creek.

Goes to Nashville to manage Grammer Guitar Company for two years, commuting to North Carolina.

1970: Establishes Skyland Musical Instrument Company in Piney Creek, with sons Danny Sturgill and Johnny Sturgill, making hand-crafted mountain and bluegrass banjos, fiddles, mandolins, guitars, and dulcimers. Over the years will sell hundreds of instruments to customers including Del Reeves and Doc Watson, and clients as far away as Africa, Australia, Germany, Iceland, Ireland, and New Zealand.

Performs at regional fiddlers' conventions, ultimately winning over seventy-five awards, including "Best Performer" nine times, at such places as Mount Airy and Bluefield. Acts as judge at fiddlers conventions in several states, from Pennsylvania to Florida.

Lectures on instrument making at the Blue Ridge Parkway (U.S. National Park Service) and at Wilkes Community College.

Dave's band, "Skyland Strings," is recorded on albums made at conventions; and on Kyle Creed's "New River Jam" album. Also Dave plays fiddle on Rick Abrams's album "Wild Goose." See discography.

1970s and 1980s: Publishes articles in *Bluegrass Unlimited* (see bibliography).

1975: *Foxfire 3* includes "Uncle" Dave in chapter on banjo making (see bibliography).

1983: Publication of revised edition of David A. Sturgill and Mack H. Sturgill, *History of the Sturgill Family* (see bibliography)

1987: Nominated for National Heritage Fellowship, National Endowment for the Arts.

1988: Skyland Musical Instrument Company closed due to damage by Hurricane Hugo. Dave continues to make instruments in shop in home basement.

1990: Brown-Hudson Award of North Carolina Folklore Society, presented at Duke University, Durham, North Carolina.

1993: Publication of David A. Sturgill, *A Branch of the Sturgill Family*, vol. 1: *Descendants of Francis Sturgill Sr., and Rebecca Hash* (Piney Creek, N.C.: Carolina Printing Co.).

1995: Dave and a small group organize Alleghany Fiddler's Convention in Sparta, North Carolina; it has been very popular.

Virgil Leon Sturgill

1897: Born in Carter County, Kentucky, on the farm of his mother's family, on the waters of Sutton's Branch. Will live there in extended family until age fourteen. Father's ancestors came to Kentucky from the New River Valley of North Carolina. Mother's family has strong singing tradition, no use of instruments. Father plays banjo. Virgil will grow up singing in the family on all occasions.

1918: Serves in U.S. Navy in World War I. He adds the name "Virgil" because the military requires three names and he only has two.

1926: Receives B.A. degree in English, University of Kentucky.

Marries Ruth Norton of Maryland.

1935: Son Jack born.

1937: Receives M.A. degree in education, University of Kentucky.

1939: Son Lee born.

Teaches in public schools of Kentucky for a few years before leaving the state again.

Serves as psychometrician in hospitals of the U.S. Veterans Adminstration, including Swannanoa Division, Oteen, North Carolina, near Asheville.

C. 1947: First performs in public, singing and playing dulcimer at age fifty.

C. 1950: Starts work at Armed Forces Institute of Pathology, Walter Reed Hospital, Washington, D.C.

1950s: Publishes articles in *North Carolina Folklore* and *Kentucky Folklore Record* (see bibliography).

1962: Retires from Veterans Administration hospitals.

As part of the civil rights movement, teaches in a black college in Baltimore.

1965: Moves back to Asheville, North Carolina.

1965–66: Teaches English (literature and drama) at Montreat-Anderson College (Presbyterian), Montreat, North Carolina. Several years on the faculty there. Also teaches at other colleges.

1950s and 1960s: Performs at many folk festivals, including Festival of American Folklife, Smithsonian Institution, Washington, D.C.; Asheville (North Carolina) Folk Festival; and Swarthmore (Pennsylvania) Folk Festival.

Plays at such colleges as George Washington University; Johns Hopkins University; University of North Carolina, Chapel Hill; and University of Virginia, Charlottesville.

Heard on CBS Network Programs; WHYY-TV, Philadelphia; and WNYC, New York.

Plays at numerous museums, art galleries, and other venues, including Blue Dog Cellar, Baltimore, Maryland; Cafe Expresso, Baltimore, Maryland; Cafe Rafio, New York City; Gerde's Folk City, New York City; Peabody Book Shop, Baltimore; Phillips Gallery, Washington, D.C.; and Second Fret, Philadelphia (flyer in his file, Library of Congress).

1981: Dies. Buried in Asheville, North Carolina.

Wayne Henderson

May 3, 1947: Born Ashe County Hospital (North Carolina). Son of Walter Byrom Henderson and Sylvia Reedy Henderson. Their home is in Virginia, very close to the North Carolina line.

As a boy, attends Galax Fiddlers Convention with his father.

Graduates from Virginia-Carolina High School.

Works in Abingdon, Virginia, for a time but comes back to home county. Studies guitar making under Albert Hash. Wayne will always work in his own shop in his home.

1952: First recording (Wilcox-Gary Records). Sings "Hey Good Looking."

1967: Attends revival of the White Top Festival.

1968: Enters Galax Fiddlers Convention for first time.

1969: Begins work for United States Postal Service.

Late 1960s: Starts band "Virginia-Carolina Boys" with his brother Max Henderson, Boyd Spencer, and Albert Hash.

"Virginia-Carolina Boys" play on WKSK, Jefferson, North Carolina, for eight years in the late 1960s and 1970s.

1970: Wins first place in guitar at Galax Fiddlers Convention, at age twenty-three. Has won this a total of twelve times.

1971: Performs at exhibition of American Folklife, Montreal, Quebec, Canada, sponsored by Smithsonian Institution.

1972: Opens "Henderson Guitar Shop" at Rugby, Virginia.

Forms the band "Rugby Gullyjumpers" with Greg Cornett and Butch Barker.

1979–80: Performs at National Park Service Festival, El Paso, Texas.

1982: Performs in tour of Southeast Asia, sponsored by National Council for Traditional Arts.

1982: Performs at World's Fair, Knoxville, Tennessee.

1986: Nominated for National Heritage Fellowship, National Endowment for the Arts.

1990: Concert in Carnegie Hall, New York City, in Folk Masters Series.

1990, 1991, and 1993: Performs in Masters of the Steel-String Guitar Tours.

1991: Concert at Wolf Trap Farm, near Washington, D.C., in Folk Masters Series.

1991: Performs at Mountain Stage, Charleston, West Virginia.

1992: Performs at inauguration of U.S. President Bill Clinton, Washington, D.C.

1994: Instruments displayed in traveling exhibition sponsored by National Council for the Traditional Arts.

1994: Wins twenty-five-year service award, United States Postal Service.

1994: Wins first place in guitar at the 79th Laurel Bloomery Fiddlers Convention, Mountain, Tennessee (nation's oldest for old-time music only).

1995: Awarded National Heritage Fellowship, National Endowment for the Arts.

1996: Tour of Africa and Sri Lanka, sponsored by National Council for Traditional Arts. Performance and display of Wayne's instruments.

1996: Performs at "Southern Crossroads," musical venue at Olympic Games.

Guest recordings include those with E. C. Ball, 1960 (Wayne played "Home, Sweet Home"); the bluegrass band "Once Again from the Top," on Hay Holler label; Olen Gardner and Frances Gardner, on Heritage label; Gus Ingo, on Heritage label; the "Konnarock Critters," *Old Favorites,* on Heritage label (1995); Jeff Robbins on a gospel album; and on the *Virginia-Carolina Sampler* on the Flying Cloud label.

Current Band: "Wayne Henderson and Friends." Wayne on guitar; Gerald Anderson on mandolin; Helen White, fiddle; Herb Key, bass; and Tim Lewis, banjo.

Has won over three hundred ribbons at fiddlers conventions. Twenty-two are from Galax Fiddlers Convention, including twelve first-place awards.

Performs often at Rocky Gap Folk Festival, Cumberland, Maryland; Grayson Highlands State Park, Rugby, Virginia; Seattle Folk Festival, Seattle, Washington; Smithsonian Institution, Washington, D.C.

Wayne has made more than 160 guitars, 60 mandolins, 12 banjos, and 1 fiddle. His instruments have been displayed at various festivals and museums not mentioned above, including Blue Ridge Institute Museum, Ferrum College, Ferrum, Virginia; and Festival of American Folklife, Smithsonian Institution, Washington, D.C.

Gerald Anderson

December 12, 1953: Born in Grayson County, Virginia. Born at home. Son of Stephen and Catherine Anderson.

In late teens, studies guitar with Wayne Henderson.

1972–76: Attends Emory and Henry College, Emory, Virginia. This experience increases awareness of Appalachian heritage.

During summers between college, studies instrument making with Wayne Henderson.

1976: Receives B.A. degree in anthropology and sociology at Emory and Henry College.

Joins United States Postal Service as mailman. Drives routes until mid-afternoon, then works on instruments at shop.

September 1976: Sets up shop in building with Wayne Henderson at Rugby, Virginia. Each will work independently.

Makes many instruments but specializes in mandolins. Craftsmanship recognized in magazines on music (see bibliography).

Instruments displayed at various festivals and museums, including: Blue Ridge Institute Museum, Ferrum, Virginia; Visitor's Center, Grayson Highlands State Park, Rugby, Virginia; Hunter Museum of Art, Chattanooga, Tennessee, 1994, in an exhibition sponsored by the National Council for the Traditional Arts; National Folklife Festival, Washington, D.C.; the Abby Aldrich Rockefeller Folk Art Center at Colonial Williamsburg, Virginia; Virginia Historical Society, Richmond; and William King Regional Arts Center, Abingdon, Virginia.

As a performer, specializes in guitar. Has made tapes and records.

Radio performances include WBRF, Galax, Virginia; WPAQ, Mount Airy, North Carolina; and WETS, Johnson City, Tennessee.

Television performances include: WCYB Television, Channel 5, Bristol, Tennessee, c. 1980; Channel 8, Winston-Salem, North Carolina, c. 1991; Virginia Public Television, Richmond, Virginia, 1994; and Public Television, Channel 2, Boone, North Carolina, July 1994.

Has performed for the National Park Service (many times); for National Council for the Traditional Arts; at Rocky Gap Festival (annual), Cumberland, Maryland; at Blue Ridge Folklife Festival (annual), Ferrum, Virginia; and at Grayson Highland State Park (annual), Rugby, Virginia.

Has won some one hundred awards at fiddlers conventions in Virginia, Tennessee, West Virginia and North Carolina, including eight ribbons at Galax Fiddlers Convention and second place in guitar at the 79th Laurel Bloomery Fiddlers Convention, Mountain City, Tennessee (nation's oldest for old-time music only), 1994.

Appendix D
Identification
of Repertoires

Ola Belle Campbell Reed

Reed Family Songbook

The Reed Family Songbook (Wilmington, Delaware: Zeta Nu Upsilon Sorority, Goldey Beacom College, n.d.) contains two sections. The first section is "Original Compositions" by Ola Belle Campbell Reed. The second section of the book contains the main body of her repertoire, introduced by Jason David Pate. What is presented below contains traditional songs from the second section of the songbook.

1. "Orange Blossom Special": Railroad. Cohen, *Long Steel Rail,* 454: "Chubby Wise and Ervin Rouse put together the instrumental part; recorded by Rouses, 1939."
2. "Poison Love": Malone, *Country Music,* 216: late 1940s, Grand Ole Opry, Nashville; written by brother and husband of Kitty Wells.
3. "Rosewood Casket": Laws, *Native American Balladry,* 264, identifies this among "ballad-like pieces"; Roberts and Agey 202, attribute it to an "unknown author"; published 1870, in collections from Appalachia to Ozarks; also see Malone, *Southern Music,* 23.
4. "Great Reaping Day": Hymn; see Lornell, *Virginia's Blues,* 96 and 188, concerning Ernest Stoneman.
5. "While Eternal Ages Roll": Hymn
6. "Home of Light and Love"
7. "Six Feet of Earth"
8. "Thank God I'm Free"
9. "Guiding Light": Hymn
10. "Life's Railway to Heaven" (also called "The Faithful Engineer"): Railroad hymn; Malone, *Country Music,* 132; Cohen, *Long Steel Rail,* 611–18, says it was copyrighted in 1890 by Abbey and Tillman and modeled after a poem by William S. Hays, published in 1886. Hays, who also wrote "Molly Darling," was prominent in the 1860s–1880s.
11. "Man Born to Die": Probably same as "Am I Born to Die?" Alan Lomax, *Folk Songs of North America,* under "White Spirituals," 246; words by Charles Wesley, tune by Davidson in *Original Sacred Harp.*

12. "Just Over in the Gloryland": Hymn; Lornell, *Virginia's Blues,* 99.
13. "Tramp on the Street": "The Tramp" is in *Checklist of Recorded Songs* (hereafter cited as *Checklist AAFC*).
14. "Going Through": Lornell, *Virginia's Blues,* 169: "I'm Going Through with Jesus."
15. "Kitty Wells": "Katy Wells" is in *Checklist AAFC*; Laws, *Native American Balladry,* 264: "Ballad-like pieces."
16. "Single Girl [Wish I Was]": *Checklist AAFC* 131; Roberts and Agey 225, no. 98, mid-19th-century England.
17. "Banks of the Ohio": Laws F5, Murder Ballads.
18. "Are You Happy?"
19. "Miner's Song": Could be "Miner's Fate" (Laws G10, re Pittston, Pennsylvania) or "The Happy Miner" (John Lomax and Alan Lomax, *Cowboy Songs,* 383).
20. "Ranger's Song": Could be "The Dying Ranger" (Laws A14).
21. "Orphaned Girl" ("Orphan Gal"): *Checklist AAFC* 131; Thede 58: "Old English ballad has been published numbers of times, gives fiddle accompaniment in 'crosskey.'"
22. "Handsome Molly" ("Handsome Holly"): Lornell, *Virginia's Blues,* 213–14: sung by Whitter of Fries, Grayson County, Virginia.
23. "Little Mohee": Chase 128 says this is adapted from an English broadside; widely known in the South, Appalachia, Midwest, and New England.
24. "Wild Bill Jones": Laws E10, ballads about criminals; also *Checklist AAFC* 132.
25. "Black Jack Davy" ("Gypsy Davey," "Gypsy Laddie"): Child ballad 200.
26. "Sweet Fern": Roberts and Agey say it also is called "Sweet Bird," 239; seems to be found only in Southern Appalachia, Kentucky, North Carolina, Virginia; not in other collections.
27. "Wildwood Flower": Rosenberg 158, "from Southern Appalachian tradition."
28. "T for Texas" ("Blue Yodel"): Jimmie Rodgers recorded on Victor, 1927; John Lomax and Alan Lomax, *Cowboy Songs,* says vaudeville, string bands.
29. "I've Always Been a Rambler": Probably country-western category. John Miller heard it as a boy around Lansing, North Carolina, 1940s.
30. "Reuben's Train": Cohen, *Long Steel Rail,* 503–18, says that, musically, it recalls "Train 45," recorded by Grayson and Whitter; also recorded by Mainer, Morris, and Ledford in South Carolina about 1905.
31. "Darling I Still Remember"
32. "Dark as a Dungeon" ("Down in the Mine"): Malone, *Country Music,* 221. Merle Travis composed and recorded this song in 1949, based on traditional sources; his Kentucky family was in coal mining.
33. "Letter Edged in Black": Richardson 35, text and music; it "once had a wide vogue all over America but may well have been of mountain origin; its melody suggests 'Prisoner's Song.'" (107).
34. "Now Is the Hour": Performed on Grand Ole Opry; hymn?

Ola's Recollections in 1984 Interview

Below are traditional titles in Ola's repertoire that she remembered from childhood days as having been sung frequently in the Ashe-Grayson area. Source: Ola Belle Campbell Reed interview by Anderson-Green, Rising Sun, Maryland, August 1, 1984.

1. "Arkansas Traveler": Bayard, *Dance to the Fiddle,* no. 316; Cauthen 20; Laws 1.
2. "Barbara Allen": Child ballad 84. This ballad was one of those sung most widely in the Upper New River area. Known to have been sung by Miriam Perkins Hash, playing dulcimer, in Major (Grayson County), Virginia, in the 1880s (Anderson-Green, oral tradition notes). Also noted as sung in 1914 in Baywood (Grayson County) and Hillsville (Carroll County), Virginia; and in Wythe County, Virginia; and sung in 1921 by J. W. Wyatt of Russell County, Virginia, and J. W. Fields of Wise County, Virginia; also in Smyth and Washington Counties, Virginia (Arthur Davis, *Traditional Ballads*; Leach, *Ballad Book*).
3. "Bile Em Cabbage Down": Bayard, *Dance to the Fiddle,* no. 219.
4. "Billy in the Low Ground": Traditionally British; Bayard, *Dance to the Fiddle,* no. 234.
5. "Black Jack Davy" ("Gypsy Davey," "Gypsy Laddie"): Child ballad 200.
6. "Blue Grey Eagle": Ira Ford 86.
7. "Buffalo Girls": Bayard, *Hill Country Tunes,* no. 1; British and German.
8. "Columbus Stockade Blues": Cohn 245: recorded by Darby on Columbia, 1927.
9. "Cripple Creek": *Checklist AAFC*; also Lornell, *Virginia's Blues,* 103.
10. "Cumberland Gap": *Checklist AAFC* 131; Malone, *Country Music,* 46.
11. "Flop Eared Mule": Bayard, *Hill Country Tunes,* no. 56.
12. "Fly Around My Pretty Little Miss": *Checklist AAFC* 131; Laws N42; Coffin 199; Lornell, *Virginia's Blues,* 26, reports that Frank Blevins and Tar Heel Rattlers of Lansing, North Carolina, recorded this song in Atlanta, 1927.
13. "Good Ole Mountain Dew": John Lomax and Alan Lomax, *American Ballads and Folk Songs,* 180–82.
14. "John Hardy": Laws I2; Leach says often confused with "John Henry."
15. "John Henry": Laws I1.
16. "Little White Church": Gospel hymn.
17. "Little Moses": Gospel hymn; Lornell, *Virginia's Blues,* 42: Carter Family.
18. "New River Train": *Checklist AAFC* 130; Cohen, *Long Steel Rail,* 55, calls it a "lyric folksong"; Roberts and Agey 241; Lornell, *Virginia's Blues,* 210: Whitter of Fries, Virginia.
19. "The Ninety and Nine": Traditional hymn: T. E. Ford 26.
20. "Old Joe Clark": *Checklist AAFC* 132.
21. "Old Pal of Yesterday": Country-western; similar to Jimmie Rodgers, "Old Pal of my Heart."
22. "Paul and Silas": Gospel hymn.
23. "Picture from Life's Other Side": John Miller calls this a Carter Family song; may be same as "Picture on the Wall," which Lornell, *Virginia's Blues,* 46, lists under Carter Family.
24. "Pretty Polly": Laws P36, from England c. 1750 or earlier; Arthur Davis, *Traditional Ballads,* same as Child ballad 4, "Lady Isabel and the Elf-Knight"; Combs, no. 133, found in Marion County, West Virginia, 1924; murder ballad.
25. "Saint Louis Blues": Blues and jazz tradition; Cohn 19: recorded by W. C. Handy.
26. "Sally Goodin": Bayard, *Dance to the Fiddle,* no. 273: constant throughout South; Rosenbaum 210: "Almost universally known as fiddle tune in the South"; Lornell, *Virginia's Blues,* 214: Whitter performs "Sally Gooden."

27. "The Soldier and the Lady": Laws, *American Balladry from British Broadsides*, 193, M27: variant title from the words of "The Bold Soldier."
28. "Soldier's Joy": Bayard, *Hill Country Tunes,* no. 21, a version of the British song "The King's Head."
29. "There's a Blue Sky Way Out Yonder": Country-western, sung by Blue Sky Boys.
30. "Time Changes Everything": Malone, *Country Music,* 180, attributes this to Bob Wills.
31. "Tom Cattin' Around": Country-western; Malone, *Country Music,* 123: "Tom Cat Blues"; "rowdy."
32. "Uncloudy Day": Gospel hymn.
33. "Wayfaring Pilgrim" ("I'm Just a Poor Wayfaring Pilgrim [Stranger]"): Rosenbaum 68: "One of the best-known camp-meeting spirituals"; early publications of text, without tune, 1858 and 1867; first published with tune, 1893; Chase 162.
34. "Whoa Back, Buck" ("Whoa, Mule"): Ira Ford 295.

Performance at New River Ranch, 1955 or 1956

A set performed by Ola Belle Campbell Reed, Kenny Miller, and Alex Campbell. Taped by Henry Glassie, 1955 or 1956. File of Ola Belle Reed, American Folklife Center, Library of Congress. Note that certain titles in the set are in other lists also.

1. "John Henry": Laws I1.
2. "Cripple Creek": *Checklist AAFC* 129.
3. "I Ain't Going to Work Tomorrow" ("Roll in My Sweet Baby's Arms"): Malone, *Southern Music,* 145.
4. "Roll On, Buddy": Alan Lomax, *Folk Songs of North America,* 284.
5. "Davy Crockett": Performed by Ralph Reed, Ola's son.
6. "Foggy Mountain Top": Malone, *Country Music,* 321: "Foggy Mountain Breakdown," Flatt and Scruggs popularized in the 1950s.
7. "Traveling the Highway Home": Could be "Traveling Blues"; Malone, *Country Music,* 98: Jimmie Rodgers.

Titles from Library of Congress Tapes

These are titles from audiotapes in the Archive of American Folk Song, Library of Congress, which are not included in *Reed Family Songbook* or in the list from the Anderson-Green interview of August 1, 1984. These are mostly in the country-western or Nashville category.

1. "All the World Is Lonely Now": Malone, *Country Music,* 204, popularized by Roy Acuff.
2. "Build Me a Cabin in Gloryland": Composer is Curtis Stuart; Flatt and Scruggs performed and used as title of an album.
3. "Gal I Left Behind Me": John Lomax and Alan Lomax, *American Ballads and Folk Songs,* 280–83.
4. "God Put a Rainbow in the Sky": Malone, *Country Music,* 61: *sky* is *clouds*; 1920s.

5. "Gonna Have a Big Time Tonight"
6. "Gonna Lay Down My Old Guitar"
7. "I'll Be All Smiles Tonight": Ford 414.
5. "I'm Thinking Tonight of My Blue Eyes": Malone, *Country Music,* 203: A. P. Carter.
8. "Just Because": Could be "Just Because You Think I'm So Lonesome."
9. "Lamplighting Time in the Valley": Malone, *Country Music,* 161; Lornell, *Virginia's Blues,* 96.
10. "Life I Love the Best"
11. "The Little Adobe Shack Way Out West": Lornell, *Virginia's Blues,* 50; Carter Family recorded in New Jersey, 1934.
12. "Longing for a Love"
13. "Love Please Don't Come Home"
14. "My Doney, Where You Been So Long?" ("My Honey, Where You Been So Long?"): Lornell, *Virginia's Blues,* 76: "Darling, Where You Been So Long?"; Lornell, *Virginia's Blues,* 210: sung by Whitter.
15. "Oloha"
16. "Out on Montana's Plains": Country-western; Malone, *Country Music,* 108.
17. "Sing Me a Song": Composed by Ola Belle Campbell Reed.
18. "Still the Same"
19. "Tell Me Why That I'm So Lonesome"
20. "Those Brown Eyes": Could be "Let Those Brown Eyes Smile at Me," by R. Hail.
21. "Two Little Rosebuds Taken from Their Home"
22. "We Are Drifting": Probably Charles Moody hymn, "Drifting Too Far From the Shore," in Eggett 68.
23. "Where Was You When the Train Left Town?"
24. "You Led Me to the Wrong"

Albert Hash

1. "Alabama Gal": Cauthen, app. 1, p. 219.
2. "Angel Band" ("O Come Angel Band"): Malone, *Country Music,* 326: hymn, dates back to the 19th-century shaped-note tradition.
3. "Arkansas Traveler": Laws 1.
4. "Cackling Hen": Lornell, *Virginia's Blues,* 103: recorded by a Galax band, "The Hillbillies," in 1926.
5. "Cluck Old Hen": Recorded by Galax band "The Hillbillies" in 1927.
6. "Cripple Creek": *Checklist AAFC*; Lornell, *Virginia's Blues,* 103.
7. "Coming Down from God": Hymn
8. "Did You Ever See the Devil, Uncle Joe?": Lornell, *Virginia's Blues,* 151: "Don't Whip Your Wife on Sunday."
9. "Down Among the Budded Roses": Lornell, *Virginia's Blues,* 93 and 144: "Budded Roses."
10. "Dream of the Miner's Child": Richardson 40.
11. "Dugannon"
12. "Dusty Miller": Christeson 31: "Only a few of the many fiddlers I have known could play this tune . . . was played live occasionally over WSM, Nashville."
13. "Flop-eared Mule": Bayard, *Hill Country Tunes,* no. 56.

14. "Gathering Flowers from the Hillside": Lornell, *Virginia's Blues,* 51: Carter Family.
15. "Gold Hill Waltz": Local tune in Grayson County, Virginia; music by Thornton and Emily Spencer, words by Carol Holcomb.
16. "Great Physician": Hymn (Albert Hash's favorite).
17. "Green Valley Waltz": Thede 146.
18. "Hangman's Reel": Albert Hash learned from a French Canadian fiddler.
19. "I Never Will Marry": Lornell, *Virginia's Blues,* 48: Carter Family.
20. "I Saw the Light": Hymn; Horstman 50; by Hank Williams, 1948.
21. "I'll Fly Away": Hymn; Malone, *Southern Music,* 7, 78.
22. "Intoxicated Rat": Malone, *Country Music,* 124: Dixon Brothers performed and recorded it in the 1930s.
23. "Kentucky"
24. "Leather Britches": Bayard, *Hill Country Tunes,* no. 16.
25. "Little Brown Hand": Albert Hash learned it from a commercial recording.
26. "Lost John": Lornell, *Virginia's Blues,* 212: done by Whitter.
27. "'Mid the Greenfields of Virginia": Lornell, *Virginia's Blues,* 46: Carter Family.
28. "Mississippi Sawyer": Bayard, *Dance to the Fiddle,* no. 329; Ford 32.
29. "My Child Is Going to Be a Miner": Composed by Albert's older cousin, Nancy Blevins (liner notes to *Old Originals*).
30. "No Hiding Place Down Here": Lornell, *Virginia's Blues,* 50: Carter Family.
31. "Old Molly Hare": Lornell, *Virginia's Blues,* 151.
32. "Old Sport"
33. "Pretty Little Indian": Probably what others in area called "Napanee."
34. "Rabbit Up a Gum Stump": Lornell, *Virginia's Blues,* 103: "Possum Up a Gum Stump" performed by "The Hillbillies" of Galax, recorded in New York on Okeh Records.
35. "Raggedy Ann": Same as "Ragtime Annie," according to Dean Sturgill; Lornell, *Virginia's Blues,* 65.
36. "Rake and Rambling Boy": "Rambling Boy" in Laws, *Native American Balladry,* 280, traced to Britain.
37. "Rambling Hobo": Malone, *Southern Music* 110; "Rambling Man"; Lornell, *Virginia's Blues,* 195.
38. "Sally Ann": Rosenbaum 82.
39. "Sally Goodin": Bayard, *Dance to the Fiddle,* no. 273; Lornell, *Virginia's Blues,* 214: Whitter.
40. "Shortening Bread": John Lomax and Alan Lomax, *American Ballads and Folk Songs,* 234–36; Lornell, *Virginia's Blues,* 62.
41. "Silver Bells": Lornell, *Virginia's Blues,* 187: Ernest Stoneman does "Silver Bell."
42. "Single Girl": Lornell, *Virginia's Blues,* 39: Carter Family.
43. "Soldier's Joy": Bayard, *Hill Country Tunes,* no. 21.
44. "Sourwood Mountain": Rosenbaum 216; Chase 148.
45. "Spencer's Reel": Composed by Albert Hash's relative, Thornton Spencer.
46. "Storms Are on the Ocean": Lornell, *Virginia's Blues,* 39: Carter Family.
47. "Sweet As the Flowers in May": Lornell, *Virginia's Blues,* 46: Carter Family.
48. "Sweet Fern": Roberts and Agey 239.
49. "When the Snowflakes Fall": Lornell, *Virginia's Blues,* 161.
50. "Whistling Rufus": Cauthen 15.
51. "Wildwood Flower": Rosenberg 158.
52. "Winefarger's Mill"

David Andrew ("Uncle" Dave) Sturgill

Songs Included in Records and Tapes

1. "Amazing Grace": John Lomax and Alan Lomax, *American Ballads and Folk Songs,* 573–74.
2. "Arkansas Traveler": Bayard, *Dance to the Fiddle,* no. 316 (American amalgam).
3. "Bear Tracks"
4. "Black Mountain Rag": Rosenberg 80: in 1930s near Bristol, Leslie Keith "put together" a fiddle tune called "Black Mountain Blues," based on an old Alabama tune, "The Lost Child"; played it on radio and at contests. It was picked up by Magness and Fox, who played it on Grand Ole Opry as "Black Mountain Rag"; later Doc Watson made it famous, a "most copied piece."
5. "Chicken Pie": Thede 126.
6. "Cindy": Rosenbaum 12; Ford 58: "Get Along, Cindy."
7. "Cluck Old Hen": Bayard, *Dance to the Fiddle,* no. 284 (floating title: "Old Aunt Katie"); Lornell, *Virginia's Blues,* 105; Thede 122: "Cluckin' Hen."
8. "Cotton-Eyed Joe": Bayard, *Dance to the Fiddle,* no. 10 (part 1, 16th century; has other names).
9. "Cumberland Gap": *Checklist AAFC* 128.
10. "Danny Boy" ("Londonderry Air"): Malone, *Country Music,* 228.
11. "Devil in a Briar Patch": Ford 124, lists "Devil in a Canebrake."
12. "Fire in (on) the Mountain": Bayard, *Hill Country Tunes* (floating title).
13. "Fireball Mail": Cohen, *Long Steel Rail,* 55: written by Fred Rose; Cohen, *Long Steel Rail,* 653: Roy Acuff, 1940s.
14. "Fraulein": "Pop country"; Malone, *Country Music,* 250.
15. "Jesse James": Laws E1, identified by Rosenbaum 196.
16. "John Henry": Laws I1; Rosenbaum 188 gives history, calls it "America's most important indigenous ballad" . . . the legendary black worker who died in building Big Bend Tunnel, West Virginia, early 1870s.
17. "Kentucky Waltz": Rosenberg 62: composed by Bill Monroe in 1930s, later released on Columbia in 1946; Rosenberg 73: "Kentucky Waltz" and others established Monroe as a singer of "folk"—previously "hillbilly," soon to be "country and western"—hit tunes; also see Malone, *Country Music,* 231.
18. "Lonesome Road": *Checklist AAFC* 130; "Lonesome Road Blues" is in Cohen, *Long Steel Rail,* 496; Lornell, *Virginia's Blues,* 210: also by Henry Whitter of Fries on his first record, 1923; Cohn 238: "No one knows where Whitter learned 'Lonesome Road Blues' with its famous opening line . . . or if, in fact, he had composed it himself. With its incessant guitar and high, nasal voice, Whitter's record sounded little like any black blues, but the song was in the standard blues form and stanzas of it had apparently been circulating in black and white folk traditions."
19. "Love Somebody": Same as "Soldier's Joy," according to Dave Sturgill; Thede 47, states that in Oklahoma it is the same as "Old Lady Tucker."
20. "Mississippi Sawyer": Bayard, *Dance to the Fiddle,* no. 329 (derivative, "Downfall of Paris"); also Ford 32.
21. "Mole in the Ground" ("I Wish I Was"): Rosenbaum 167: recorded by Bascom Lunford in the 1920s; native to his Blue Ridge area of Haywood County, North Carolina. Also see Erbsen 51.

22. "Old Joe Clark": Bayard, *Dance to the Fiddle*, no. 161: original song was a tune for play party. Roberts and Agey 289: traced to 1840s in English play parties, later used for hoe-downs. Jabbour, "Fiddle in the Blue Ridge," in *Blue Ridge Folk Instruments*, ed., Moore, 1993.
23. "Pig in a Pen": Played in key of A; if played in key of D, it is called "Lost Indian" source; Malone, *Country Music*, 326.
24. "Raggedy Ann": According to Dave Sturgill and Gerald Anderson, this is "Ragtime Annie"; in Ford 44.
25. "Red Wing": Carter Family song; Lornell, *Virginia's Blues*, 31.
26. "Sail Away Ladies": Ford 35; also Lornell, *Virginia's Blues.*
27. "Sally Ann": Rosenbaum 82: black origin, moved into white repertoire; Wade Ward recorded this on Folkways Records FA2363.
28. "Shady Grove": Rosenbaum 138: usually played in Dorian key; this title is used for several tunes; Wilkinson identifies "Shady Grove" as American variant of "London Pride," an English Morris-dance tune.
29. "So Lonesome I Could Die": Hank Williams song.
30. "Sugar Hill": Lornell, *Virginia's Blues*, 206: Crockett Ward and Fields Ward recorded this on OK45179.
31. "Sourwood Mountain": Rosenbaum 216: "old mountain hoe-down," fast tempo; Chase 148: "Country dance tune: jig song . . . comic couplets that wander from one jig tune to another, but this particular one has established a sequence all its own. It is usually associated with the Southern mountains."
32. "Wabash Cannon Ball": Cohen, *Long Steel Rail*, 373–81: in print 1904, text based on earlier song pub. 1882; Old Wabash Railroad was part of the Norfolk & Western Railroad.
33. "Wild Goose": Cauthen 217; may be played in different keys.
34. "Wreck of the Old Ninety-Seven": Laws G2, 205: refers to railroad disaster in 1903; train left Monroe, Virginia, and, after passing Lynchburg, was heading to Danville, and plunged off trestle; song recorded by V. Dalhart, 1925; Cohen, *Long Steel Rail*, 197–226, based on earlier "Ship That Never Returned," 1865.
35. "Wreck of the Old Number Nine" ("On a Cold Winter Night"): Cohen, *Long Steel Rail*, 267–71; Robison copyrighted and Dalhart recorded in 1927.

Songs Played at Old-time Fiddlers Conventions

1. "Bill Cheatam": Dave played this on fiddle at Galax Fiddlers Convention in 1997.
2. "Bonaparte's Retreat": Bayard, *Hill Country Tunes*, no. 86: in all probability is Scots-Irish.
3. "Cripple Creek": Combs 231 cites Brown, 3:354ff.; 5:213ff.
4. "Eighth of January" ("Battle of New Orleans"): Malone, *Country Music*, 26, 302.
5. "Golden Slippers": Ford 113.
6. "Ida Red": *Checklist AAFC* 131; John Lomax and Alan Lomax, *American Ballads and Folk Songs*, 110–11.
7. "John Hardy": Laws I2.
8. "Leather Britches": Bayard, *Hill Country Tunes*, no. 16.

9. "Orange Blossom Special": Cohen, *Long Steel Rail,* 454.
10. "Sally Goodin": Bayard, *Dance to the Fiddle,* no. 273.
11. "Turkey in the Straw": *Checklist AAFC*; Bayard, *Dance to the Fiddle,* no. 320: this tune "is the one most often found in fiddle-tune books," comes from the blackface minstrel tradition, is probably a composite, and is close to an "Irish reel tune."
12. "When You and I Were Young, Maggie": Dave Sturgill played this on dulcimer at Galax Fiddlers Convention, 1997.
13. "Wildwood Flower": Rosenberg 158.

"Wandering Around" Songs

"Uncle" Dave Sturgill's repertoire also included the following songs that he played when "wandering around during the 1930s" out West and during winters in the Civilian Conservation Corps camps. He played both guitar and banjo.

1. "All the old Carter Family songs"
2. "The Cowboy's Lament"
3. "Harbor Lights"
4. "Lamplighting Time in the Valley"
5. "The Last Roundup"
6. "Little Stream of Whiskey" ("Big Rock Candy Mountain")
7. "Night Time in Nevada"
8. "The Old Spinning Wheel"
9. "Red River Valley"
10. "San Antone"
11. "Silver-haired Daddy"
12. "Wagon Wheels"
13. "Weary Man"
14. "When the Roses Bloom Again"
15. "The Yellow Rose of Texas"

Virgil Leon Sturgill

Since Virgil Sturgill created no commercial recordings, it is necessary to discover his repertoire from other sources. These include an extensive list of songs now housed at Appalachian State University, archival tape recordings now housed in the Library of Congress, and the program for a concert he presented at the Phillips Gallery in Washington, D.C.

Appalachian State University List

Virgil Sturgill listed the following songs in notes filed in the Virgil Sturgill Collection, W. L. Eury Appalachian Collection, Appalachian State University (ASU), Boone, North Carolina. It seems likely that he chose from among these songs for his many performances, but this was not always the case (see Phillips Gallery list below). Nor is it clear that he sang all of them. Some of these he recorded on tapes that are in his file at the Library of Congress (see below).

* = Also recorded on Library of Congress tapes
** = Also included in Phillips Gallery performance

1. "Abide With Me": Hymn
2. **"Amazing Grace": Hymn; John Lomax and Alan Lomax, *American Ballads and Folk Songs,* 573–74.
3. *"Ashland Tragedy": Laws 26 (also variants F25, F27).
4. "Ballad of Lord Bateman": Arthur Davis, *Traditional Ballads,* 158 and 565.
5. "Bar the Door" ("Get Up and Bar the Door"): Arthur Davis, *Traditional Ballads,* 495.
6. "Barbara Allen": Child ballad 84; Arthur Davis, *Traditional Ballads,* cites many performed in Virginia.
7. "The Battle of New Orleans" (also called "Eighth of January"): Malone, *Southern Music,* 9.
8. "Beautiful Brown Eyes"
9. "Black Is the Color of My True Love's Hair": Alan Lomax, *Folk Songs of North America,* 206, cites Sharp; Lindsey 72 ("old American").
10. "Blow Ye Winds of Morning" ("Peter Grey"): Agay 80.
11. "Blue Tail Fly" ("Jim Crack Corn," no. 69 below in ASU list): Malone, *Country Music,* 22; Agay 383: minstrel song of the 1840s; Ronald Davis: white composer, Dan Emmett, in the "blackface" tradition.
12. "The Boll Weevil": John Lomax and Alan Lomax, *American Ballads and Folk Songs,* 112–17.
13. "The Boston Burglar": Malone, *Country Music,* 46.
14. "Bound for the Promised Land": Hymn; Bock 72.
15. "The Braes of Yarrow": Child ballad 214; Coffin 195, 219, 258–60.
16. "The Butcher's Boy": Laws P24; Coffin 235; Lornell, *Virginia's Blues,* 84.
17. **"Careless Love": Laws, *Native American Balladry,* 277; Lornell, *Virginia's Blues,* 118.
18. "Casey Jones": Malone, *Country Music,* 132.
19. "The Cat and the Fiddle": Nursery rhyme
20. "Charles Guiteau": Malone, *Country Music,* 55; Lornell, *Virginia's Blues,* 85.
21. "Chicken McCraney Crow"
22. "Cindy": Rosenbaum 12; Ford 58.
23. "Clementine": Agay 200.
24. *"Clinch Mountain" ("Rye Whiskey" is no. 110 below in ASU list; "On Top of Clinch Mountain"): John Lomax and Alan Lomax, *American Ballads and Folk Songs,* 625.
25. "Come Friends Go With Me"
26. **"Come, O My Love"
27. "The Cowboy's Lament" ("Streets of Laredo," no. 119 in ASU list below): John Lomax and Alan Lomax, *Cowboy Songs,* 417–22.
28. "The Crawdad Song"
29. "Cripple Creek": *Checklist AAFC* 129.
30. "The Cuckoo": Malone, *Country Music,* 55.
31. "Dark as a Dungeon": Malone, *Country Music,* 221.
32. "Darling Cory": Downes and Siegmeister 250.
33. "Devilish Mary": Thede 101.
34. "The Doney Song": Could be "Doney Where You Been So Long."

35. **"Down in the Valley": Laws, *Native American Balladry,* 277.
36. *"Down in a Willow Garden" (also "Rose Connoley"): Laws F6.
37. "Drowsy Sleepers"
38. "The Dying Cowboy": John Lomax and Alan Lomax, *Cowboy Songs,* 48–51.
39. "East Virginia"
40. **"Fair and Tender Ladies": Alan Lomax, *Folk Songs of North America,* 205; Roberts and Agey, no. 102.
41. "The Farmer's Curst Wife": Arthur Davis, *Traditional Ballads,* 505 and 598.
42. "Free as a Bird"
43. "Foggy, Foggy Dew": Laws, *American Balladry,* 20, 96, 100, 227, and 299.
44. "Four Marys"
45. "Frankie and Johnnie": Malone, *Country Music,* 96.
46. "French Broad"
47. "Frog Went A-Courtin": John Lomax and Alan Lomax, *American Ballads and Folk Songs,* 310–13.
48. "The Frozen Logger": Alan Lomax, *Folk Songs of North America,* 120.
49. "Get Up and Bar the Door" (same as "Bar the Door"): Arthur Davis, *Traditional Ballads,* 495.
50. "Git Along Little Dogies": John Lomax and Alan Lomax, *Cowboy Songs,* 4.
51. "Go In and Out the Window": Children's play party
52. "Go 'Way From My Window": John Lomax and Alan Lomax, *American Ballads and Folk Songs,* 198.
53. "Good Ol' Mountain Dew": John Lomax and Alan Lomax, *American Ballads and Folk Songs,* 180–82.
54. **"Goodman Comes Home" (same as "Our Goodman"?): Child ballad 274; Arthur Davis, *Traditional Ballads.*
55. **"Greenfields": Lornell, *Virginia's Blues,* 46.
56. "Green Gravel"
57. "Greensleeves": Agay 10.
58. **"Gypsy Davey" ("Gypsy Laddie," "Black Jack Davy"): Child ballad 200; Arthur Davis, *Traditional Ballads.*
59. **"The Hangman": Arthur Davis, *Traditional Ballads,* 360 and 583.
60. "Hattie Ray": Could be "Hattie Belle" in Alan Lomax, *Folk Songs of North America,* 584.
61. "The House Carpenter": Arthur Davis, *Traditional Ballads,* 439 and 592.
62. "I Love Little Willie": John Lomax and Alan Lomax, *American Ballads and Folk Songs,* 327.
63. "I'm Goin' Down the Road Feelin' Bad": Downes and Siegmeister 400.
64. "I'm Thinking Tonight of My Blue Eyes": A. P. Carter; Malone, *Country Music,* 203.
65. *"In the Pines": Malone, *Country Music,* 87.
66. "I Will Arise and Go to Jesus": Hymn
67. *"Jackie Went A-Sailin'" ("Jack, the Sailor Boy"): Laws 279.
68. "Jesse James": John Lomax and Alan Lomax, *American Ballads and Folk Songs,* 128–31.
69. "Jim Crack Corn" ("Blue Tail Fly," no. 11 in ASU list above): Malone, *Country Music,* 22; Agay 383: minstrel song of the 1840s; Ronald Davis: white composer, Dan Emmett, in the "blackface" tradition.
70. "John Hardy": Laws I2.

71. "John Henry": Laws I1; Rosenbaum 188.
72. "Johnny, I Hardly Know Ye": Bayard, *Dance to the Fiddle,* 557.
73. "Johnny, So Long at the Fair"
74. "Jordan": Could be "Jordan Is a Hard Road to Travel," in Ronald Davis 223.
75. "Joseph and Mary"
76. "Knoxville Girl" ("Wexford Girl"): Malone, *Country Music,* 285; also Laws 35, 267.
77. "Leatherwing Bat"
78. ***"Little Mohee" ("Pretty Mohee," "The Pretty Mohee" below, no. 103 in ASU list): Chase 128; Laws 8; Cox 147.
79. *"London Bridge": Children's play party
80. ***"Lord Lovel" ("Lord Lovel and Lady Nancy"): Child ballad 75; Coffin 233–34, 240.
81. "Lord Randall" (also "Jacky My Son"): Arthur Davis, *Traditional Ballads,* 105 and 556.
82. "Loving Nancy"
83. ***"Mary Hamilton": Child ballad 173; Arthur Davis, *Traditional Ballads,* 421 and 590.
84. "Methodist Pie": Methodist Youth Fellowship song, "I'm a Methodist 'Til I Die."
85. "Midnight Special"
86. "Mollie Malone"
87. ***"Molly Vaughn" ("Mollie Vaughan"): Could be "Molly Bawn," Laws O36.
88. "The Murder of Lottie Yates": See Virgil Sturgill, "Murder."
89. "Muskrat"
90. "My Parents Raised Me Tenderly"
91. "Needle's Eye": Play party
92. "New River Train": Cohen, *Long Steel Rail,* 55.
93. ***"Old Dan Tucker": John Lomax and Alan Lomax, *American Ballads and Folk Songs,* 258–62; Ronald Davis: composed by Dan Emmett in the minstrel tradition.
94. "Old King Cole": Nursery rhyme
95. *"Old Smokey" ("On Top of Old Smoky"): Laws, *Native American Balladry,* 278; Alan Lomax, *Folk Songs of North America,* 60.
96. "Old Time Religion": Hymn; Lornell, *Virginia's Blues,* 81.
97. ***"Ol' Joe Clark" ("Old Joe Clark"): Roberts and Agey 289: English play party song; *Checklist AAFC* 132; Bayard, *Dance to the Fiddle,* no. 161.
98. "On the Banks of the Ohio": Laws F5.
99. "The Orphan Girl": *Checklist AAFC* 131.
100. * and ***"Pearl Bryant" ("Pearl Bryan"): Coffin 199; Laws F1 or F2.
101. "Peter Gray" ("Blow Ye Winds of Morning"): Agay 80.
102. "Pretty Little Miss" ("Fly Around My Pretty Little Miss"): Laws N42; Malone *Country Music,* 46.
103. * and ***"The Pretty Mohee" ("Little Mohee" is no. 78 above in ASU list; "Pretty Mohee"): Chase 128; Laws 8; Cox 147.
104. ***"Pretty Polly": Child ballad 4, calls it "Lady Isabel"; Laws P36; Arthur Davis, *Traditional Ballads,* 62.
105. "The Prisoner's Song": Malone, *Country Music,* 56, 58, 230.
106. ***"Ram of Darby"

107. "Rolly Dru Dum"
108. "Rolly Trudum" (probably same as above)
109. "Rowan County Crew": Roberts and Agey, no. 52, 128.
110. *"Rye Whiskey" ("Clinch Mountain" is no. 24 above in ASU list; "On Top of Clinch Mountain"): John Lomax and Alan Lomax, *American Ballads and Folk Songs,* 625.
111. "Sally Goodin": Bayard, *Dance to the Fiddle,* no. 273.
112. "Santa Anna"
113. "Seeds of Love"
114. "Shenandoah": John Lomax and Alan Lomax, *American Ballads and Folk Songs,* 546.
115. "Skip to My Lou": Children's play party
116. *"Soldier and the Lady": Laws, *American Balladry from British Broadsides,* 193: variant title of M27, "The Bold Soldier."
117. "The Soldier Boy"
118. "Sourwood Mountain": Rosenbaum 216; Chase 148.
119. "The Streets of Laredo" ("The Cowboy's Lament," no. 27 in ASU list above): John Lomax and Alan Lomax, *Cowboy Songs,* 417–22.
120. "Turkey in the Straw": *Checklist AAFC*; Agay 396: 1830s, minstrel tradition; Ronald Davis, 204; also in Dave Sturgill's repertory.
121. * and **"The Two Ravens" ("The Twa Corbies"): Child ballad 26; Coffin 222.
122. "The Two Sisters ("Twa Sisters"): Arthur Davis, *Traditional Ballads,* 93, 552.
123. "The Unclouded Day": Hymn
124. "Wabash Cannon Ball": Malone, *Southern Music,* 92.
125. "The Wagoner's Lad": Alan Lomax, *Folk Songs of North America,* 220.
126. *"Wailie, Waillie!!" ("Whalie, Whalie"): Coffin 257: resembles passages in Child ballad 204.
127. *"Wayfaring Stranger" ("Wayfaring Pilgrim"): Ballad hymn; Rosenbaum 68.
128. "Weeping Willow" ("Bury Me Under the Weeping Willow"): Lornell, *Virginia's Blues,* 39, 213, sung by Whitter and by Carter Family.
129. "Were You There?": Hymn
130. "Wexford Girl" ("Knoxville Girl"): Laws P35.
131. "When I Can Read My Title Clear": Bock 61: Isaac Watts hymn; also Alan Lomax, *Folk Songs of North America.*
132. "When Johnny Comes Marching Home": Downes and Siegmeister 188.
133. "Whistle Daughter, Whistle"
134. "Who Mule!" [probably "Whoa Mule"]: Ford 295.
135. ***"The Wife of Usher's Well": Child ballad 79.
136. *"William-A-Trimmy-Toe": Children's play party
137. "Wreck of the Old Ninety-Seven": Laws G2; Lornell, *Virginia's Blues,* 84.

Recordings in the Library of Congress

There is no record of commercial recordings by Virgil Sturgill. However, unpublished recordings of ballads and songs collected and sung by Virgil Sturgill form part of the holdings of the Archive of Folk Culture, American Folklife Center, Library of Congress, Washington, D.C. There were two sittings for these recordings, one (LWO 1821) in June 1951 and the other (LWO 2586) on July 31, 1957. In addition to playing music, Virgil gave an introduction and

discussed playing the dulcimer. The combined repertoire on these two recordings follows. Songs marked with an asterisk also appear in the Appalachian
State University list (see above). Songs marked with a pound sign (#) also
appear in the Phillips Gallery performance program list.

1. *"Ashland Tragedy": Laws 26 (also variants F25, F27).
2. "Bury Me Beneath the Willow": Lornell, *Virginia's Blues,* 213 (Henry
   Whitter).
3. *"Down in a Willow Garden" (also "Rose Connoley"): Laws F6.
4. *"In the Pines": Malone, *Country Music,* 87.
5. *"Jackie's Gone A-Sailing": Laws 279, identifies this as "Jack, the Sailor
   Boy."
6. #"Jesus Lover of My Soul": Charles Wesley hymn. Note that this song is
   in the Phillips Gallery performance program (below).
7. *"London Bridge": Children's play party
8. * and #"Lord Lovel and Lady Nancy": Child ballad 75; Arthur Davis, *Traditional Ballads,* 240; Coffin 233–34, 240.
9. *"On Top of Clinch Mountain" ("Rye Whiskey," "Clinch Mountain"): John
   Lomax and Alan Lomax, *American Ballads and Folk Songs,* 625.
10. *"On Top of Old Smoky" ("Old Smokey"): Laws, *North American Balladry,*
    278; Alan Lomax, *Folk Songs of North America,* 60.
11. * and #"Pearl Bryan" ("Pearl Bryant"): Coffin 199; Laws F1 or F2.
12. * and #"Pretty Mohee" ("Little Mohee"): Chase 128; Laws 8; Cox 147.
13. *"The Soldier and the Lady": Laws 193: variant title of M27, "The Bold
    Soldier."
14. #"Tap Each Other on the Shoulder": Children's play party. Note that this
    song is in the Phillips Gallery performance program (below).
15. * and #"The Two Ravens" ("The Twa Corbies"): Child ballad 26; Coffin 222.
16. *"Wayfaring Stranger" ("Wayfaring Pilgrim"): Ballad hymn; Rosenbaum 68.
17. *"Whalie, Whalie": Coffin 257: resembles passages in Child ballad 204.
18. *"William-A-Trimmy-Toe": Children's play party.

The following songs were included in recordings at the Library of Congress
but are not on the list at Appalachian State University:

1. "Bury Me Beneath the Willow": Lornell, *Virginia's Blues,* 213: Henry Whitter
   performed this.
2. "Jesus Lover of My Soul": Charles Wesley hymn. This song is included in
   the Phillips Gallery performance program.
3. "Tap Each Other on the Shoulder": Children's play party. This song is
   included in the Phillips Gallery performance program.

Program at Phillips Gallery

Virgil Sturgill gave a concert at the Phillips Gallery, Washington, D.C., on June
20, 1960. The program for that event is presented here. Those also included in
the list at Appalachian State University are marked with a double asterisk. Those
also included in the Library of Congress tapes are marked with a pound sign (#).

British and Early American Ballads

1. **"Come, O My Love"
2. **"Fair and Tender Ladies": Alan Lomax, *Folk Songs of North America.*
3. **"The Gypsy Davey" ("The Gypsy Laddie," "Black Jack Davy"): Child ballad 200; Arthur Davis, *Traditional Ballads.*
4. ** and #"Lord Lovel and Lady Nancy" ("Lord Lovel"): Child ballad 75; Coffin 233–34, 240.
5. #"Tap Each Other on the Shoulder"

The Supernatural

6. "The Cruel Mother": Child ballad 20.
7. **"Mollie Vaughan" ("Molly Vaughn"): Could be "Molly Bawn," Laws O36.
8. ** and #"The Twa Corbies" ("The Two Ravens"): Child ballad 26; Coffin 222.
9. **"The Wife of Usher's Well": Child ballad 79.

Humor

10. **"Old Dan Tucker": John Lomax and Alan Lomax, *American Ballads and Folk Songs,* 258–62; Ronald Davis: composed by Dan Emmett in the minstrel tradition.
11. **"Old Joe Clark" ("Ol' Joe Clark"): Roberts and Agey 289: English play party song; *Checklist AAFC* 132; Bayard, *Dance to the Fiddle,* no. 161.
12. **"Our Goodman" (same as "Goodman Comes Home"?): Child ballad 274; Arthur Davis, *Traditional Ballads.*
13. **"The Ram of Darby"

Folk Hymns

14. **"Amazing Grace": John Lomax and Alan Lomax, *American Ballads and Folk Songs,* 573–74.
15. **"Greenfields": Lornell, *Virginia's Blues,* 46.
16. #"Jesus Lover of My Soul": Charles Wesley hymn. This song is included in the Library of Congress recordings.

Rewarded Love/Unrequited Love

17. **"Careless Love": Laws, *Native American Balladry,* 277; Lornell, *Virginia's Blues,* 118.
18. **"Down in the Valley": Laws, *Native American Balladry,* 277.
19. **"The Hangman": Arthur Davis, *Traditional Ballads,* 360 and 583.
20. "Jackie Frazier": L205.
21. ** and #"Pretty Mohee" ("Little Mohee"): Chase 128; Laws 8; Cox 147.
22. "Shady Grove": Rosenbaum 138.
23. "Wildwood Flower": Malone, *Southern Music,* 64.

Crimes Old and New

24. **"Mary Hamilton": Child ballad 173.
25. ** and #"Pearl Bryan" ("Pearl Bryant"): Coffin 199; Laws F1 or F2.
26. **"Pretty Polly": Child ballad 4, calls it "Lady Isabel"; Laws P36; Arthur Davis, *Traditional Ballads,* 62.

The following songs were included in Virgil Sturgill's program at the Phillips Gallery, Washington, D.C., June 20, 1960, and are not on the Appalachian State University list or Library of Congress list.

1. "The Cruel Mother": Child ballad 20; Coffin 198, 204, 221.
2. "Jackie Frazier": L205.
3. "Shady Grove": Rosenbaum 138.
4. "Wildwood Flower": Malone, *Southern Music*, 64.

Wayne Henderson and Gerald Anderson

W = Wayne Henderson
G = Gerald Anderson
No initial = Both performed a tune, together or separately

1. "Alabama Jubilee"
2. "Back Up and Push"
3. "Banks of the Ohio": Laws F5.
4. "Battle Hymn of the Republic": Agay 128.
5. "Bill Baily": Agay 245.
6. "Billy in the Lowground": Bayard, *Dance to the Fiddle*, no. 234.
7. "Black Jack Davy" ("Gypsy Davey," "Gypsy Laddie"): Child ballad 200; Arthur Davis, *Traditional Ballads*.
8. "Blackberry Blossom": Christeson, no. 142.
9. "Blue Ridge Mountain Blues" (G): Ford 45; Lornell, *Virginia's Blues*, 185.
10. "Can't Take it With You" (G)
11. "Carter Family Medley": Lornell, *Virginia's Blues*, 37–58.
12. "The Cat Came Back": Christeson, no. 10 ("seldom heard anymore").
13. "Cherokee Shuffle" (W)
14. "Dandelion Wine"
15. "Devilish Mary": Thede 101.
16. "East Tennessee Blues" (W): Lornell, *Virginia's Blues*, 103.
17. "Eight More Miles to Louisville" (G): Lornell, *Virginia's Blues*; Horstman 11.
18. "Fisher's Hornpipe" (W): Christeson, no. 75.
19. "Florida Blues": Lornell, *Virginia's Blues*.
20. "Flop-eared Mule" (W): Bayard, *Hill Country Tunes*, no. 56.
21. "Forked Deer": Ford 45; also Christeson, no. 89.
22. "Georgia"
23. "Going Home" (G)
24. "Handsome Molly: Lornell, *Virginia's Blues*, 213–14 (sung by Whitter of Fries, Virginia).
25. "Hangman's Reel"
26. "Hey Good-Looking": Hank Williams song.
27. "I Am a Pilgrim" (G): Hymn; Malone, *Country Music*, 221.
28. "I'll Get Over You" (G)
29. "John Henry": Laws I1.
30. "Leather Britches": Bayard, *Hill Country Tunes*, no. 16; Christeson, 123.
31. "Little Rock Getaway" (W)

32. "Lisa Jane Medley": John Lomax and Alan Lomax, *American Ballads and Folk Songs,* 284–86.
33. "Mississippi Sawyer" (W): Bayard, *Dance to the Fiddle,* no. 329; Christeson, no. 88.
34. "My Window Faces South" (G)
35. "New River Train": *Checklist AAFC* 130.
36. "Old Joe Clark": *Checklist AAFC* 132.
37. "Peace in the Valley": Hymn; Horstman 58.
38. "Pretty Polly": Laws P36.
39. "Ragtime Annie" (W): Lornell, *Virginia's Blues,* 65; Christeson, no. 218.
40. "Redwing": Lornell, *Virginia's Blues,* 31; Carter Family song.
41. "Saint Anne's Reel"
42. "Saddle Up the Grey"
43. "Salty"
44. "Speedin' West"
45. "Spinning Wheel": Dave Sturgill has this listed as "country-western."
46. "Streamline Cannonball" (G): Malone, *Country Music,* 204.
47. "Sweet Fern": A. P. Carter performed; Roberts and Agey 239.
48. "Sweet Georgia Brown" (W): Malone, *Southern Music,* 82.
49. "Sweet Sunny South": Lornell, *Virginia's Blues,* 91 and 146.
50. "Temperance Reel" (W): Bayard, *Dance to the Fiddle,* 286.
51. "Tennessee Waltz": Malone, *Southern Music,* 95.
52. "Turkey in the Straw" (W): Malone, *Southern Music,* 35 (see chap. 3).
53. "Whiskey Before Breakfast"
54. "Whistlin Rufus": Cauthen 15.
55. "Will the Circle Be Unbroken?": Old-time hymn; Malone, *Southern Music,* 65.

Notes

Chapter 1

1. For this Virginia-Carolina area, regional and subregional labels vary among both musicians and writers. The term "Upper New River Valley," as used by geographers, seems most appropriate; however, musicians and writers (both journalists and scholars) more frequently use "the Whitetop region." The meaning of that term, too, varies. Although Galax and Fries, Virginia, are on the edge of the territory, the center generally is considered to be west of Independence, Virginia. The Whitetop region usually is thought to include western Grayson County, Virginia; some of Washington County, Virginia; and those parts of Ashe County and Alleghany County, North Carolina (including Lansing, Jefferson, Piney Creek, etc.), that lie near Whitetop Mountain, Haw Orchard Mountain, and Mount Rogers. This is where Ola Belle Campbell Reed, Albert Hash, and the parents of "Uncle" Dave Sturgill were born, and where Dave also grew up. It is where Gerald Anderson, Wayne Henderson, and most of the musicians discussed in chapter 5 and the appendices were born and raised. Also see app. A.

Chapter 2

1. For further discussion of this migration pattern from the southern mountains to the Washington, D.C.–Maryland area, see Ivan M. Tribe, *The Stonemans: An Appalachian Family and the Music That Shaped Their Lives* (Urbana: Univ. of Illinois Press, 1993).
2. This song title was listed incorrectly in the Library of Congress entry as "Take My Mother's Hand for Me," but a close analysis of the sound verifies the word *shake,* also verified by checking listings of titles in hymnals.
3. One of Ola's band members, Ted Lundy, who also moved from the New River homeland to the tri-state area, later committed suicide by jumping off the Delaware Bay Bridge. Some friends said that his conversations indicated an inner anguish concerning the transition from Appalachia to urban life. Whatever the causes of Ted's death, Ola realized that this migration created many problems for all those involved.

Chapter 5

1. For complete discographies on musicians of this chapter, see Marty McGee, *Traditional Musicians of the Central Blue Ridge: Old-time, Early Country, Folk, and Bluegrass Label Recording Artists, with Discographies* (Jefferson, N.C.: McFarland and Company, 2000).
2. See works by Charles Perdue and Nancy Martin-Perdue on the Shenandoah Valley land removals to create the Shenandoah National Park, similar to what happened at Mount Rogers. Also see their work on Virginians in the Great Depression: Charles L. Perdue and Nancy J. Martin-Perdue, eds., *Talk About Trouble: A New Deal Portrait of Virginians in the Great Depression* (Chapel Hill: Univ. of North Carolina Press, 1996).

Bibliography

Published and Unpublished Sources

Abrams, Rick. "Frets Visits . . . Piney Creek, North Carolina, Skyland Musical Instruments." *Frets Magazine* 5, no. 2 (Feb. 1983): 14–16.

_____, Letter nominating Dave Sturgill for the North Carolina Folklore Society Brown-Hudson Award, 1989.

Agay, Denes. *Best Loved Songs of the American People.* New York: Doubleday, 1975.

"Albert Hash." In Program, 39th National Folk Festival, Washington, D.C., 1977, p. 19.

Alleghany County Historical and Genealogical Society. *Alleghany County Heritage.* Winston-Salem, N.C.: Hunter Publishing Company, 1983.

Anderson, Charles ("Charlie"). "Going to Galax." *Calliope House Newsletter of Traditional Music and Arts in Western Pennsylvania* 7, no. 8 (Aug. 1988): 1–3.

Anderson-Green, Paula H. "David A. Sturgill: Brown-Hudson Award." *North Carolina Folklore Journal* 37 (1990): 71–72.

_____. "The New River Frontier Settlement on the Virginia–North Carolina Border, 1760–1820." *Virginia Magazine of History and Biography* 86 (Oct. 1978): 413–32.

_____. "New River Musician: Ola Belle Campbell Reed." In *Proceedings of the New River Symposium, 1986,* ed. William Cox, pp. 27–37. Washington, D.C.: National Park Service, U.S. Department of the Interior, 1986.

_____, to Folk Arts Panel, National Endowment for the Arts, nominating Dave Sturgill for a National Heritage Fellowship, Sept. 18, 1987. Files of the National Endowment for the Arts.

_____, to Folklife Section, North Carolina Council for the Arts, Raleigh, North Carolina, nominating Dave Sturgill for Brown-Hudson Award, Feb. 28, 1989.

_____, ed. *Pioneer Settlers in Grayson County, Virginia: From the Colonial Days to the Early County Formation, 1760–1800.* Atlanta: Pro-Graphics, 1993.

Anonymous article on Ola Belle Campbell Reed, *Baltimore Sun,* Aug. 24, 1975, magazine section.

Anonymous article on Ola Belle Campbell Reed, *Franklin Times* [Louisburg, North Carolina], Apr. 12, 1981.

"Artist [Ola Belle Campbell Reed] Recognized." *Independence (Va.) Declaration,* Aug. 20, 1986.

"Asheville Folklore Expert [Virgil Sturgill] To Be Heard on CBS Network. *Asheville (N.C.) Citizen-Times,* Mar. 11, 1951.

"Baliles Visits Old Fiddlers' Convention." *Galax (Va.) Gazette,* Aug. 15, 1988. Photo of "Uncle" Dave Sturgill, with caption.

Bamberg, Bob. "Dave Sturgill: Musician, Engineer, Historian, and Free Spirit." *Alleghany News* [Sparta, North Carolina], p. 1, Oct. 23, 1983.

_____. "Folklore Society Honors Sturgill." *Alleghany News* [Sparta, North Carolina], Apr. 12, 1990.

Banes, Ruth A. "Mythology in Music: The Ballad of Loretta Lynn." *Canadian Review of American Studies* 16, no. 3 (1985): 284–86.

Batteau, Allen. "The Contradictions of a Kinship Community." In *Holding onto the Land and the Lord: Kinship, Ritual, Land Tenure, and Social Policy in the Rural South,* ed. Robert Hall and Carol Stack. Athens: Univ. of Georgia Press, 1982.

_____. *Invention of Appalachia.* Tucson: Univ. of Arizona Press, 1990.

Bauman, Richard. "Differential Identity and the Social Base of Folklore." *Journal of American Folklore* 84 (1971): 31.

Bayard, Samuel P., ed. *Dance to the Fiddle, March to the Fife.* University Park: Pennsylvania State Univ. Press, 1982.

_____. *Hill Country Tunes.* Philadelphia: American Folklore Society, 1944.

Beaver, Patricia Duane. *Rural Community in the Appalachian South.* Lexington: Univ. Press of Kentucky, 1986.

Blanton, Bill. "Albert Hash." In *The Plow Reader: Selections from an Appalachian Alternative Newsmagazine of the Late 1970s,* ed. Ann Richmond. Abingdon, Va.: Sow's Ear Press, 1996.

Blaustein, Richard J. "Traditional Music and Social Change: The Old-time Fiddlers Association Movement in the United States." Ph.D. diss., Indiana Univ., 1975.

Blethen, Tyler, and Curtis Wood. "Community and Perceptions of Community in Western North Carolina, 1830–80." Paper delivered at Appalachian Studies Conference, Western Carolina Univ., Cullowhee, N.C., 1992.

Bock, Fred, ed. *Country and Western Gospel Hymnal.* Grand Rapids, Mich.: Singspiration Music, Zondervan Corp., 1972.

Brown, Robert. "Fiddle Maker, Dave Sturgill, Is Master Craftsman." *North Wilkesboro (N.C.) Journal-Patriot,* Aug. 4, 1980.

Bryant, F. Carlene. *We're All Kin: A Cultural Study of a Mountain Neighborhood.* Knoxville: Univ. of Tennessee Press, 1981.

Burrelle. "Bluegrass Concert Will Reunite Alex, Ola Belle, and the Original New River Boys." *Chester County Press* (Oxford, Pennsylvania), Jan. 8, 1984.

Camp, Charles, and David Whisnant. "A Voice from Home: Southern Mountain Musicians on the Maryland-Pennsylvania Border." *Long Journey Home: Folklife in the South. Southern Exposure* 5, nos. 2–3 (1977): 80–90.

Cash, W. J. *The Mind of the South.* New York: Knopf, 1941.

Cauthen, Joyce H. *With Fiddle and Well-Rosined Bow: Old-time Fiddling in Alabama.* Tuscaloosa: Univ. of Alabama Press, 1989.

Chase, Richard. *American Folk Tales and Songs.* New York: Signet Books, 1956. Rpt. 1971.

Checklist of Recorded Songs in the English Language. Archive of American Folk Song, Library of Congress, 1940. Rpt. New York: Arno Press, 1971. Cited as *Checklist AAFS.*

Christeson, R. P. *The Old-time Fiddlers Repertory.* Columbia: Univ. of Missouri Press, 1973.

Clark, Debby Tillson. "Henderson Provokes Big Smiles." *Independence (Va.) Declaration,* Nov. 6, 1991.

Coffin, Tristan P. *The British Traditional Ballad in North America.* Bibliographical and Special Series, vol. 2. 1950. Rev. ed. Philadelphia: American Folklore Society, 1963.

Cohen, Norman. "Folk Music Discography: Norman Cohen." *Western Folklore* 30 (1971): 235.

_____. *Long Steel Rail: The Railroad in American Folk Song.* Urbana: Univ. of Illinois, 1981.

Cohn, Lawrence, ed. *Nothing But the Blues: The Music and the Musicians.* New York: Abbeville Press, 1993.

Coles, Robert. *Children of Crisis.* Vol. 2: *Migrants, Sharecroppers, and Mountaineers.* Boston: Little, Brown, 1967.

Combs, Josiah H. *Folk-Songs of the Southern United States.* Ed. K. K. Wilgus. Austin: Univ. of Texas Press, for the American Folklore Society, 1967.

Conway, Cecelia. *African Banjo Echoes in Appalachia: A Study of Folk Traditions.* Knoxville: Univ. of Tennessee Press, 1995.

_____, and Tommy Thompson. "Talking Banjo." *Southern Exposure* 2 (1974): 63–66.

Corrigan, Ann. "Apprentices Beat Path to Alleghany Guitar Maker." *Winston-Salem (N.C.) Journal,* Sept. 14, 1975.

Cotton, Cay. "Albert Hash: Fiddle Master, Fiddle Maker." *Bluegrass Unlimited* 13, no 10 (Apr. 1979): 88–92.

Cox, John Harrington II. *Traditional Ballads and Folksongs Mainly from West Virginia.* Philadelphia: American Folklore Society, 1939. Rpt. 1964.

Crawford, Martin. "Political Society in a Southern Mountain Community: Ashe County, North Carolina, 1850–1861." *Journal of Southern History* 55, no. 3 (Aug. 1989): 373–90.

Davidson, Eric. Liner notes for "Traditional Music from Grayson and Carroll Counties." Folkways Album FS 3811, 1962.

Davis, Arthur Kyle. *More Traditional Ballads of Virginia.* Chapel Hill: Univ. of North Carolina Press, 1960.

_____. *Traditional Ballads of Virginia.* Cambridge, Mass.: Harvard Univ. Press, 1929.

Davis, Ronald L. *A History of Music in American Life.* Vol. 1: *The Formative Years, 1620–1865.* Malabar, Fla.: Robert Krieger Publishing Company, 1982.

Denson, Paine, ed. *Original Sacred Harp.* 1884. Rev. ed. Kingsport, Tenn.: Kingsport Press, 1971.

Downes, Olin, and Elie Siegmeister. *A Treasury of American Song.* 2d ed. New York: Knopf, 1943.

Eggett, E. Charles, ed. *Tennessee Ernie Ford's Book of Favorite Hymns.* New York: Bramhall House, 1962.

Erbsen, Wayne. *Backpocket Old Time Song Book: Words and Music to Forty Timeless Mountain Tunes.* Asheville, N.C.: Erbsen Music, 1981.

Fairfield, John H. *Known Violin Makers.* 1942. Rpt. St. Clair Shores, Mich.: Scholarly Press, 1977.

Fant, Rebecca. "Grayson Star Shines Brightly at Carnegie Hall." *Independence (Va.) Declaration,* Dec. 22, 1990.

Farrell, Susan Caust. *Directory of Contemporary American Musical Instrument Makers.* Columbia: Univ. of Missouri Press, 1981.

Fields, Bettye-Lo, ed. *Grayson County: A History in Words and Pictures.* Independence, Va.: Grayson County Historical Society, 1976.

"Fifty Years Ago: 500 Miles on a Bicycle." *Bel Air (Md.) Aegis,* Oct. 13, 1983. About Dave Sturgill.

Fletcher, Arthur L., ed. *Ashe County: A History.* Charlotte, N.C.: Heritage Printers, 1963.

Ford, Ira W. *Traditional Music in America.* Hatboro, Pa.: Folklore Association, 1965.

Gallanter, Marty. "Arlo Guthrie." In *Artists of American Folk Music,* ed. Phil Hood. New York: GPI Publications, 1986.

_____. "Pete Seeger." In *Artists of American Folk Music,* ed. Phil Hood. New York: GPI Publishers, 1986.

Genealogical Files. Grayson County Historical Society. Independence, Va.

Gerrard, Alice, and Andy Cahan to Folk Arts Panel. National Endowment for the Arts, nominating Albert Hash for National Heritage Fellowship, Dec. 8, 1982. Albert Hash file, American Folklife Center, Library of Congress.

Glassie, Henry. Notes for LWO 9080 ("New River Boys and Girls") and for LWO 15509 (Henry Glassie's field recordings in North Carolina–Virginia) are in Archive of Folk Song, Library of Congress, Washington, D.C. See discography for details on LWO 9080 and LWO 15509.

_____. *Pattern in the Material Folk Culture of the Eastern United States.* Philadelphia: Univ. of Pennsylvania Press, 1968.

Golladay, Nadine. "David A. Sturgill: Creator of Music and Beauty." *Transmitter* [magazine of Bell System] (1954): 23–25.

"Guitar [made by Dave Sturgill] Is Given to [Governor] Holshouser." *Raleigh (N.C.) Journal,* Aug. 1976.

Hash Family Genealogical File. Grayson County Historical Society. Independence, Virginia.

Hash Family Historian Newsletter 7, no. 3 (Jan. 1987); 12, no. 3 (Sept. 1992); and 14, no. 1 (Jan. 1994). Newsletter edited by Richard O. Johnson, Grass Valley, Calif.

Hauslohner, Amy Worthington. "Henderson Hand-crafted Guitars: Putting Rugby on the Map." *Bluegrass Unlimited* 23, no. 12 (June 1989): 34–37.

_____. "Twenty-nine Hours: A Day (and More) in the Life of the Konnarock Country Critters." *Bluegrass Unlimited* 40 (Mar. 1991): 38–45.

Hawthorne, Ann. "Appalachian Scene: Young and Old Share Music in Galax." *Appalachia: Journal of the Appalachian Regional Commission* 22, no. 4 (Fall 1989): 34–38.

Hobbs, Samuel Huntington. *North Carolina: Economic and Social.* Chapel Hill: Univ. of North Carolina Press, 1930.

Hood, Phil, ed. *Artists of American Folk Music.* New York: GPI Publishers, 1986.

Horstman, Dorothy. *Sing Your Heart Out, Country Boy.* Nashville: Country Music Foundation, 1975; rev. ed. 1986.

Hurst, Jack. "She's [Ola Belle Campbell Reed] No Amateur at Music or Life." *Philadelphia Inquirer,* Sept. 15, 1974.

Jabbour, Alan. "The Fiddle in the Blue Ridge." In *Blue Ridge Folk Instruments and Their Makers,* ed. J. Roderick Moore. Ferrum, Va.: Blue Ridge Institute, Ferrum College, 1993.

Jackson, George Pullen. *White Spirituals in the Southern Uplands.* New York: Dover, 1965.

Johnson, Patricia Givens. *The New River Early Settlement.* Pulaski, Va.: Edmonds Printing, 1983.

Jones, Louis M. "Grandpa," and Charles K. Wolfe. *Everybody's Grandpa: Fifty Years Behind the Mike.* Knoxville: Univ. of Tennessee Press, 1984.

Jones, Robert. "People of the New River" [Sturgills, Osbornes, Andersons, Jack Phipps, Maggie Speeks]. *The Plow* [Saltville, Virginia], June 1976, pp. 11–14.

Joyner, Charles. "African and European Roots of Southern Culture: The 'Central Theme' Revisited." In *Dixie Debates: Perspectives on Southern Culture,* ed. Richard H. King and Helen Taylor. New York: New York Univ. Press, 1996.

Kenzer, Robert C. *Kinship and Neighborhood in a Southern Community: Orange County, North Carolina, 1849–1881.* Knoxville: Univ. of Tennessee Press, 1987.

Kephart, Horace. *Our Southern Highlanders.* New York: Macmillan, 1922.

Laws, G. Malcolm, Jr. *American Balladry from British Broadsides.* Bibliographical and Special Series, vol. 8. Philadelphia: American Folklore Society, 1957.

———. *Native American Balladry.* Rev. ed. Philadelphia: American Folklore Society, 1964.

Leach, Mac Edward, ed. *The Ballad Book.* New York: A. S. Barnes & Co., 1955. (Contains Child Ballads from collection of F. J. Child, Boston, 1882.)

Leyburn, James G. *The Scotch-Irish: A Social History.* Chapel Hill: Univ. of North Carolina Press, 1962.

Lindsey, Charles, ed. *Folk Song Sing Along.* New York: Amsco Music Publishing Company, 1962.

Lomax, Alan. *The Folk Songs of North America.* New York: Doubleday, 1960.

Lomax, John, and Alan Lomax. *American Ballads and Folk Songs.* New York: 1934.

———. *Cowboy Songs and Other Frontier Ballads.* Rev. ed. New York: Macmillan, 1938.

Lomax, John, and Jean Ritchie. *Folk Songs of the Southern Appalachians as Sung by Jean Ritchie.* New York: Oak Publications, 1965.

Lornell, Kip. *Virginia's Blues, Country, and Gospel Records, 1902–1943: An Annotated Bibliography.* Lexington: Univ. Press of Kentucky, 1989.

Malone, Bill C. *Country Music, USA.* Austin: Univ. of Texas Press for American Folklore Society, 1968.

_____. *Singing Cowboys and Musical Mountaineers: Southern Culture and the Roots of Country Music.* Athens: Univ. of Georgia Press, 1993.

_____. *Southern Music, American Music.* Lexington: Univ. Press of Kentucky, 1979.

Marti, Judy. "Banjo Picking Girl: The Life and Music of Ola Belle Campbell Reed." *Old-time Herald* 3, no. 6 (1992–93): 17–22.

Martin-Perdue, Nancy J., and Charles L. Perdue Jr., eds. *Talk About Trouble: A New Deal Portrait of Virginians in the Great Depression.* Chapel Hill: Univ. of North Carolina Press, 1996.

McGee, Marty. *Traditional Musicians of the Central Blue Ridge: Old-time, Early Country, Folk, and Bluegrass Label Recording Artists, with Discographies.* Jefferson, N.C.: McFarland and Company, 2000.

Messick, Hank. *King's Mountain: The Epic of the Blue Ridge "Mountain Men" in the American Revolution.* Boston: Little, Brown, 1976.

Moore, J. Roderick, Director, Blue Ridge Institute, Ferrum College, Ferrum, Virginia, to Folk Arts Panel, National Endowment for the Arts, nominating Albert Hash for National Heritage Fellowship, Nov. 18, 1981. Albert Hash file, American Folklife Center, Library of Congress.

_____, ed. *Blue Ridge Folk Instruments and Their Makers.* Ferrum, Va.: Blue Ridge Institute, Ferrum College, 1993.

Morgan, Edmund S. *Virginians at Home.* Charlottesville: Univ. Press of Virginia, 1952.

Moyers, William J. "One Man's Ulcer Cure." *Washington Star Pictorial Magazine,* May 23, 1954, p. 23.

Mullinax, Gary. "They Brought Their Music North." *Sunday News Journal* [Wilmington, Delaware], June 5, 1977.

"Musician Gets Folklore Honor at Ceremony." *Independence (Va.) Declaration,* Apr. 25, 1990.

National Council for Traditional Arts. Notes and accompanying tape by Albert Hash. Submitted to Heritage Awards Panel, National Endowment for the Arts, 1982.

Newsome, A. R. "Twelve North Carolina Counties in 1810–1811." *North Carolina Historical Review* 5, no. 4 (1928): 413–46.

Nuckolls, Benjamin Floyd. *Pioneer Settlers of Grayson County, Virginia.* Bristol, Tenn., 1914.

Orr, Jay. "Fiddle and Fiddler's Conventions." In *Encyclopedia of Southern Culture,* ed. Charles Reagan Wilson and William Ferris. Chapel Hill: Univ. of North Carolina Press, 1989.

Owsley, F. W. "Patterns of Migration." In *The South: Old and New Frontiers,* ed. Harriet Owsley. Athens: Univ. of Georgia Press, 1969.

Patterson, Bobby. Liner notes for *Old Favorites,* audiotape recording by Konnarock Critters. Heritage Records HRC-C-113. Galax, Va.: Heritage Records, 1995.

Perdue, Charles L., Jr. "What Made Little Sister Die? The Core Aesthetic and Personal Culture of a Traditional Singer." *Western Folklore* 54, no. 2 (Apr. 1995): 141–59.

Perdue, Charles L., Jr., and Nancy J. Martin-Perdue. "Appalachian Fables and Facts: A Case Study of the Shenandoah National Park Removals." *Appalachian Journal* 7, Nos. 1–2 (Autumn–Winter 1979–80): 84–104.

Ramsey, Robert W. *Carolina Cradle: Settlement of the Northwest Carolina Frontier, 1747–1762.* Chapel Hill: Univ. of North Carolina Press, 1964.

The Reed Family Songbook. Wilmington, Delaware: Zeta Nu Upsilon Sorority, Goldey Beacom College, n.d. Introduction by Jason Pate. Ola Belle Reed file, American Folklife Center, Library of Congress.

Rehert, Isaac. "A 'Hillbilly' Doctorate." *Baltimore Sun,* June 13, 1978.

Richardson, Ethel Park. *American Mountain Songs,* ed. Sigmund Spaeth. New York: Greenburg Publishers, 1927; rev. ed., 1955.

Rinzler, Ralph. "Roots of the Folk Revival." In *The Folk Music Sourcebook,* ed. Larry Sandberg and Dick Weisman. New York: Knopf, 1976.

Roberts, Leonard, and C. Buell Agey. *In the Pines: Selected Kentucky Folksongs.* Pikeville, Kentucky: Pikeville College Press, 1978.

Rooney, James. *Bossmen: Bill Monroe and Muddy Waters.* New York: Dial Press, 1971.

Rosenbaum, Art. *Folk Visions and Voices: Traditional Music and Song in North Georgia.* Athens: Univ. of Georgia Press, 1983.

Rosenberg, Neil V. *Bluegrass: A History.* Urbana: Univ. of Illinois Press, 1985.

Sacks, Howard L., Associate Director, National Council of Traditional Arts, to Folk Arts Panel, National Endowment for the Arts, nominating Albert Hash for National Heritage Fellowship. Dec. 9, 1982. Albert Hash file, American Folklife Center, Library of Congress.

Sandberg, Larry, and Dick Weisman. "Old-time String Bands and Early Country Music." In *The Folk Music Sourcebook,* ed. Larry Sandberg and Dick Weisman. New York: Knopf, 1976.

Sandberg, Larry, and Dick Weisman, eds. *The Folk Music Sourcebook.* New York: Knopf, 1976.

Saylors, Gertrude. *Hache-Hash Family Genealogy and Allied Lines.* Published by the author, 1970.

Schoenbaum, Thomas J. *The New River Controversy.* Winston-Salem, N.C.: John F. Blair, 1979.

Scholes, Percy A. *The Puritans and Music in England and New England.* New York: Russell and Russell, 1962.

Schwarzweller, Harry K.; James S. Brown; and J. J. Mangalam. *Mountain Families in Transition: A Case Study of Appalachian Migration.* State College: Pennsylvania State Univ. Press, 1971.

Seeger, Pete. *The Incompleat Folksinger,* ed. Jo Metcalf Schwartz. New York: Simon and Schuster, 1972.

Sharp, Cecil. *English Folk Songs from the Southern Appalachians.* New York: Oxford Univ. Press, 1932. Rpt. 1966.

Shepherd, Ruth, ed. *Heritage of Ashe County, North Carolina.* Vol. 1. Winston-Salem, N.C.: Hunter Publishers, 1984.

Simpson, Sally A. "Band Hits Responsive Chord." *Independence (Va.) Declaration,* Nov. 24, 1982.

Smith, L. Allen. *A Catalogue of Pre-Revival Appalachian Dulcimers.* Columbia: Univ. of Missouri Press, 1983.

_____. "Thoughts on the Appalachian Dulcimer." In *Blue Ridge Folk Instruments and Their Makers,* ed. J. Roderick Moore. Ferrum, Va.: Blue Ridge Institute, Ferrum College, 1993.

Soulsman, Gary. "I'll Be Pickin' Again." *Wilmington (Del.) Sunday News Journal,* Apr. 30, 1989, pp. J1–J7.

Spencer, Emily. Liner Notes for *Whitetop: Albert Hash and the Whitetop Mountain Boys.* Mountain Records 311. Galax, Va.: Mountain Records, 1976.

Spencer, Thornton, and Emily Spencer. "Albert Hash and His Music." Letter and article submitted to Folk Arts Panel for National Heritage Fellowship, National Endowment for the Arts, May 20, 1981. Albert Hash file, American Folklife Center, Library of Congress.

_____. "Music of Virginia-Carolina Mountains." In *The Plow.* Saltville, Va., 1978.

"State to Buy 350 Acres on New River." *Alleghany News* [Sparta, N.C.], Feb. 15, 1990.

Sturgill, David A. "Banjo Tone." *Bluegrass Unlimited* 11, no. 5 (Nov. 1976): 18–21.

_____. *A Branch of the Sturgill Family.* Vol. 1: *Descendants of Francis Sturgill, Sr., and Rebecca Hash.* West Jefferson, N.C.: Carolina Printing Co., 1993.

_____. "Our Mountain Musical Heritage." *Alleghany News* [Sparta, N.C.], Dec. 25, 1985, p. 5.

_____. "Strings and Things: Bingo, Bongo, Banjo." *Bluegrass Unlimited* 9, no. 3 (Sept. 1974): 18–19.

_____. "Strings and Things: Hand-crafted Musical Instruments." *Bluegrass Unlimited* 8, no. 9 (1974): 13–14.

_____. "Strings and Things: The Sound of Music." *Bluegrass Unlimited* 9, no. 9 (Mar. 1975): 22–24.

Sturgill, David A., and Mack H. Sturgill, eds. *A History of the Sturgill Family.* West Jefferson, N.C.: Carolina Printing Co., 1960. Rev. ed. 1983.

Sturgill, David A., to Paula H. Anderson-Green. Jan. 21, 1993. Discusses his friendship with his cousin, Virgil Leon Sturgill.

Sturgill, Dean. "The Fiddlers, Thirty and Three." In *An Old Fiddler's Book of Rhymes,* vol. 1. Lansing, N.C.: privately published, 1992.

_____. "The Fees Branch Fiddler." In *An Old Fiddler's Book of Rhymes,* vol. 3. Lansing, N.C.: privately published, 1994.

Sturgill, Virgil. "The History of the Dulcimer." *Washington Folk Strums* 1 (Apr. 1964); 2 (May 1964).

_____. "The 'Lost' Ballad of George Collins." *North Carolina Folklore* 4, no. 1 (July 1956): 31–33.

_____. "The Murder of Lottie Yates." *North Carolina Folklore* 6, no. 2 (Dec. 1958): 26–28. Also published in *Kentucky Folklore Record* 5 (1959): 61–64.

_____. "Willy Weaver." In "A Sheaf of North Carolina Folksongs," collected or transcribed by Dan Patterson. *North Carolina Folklore* 4, no. 1 (July 1956): 23–31.

_____. Virgil Sturgill clipping file. North Carolina Collection, University of North Carolina Library, Chapel Hill.

Summers, Lewis Preston. *History of Southwest Virginia, 1746–1786*. Richmond, Virginia, 1903.

Taliaferro, Harden E. *Fisher's River (North Carolina) Scenes and Characters by "Skitt, Who Was Raised Thar."* New York: Harper and Brothers, 1859.

Tebbens, Susan. "A Gathering of Strings, Fills, Hoovens, and Dreams." *Galax (Va.) Gazette,* Aug. 9, 1995.

Thede, Marion. *The Fiddle Book.* New York: Oak Publications, 1967.

Thomas, Agnes, cousin of Ola Belle Campbell Reed. Interviews and correspondence with Paula H. Anderson-Green.

Thompson, Toby. "A True Appalachian Contralto" [Ola at Kennedy Center]. *Washington Post,* Apr. 21, 1976.

Tribe, Ivan M. *The Stonemans: An Appalachian Family and the Music That Shaped Their Lives.* Urbana: Univ. of Illinois Press, 1993.

Trivette, Robert. "Flurry Dowe and Thornton Spencer: Keeping the Clawhammer Style Alive." *The Plow* [Saltville, Va.], July 15, 1977. Rpt. in *The Plow Reader,* ed. Ann Richman. Abingdon, Va.: Sow's Ear Press, 1996.

Wall, Marilyn. "The Banjo Man." *Bluegrass Unlimited* 24, no. 8 (Feb. 1990): 23–24.

Weller, Jack E. *Yesterday's People.* Lexington: Univ. of Kentucky Press, 1965.

Weston, Frank. "Albert Hash: Fiddler and Fiddle-maker." *Old-time Music* 39 (1984): 13–19.

Whisnant, David E. *All That Is Native and Fine: The Politics of Culture in an American Region.* Chapel Hill: Univ. of North Carolina Press, 1983. Note: Whisnant interviewed Albert Hash and many other musicians; see pp. 232 and 253.

_____. Notes for *Ola Belle Reed and Family.* Rounder Record 0077. 1977.

_____. "The White Top Festival, 1931–1939: An Introduction, Annotated Bibliography and Guide to Resources." *Folklore and Folklife in Virginia* 2 (1980–81): 38–52.

White, Wallace. "Our Far-Flung Correspondents: Fiddlers' Convention." *New Yorker,* July 20, 1987, pp. 74–88.

Wigginton, Eliot, ed. *Foxfire 3.* Garden City, New York: Anchor Press, 1975. On Dave Sturgill, see pp. 168–85.

Wilkinson, Winston. "Virginia Dance Tunes." *Southern Folklore Quarterly* 6, no. 1 (1942): 1–10.

Williams, Cratis D. "The New River Valley in Settlement Days." In *Heritage of Ashe County, North Carolina,* ed. Ruth Shepherd. Winston-Salem, N.C.: Hunter Publishing, 1984.

_____. "Traditional Ballads and Folksongs from the Southern Appalachians." In *Proceedings of the Seventh Annual Marshall University English Institute.* Huntington, W.Va.: 1967.

_____. "Who Are the Southern Mountaineers?" *Appalachian Journal* 1, no. 1 (1972): 48–55.

Williamson, J. W. *Hillbillyland: What the Movies Did to the Mountains and What the Mountains Did to the Movies.* Chapel Hill: Univ. of North Carolina Press, 1995.

Wilson, Joseph T. Notes for audiotape, *Wayne C. Henderson and Company.* HHH-C-107. Blacksburg, Va.: Hay Holler Harvest Records, 1994.

Wilson, Joseph T., Executive Director, National Council for the Traditional Arts, to the Folk Arts Panel, National Endowment for the Arts, nominating Albert Hash for a National Heritage Fellowship, Nov. 4, 1981. Albert Hash file, American Folklife Center, Library of Congress.

_____, Executive Director, National Council for the Traditional Arts, to the Folk Arts Panel, National Endowment for the Arts, nominating Wayne Henderson for a National Heritage Fellowship, Sept. 26, 1986. Files of the National Endowment for the Arts.

_____, ed. *Dixie Frets: Luthiers of the Southeast.* Program for Exhibition at Hunter Museum of Art, Chattanooga, Tenn., 1994. Exhibition sponsored by National Council of Traditional Arts.

Winans, Robert B. "The Banjo: From Africa to Virginia and Beyond." In *Blue Ridge Folk Instruments and Their Makers,* ed. J. Roderick Moore. Ferrum, Va.: Blue Ridge Institute, Ferrum College, 1993.

_____. "The Black Banjo-Playing Tradition in Virginia and West Virginia." *Journal of Virginia Folklore Society* 1 (1979): 7–30.

Wolfe, Charles. *The Devil's Box: Masters of Southern Fiddling.* Nashville: Vanderbilt Univ. Press, 1997.

_____. "The Early Years." In *The Blackwell Guide to Recorded Country Music,* ed. Bob Allen. Oxford, England: Blackwell Publishers, 1994.

_____. "A Lighter Shade of Blue: White Country Blues." In *Nothing But the Blues,* ed. Lawrence Cohn. New York: Abbeville Press, 1993.

_____. "Old-Time Music." In *Encyclopedia of Country Music,* ed. Paul Kingsbury. New York: Oxford Univ. Press, 1998.

_____. "Tracking the Lost String Bands." *Long Journey Home: Folklife in the South: Southern Exposure* 5, nos. 2–3 (1977): 20.

Interviews

Anderson, Gerald. By Paula H. Anderson-Green, at the "Henderson Guitar Shop," Rugby, Virginia, Aug. 2, 1994.

Hamm, Audrey Hash, and her mother, Ethel Spencer Hash. By Paula H. Anderson-Green, at their home and shop, Cabin Creek, Rugby, Virginia, Aug. 30, 1994.

Hash, Albert. By Paula H. Anderson-Green, at Galax Fiddlers Convention, Felts Park, Galax, Va., c. 1976. Not recorded on tape, only in written notes, but later referred to in correspondence. Letters from Albert Hash (1981–82) in collection of Paula H. Anderson-Green.

Hash, Casey. By Paula H. Anderson-Green, Grayson County, Virginia, 1993.

Henderson, Wayne. By Paula H. Anderson-Green, at the "Henderson Guitar Shop," Rugby, Virginia, Aug. 4, 1994.

Hooven, Greg. By Paula H. Anderson-Green, at the Elk Creek Fiddlers Convention, Elk Creek, Virginia, June 2000.

Miller, Johnny. By Paula H. Anderson-Green, at his home, Volney, Virginia. Aug. 7, 1994.

Patterson, Dan. Telephone interview by Paula H. Anderson-Green, c. 1992.

Reed, Ola Belle Campbell. By Paula H. Anderson-Green, Rising Sun, Maryland, Aug. 1, 1984.

_____. Interviews by Henry Glassie, 1967–69. LWO-5847, Archive of Folk Song, Library of Congress, Washington, D.C. Jason David Pate worked on this project also.

_____. Interviews by Mike Seeger for "logs" on tapes, mid-1950s. Southern Folklore Collection, Univ. of North Carolina, Chapel Hill.

Spencer, Emily; Thornton Spencer; and Dean Sturgill. By Paula H. Anderson-Green, at the Spencers' home, Mount Rogers, Virginia, Aug. 19, 1994.

Sturgill family. By Paula H. Anderson-Green, Piney Creek, N.C., Aug. 5, 1982.

Selected Discography

For more detailed information, consult appendix D. Also, for complete discographies, see Marty McGee, *Traditional Musicians of the Central Blue Ridge: Old-time, Early Country, Folk, and Bluegrass Label Recording Artists, with Discographies* (Jefferson, N.C.: McFarland and Company, 2000).

Ola Belle Campbell Reed

Archive of Folk Song, American Folklife Center, Library of Congress

LWO-5847. Includes two five-inch audiotapes of the "North Carolina Ridge Runners," made late 1940s–1950s; and three tapes of Ola Belle Campbell Reed. More detail about these five tapes follows.

LWO-5847. Five-inch reel labeled "North Carolina Ridge Runners I."

Side A

1. "The Echoes from the Hills": Ola yodeling
2. "A Picture from Life's Other Side" ("Somebody has fell by the way"; "A poor old mother at home")
3. "Hold to God's Unchanging Hand"
4. "Old Pal of Yesterday"
5. "I'm Walking the Floor Over You" (Ernest Tubb)
6. "Sweet Fern" ("Fly to him singing your sweet little song"; asks for message in return)
7. "Alone and Blue" ("Got no-one to tell my troubles to")
8. "The Echoes from the Hills"
9. "Time Changes Everything"
10. "No Letter in the Mail"
11. "Shake Hands With Mother Again": Old-time hymn
12. "Will the Circle Be Unbroken?": Old-time hymn

Side B

1. "When the Saints Go Marching In": Old-time hymn

2. "There's a Blue Sky Way Out Yonder": Yodeling

3. "Saint Louis Blues": Blues and jazz tradition

4. "The Life I Love the Best"

5. "I'm Thinking Tonight of My Blue Eyes"

6. "Will the Circle Be Unbroken?": Old-time hymn

7. "We Are Drifting" ("Down the rugged streams of time"; "Our days are slipping by")

8. "Out on Montana's Plains": Country-western

9. "All That I've Got Is a Worried Mind"

10. "He Walks With Me and Talks With Me": Hymn

11. "There's a Vacant Spot in my Heart"

12. "Buffalo Girls": Old-time tradition

13. "The Little Adobe Shack Way Out West"

14. "Tom Cattin' Around": Country-western

LWO-5847. Short five-inch reel labeled "North Carolina Ridge Runners II."

Side A

1. "Soldier's Joy": Instrumental—fiddle, banjo, etc.

2. "Bile Them Cabbage Down": Male vocal; tune same as "Whoa There Mule."

3. "Life's Railway to Heaven": Vocal, Ola leads

4. "Columbus Stockade Blues": Male lead

5. "Arkansas Traveler": Instrumental, fiddle

6. "Just Because": Vocal, male lead

7. "Those Brown Eyes": Vocal

8. Concluding announcement of broadcast

9. "Take Me Back to Carolina"

Side B

1. "When the Roll Is Called Up Yonder": Hymn

2. "Take My Mother's Hand For Me": Hymn. Note: first word should be "Shake."

3. "Will the Circle Be Unbroken?": Old-time hymn

LWO-5847. Five-inch reel. "K. D. You Led Me to the Wrong." 1968. Ola Belle Campbell Reed.

1. "You Led Me to the Wrong": Vocal by Ola, banjo, guitar, bass

2. Instrumental: Fiddle, banjo, and guitar

3. Fiddle tune: Salt Creek [writing unclear]

4. "Tell Me Why That I'm So Lonesome" ("Darling What Has Gone Wrong?"): Vocal by Ola Belle

5. "Love Please Don't Come Home": Group

LWO-6596. Audiotape recording of 1950. Chesapeake label. This was the first record made by Ola Belle Campbell Reed and Alex Campbell.

Side A

"Orange Blossom Special"

Side B

"Poison Love"

LWO-9080. "New River Boys and Girls." Eight ten-inch reels recorded by Henry Glassie in 1966 and 1967. Seventy-five titles total; only some of these are listed here. Most of the titles are in The Reed Family Songbook.

Reel 3, Apr. 19, 1966

Side A

1. "Amazing Grace"

2. "Orphan Gal"

3. "Cumberland Gap"

4. "Gal I Left Behind Me"

5. "Big Kid's Bar Room"

6. "Black Jack Davy"

7. "I've Endured"

8. "Sally Goodin"

9. "Soldier's Joy"

Side B

1. "Gonna Lay Down My Old Guitar"

2. Instrumental

3. "Single Girl [Wish I Was]"

4. Instrumental

5. "Two Little Rosebuds Taken From Their Home"

6. "Where Was You When the Train Left Town?"

LWO-15509. Henry Glassie's field recordings in North Carolina–Virginia. Include one song by Ola Belle Campbell Reed, recorded on April 24, 1967.

RWA 110–116. U.S. President Jimmy Carter Inaugural Concert Duplication Project. Ola performed five songs:

"I've Endured"

"Hobo's Meditation"

"My Home Is Across the Blue Ridge Mountains"

"I'm Going to Leave Here One Day"

"A Little Circle Being Broken"

Records

North Carolina Ridge Runners. Two records out of print. 1947. Security label. Made at U.S. Recording Studio, Washington, D.C. Features Ola Belle Campbell Reed as vocalist and playing banjo; leader Arthur ("Shorty") Woods; Johnny Miller, steel guitar; and Lester Miller on fiddle; Inky Pierson, banjo; Deacon Brumfield, dobro. Each 78-rpm record has one tune on each side, two minutes and forty seconds long.

First Record:

Side A: "Orange Blossom Special": Johnny Miller, steel guitar; Lester Miller, fiddle

Side B: "You Were Only Teasing Me": Vocal

Second Record:

Side A: "Remember Me": Featuring Art Woods

Side B: "Ridge Runner Boogie": Written by John Miller

Sixteen Radio Favorites: Alex Campbell, Olabelle, and Deacon and the New River Boys. C. 1955. Starday SLP 214 (RD-3640). Band members include Ted Lundy, banjo; John Jackson, fiddle; Earl Wallace, string bass; Alex Campbell, guitar; Ola Belle Campbell Reed, banjo; Deacon Brumfield, dobro.

Side A

1. "I'll Be All Smiles Tonight"

2. "Handsome Molly"

3. "Gonna Have a Big Time Tonight"

4. "Kentucky"

5. "Little White Church"

6. "Little Moses"

7. "Deacon's Boogie"

8. "Build Me a Cabin in Gloryland"

Side B

1. "White Flower"

2. "Dobro Chimes"

3. "Still the Same"

4. "Oloha"

5. "Uncloudy Day"

6. "Longing for a Love I'll Never Know"

7. "Wildwood Flower"

8. "When My Time Comes to Go"

Travel On: Alex Campbell and Ola Belle and the New River Boys. 1955. Starday 342 (RD-9040). Band members include Deacon Brumfield, John Jackson, Ted Lundy, and Earl Wallace. The record jacket calls the music old-time country, gospel, and bluegrass style with traditional stringed instruments. Side B is mostly hymns.

Side A

1. "Travel On"

2. "All the World Is Lonely Now"

3. "I Threw Away the Key"

4. "You Don't Even Know"

5. "I Can't Be Satisfied"

6. "When It Comes My Time to Go"

Side B

1. "When I Lay My Burden Down"

2. "Just Over in the Gloryland"

3. "I Marked the Spot"

4. "Indecision"

5. "Paul and Silas"

6. "Forever I Know"

Ola Belle Reed. 1972. Rounder Records 0021. "Old-time, bluegrass, and gospel with back-up band of family members" (Sandberg and Weisman, *Folk Music Sourcebook,* 66). Record jacket reads: "Ola Belle, banjo, guitar; Bud Reed, harmonica, banjo, guitar; David Reed, banjo, guitar; John Miller, fiddle; Alan Reed, banjo, guitar."

Side A

1. "Wayfaring Pilgrim"

2. "High on a Mountain"

3. "The Soldier and the Lady"

4. "Fly Around My Pretty Little Miss"

5. "Go Home Little Girl"

6. "Blues in My Mind"

7. "God Put a Rainbow in the Clouds"

8. "Flop Eared Mule"

Side B

1. "The Springtime of Life"

2. "Billy in the Lowground"

3. "You Don't Tell Me That You Love Me Any More"

4. "I've Always Been a Rambler"

5. "Rosewood Casket"

6. "John Hardy"

7. "My Epitaph"

8. "I Believe"

My Epitaph. 1976. Folkways Records FA 2493. Audio-documentary. Ola Belle Campbell Reed, with Bud Reed and David Reed. Contains interviews by Kevin Roth and six songs, all composed by Ola. Liner notes by Ola Belle Reed.

Side A

1. Interview: "High on the Mountain"

2. Interview: "I've Endured"

3. Interview: "Sing Me a Song"

Side B

1. Interview: "My Epitaph"

2. Interview: "Springtime of My Life"

3. Interview: "Fortunes"

All in One Evening. 1977. Folkways Records FA 2329. Produced by K. Roth. Ola Belle Reed, son David Reed, other family members, and friends play dulcimer and other instruments together, on the theme that music unifies all.

Ola Belle Reed and Family. 1977. Rounder Records 0077. Ola Belle performs with husband, Bud Reed; and son, David Reed. Liner notes by David E. Whisnant: "One hears the sounds of Ashe County at the turn of the century, Maryland's hillbilly migrants in the 1930s, and a hint of the music of the late 1960s."

Side A

1. "Going to Write Me a Letter"

2. "My Doney, Where Have You Been So Long?"

3. "The Ninety and Nine"

4. "Lamplighting Time in the Valley"

5. "Only the Leading Role Will Do"

6. "Over Yonder in the Graveyard"

7. "Sing Me a Song"

<u>Side B</u>

1. "You Led Me to the Wrong"

2. "The Ranger's Command"

3. "Boat's Up the River"

4. "When Can I Read My Titles Clear?"

5. "The Butcher's Boy"

6. "Where the Wild, Wild Flowers Grow"

7. "I've Endured"

Songs by Ola Belle are included in several other albums showcasing Appalachian music.

Albert Hash

Old Originals. Vols. 1 and 2. 1976. North Carolina Folklore Archive FC1752n and 1753n. Rounder Records 0058. Featuring traditional music from "the Blue Ridge section where North Carolina borders Virginia." Includes music by Albert Hash, Nancy Blevins, Worley Hash, Thornton Spencer, Corbitt Stamper, Dean Sturgill, and others. Albert Hash plays "Cripple Creek" and "Nancy Blevins."

Whitetop: Albert Hash and the Whitetop Mountain Boys. Record album. 1976. Mountain Records 311. Recorded at Mountain Records, Route 3, Galax, Va. Features Albert Hash, fiddle; Thornton Spencer, guitar; Flurry Dowe, clawhammer banjo; and Emily Spencer, guitar and vocals. Liner notes by Emily Spencer.

<u>Side A: Albert Hash, Thornton Spencer, and Flurry Dowe:</u>

1. "Lost John"

2. "Hangman's Reel"

3. "Rabbit Up a Gum Stump"

4. "Old Sport"

5. "Little Brown Hand"

6. "Nancy Blevins"

<u>Side B: Thornton Spencer, Emily Spencer, and Flurry Dowe:</u>

1. "Storms Are on the Ocean"

2. "My Child Is Gonna Be a Miner"

3. "Single Girl"

4. "Green Valley Waltz"

5. "Dugannon"

6. "I Never Will Marry"

Cacklin' Hen. 1977. Mountain Records 313. Galax, Va. Features Albert Hash, fiddle; Thornton Spencer, second fiddle; Emily Spencer, guitar; Flurry Dowe, banjo; Becky Haga, guitar and vocals; Tom Barr, bass.

Side A

1. "Cacklin' Hen"
2. "Sweet as the Flowers in May"
3. "Whistlin' Rufus"
4. "Flop-eared Mule"
5. "Raggedy Ann"
6. "Coming Down From God"

Side B

1. "Leather Britches"
2. "Dream of the Miner's Child"
3. "Shortening Bread"
4. "Don't Whip Your Wife on Sunday"
5. "O Come Angel Band"

Albert Hash and the Whitetop Mountain Band. 1979. Heritage Records 25. Recorded at Heritage Records, Route 3, Galax, Va. A = Albert Hash, fiddle; B = Thornton Spencer, fiddle; C = Flurry Dowe, banjo; D = Emily Spencer, guitar; E = Becky Haga, guitar; F = Tom Barr, bass; G = Bobby Patterson, guitar; H = Emily Spencer, fiddle.

Side A

1. "Sally Ann" (ACDEF)
2. "I'll Fly Away" (BCDEF)
3. "Sally Goodin" (ACDEF)
4. "Rambling Hobo" (CD)
5. "Gathering Flowers from the Hillside" (BCDF)
6. "Did You Ever See the Devil, Uncle Joe?" (ABCDEF)
7. "Rake and Rambling Boy" (BCDF)

Side B

1. "Arkansas Traveler" (ACDEF)
2. "Kentucky" (BCDEF)
3. "Shortening Bread" (CD)
4. "I Saw the Light" (BCDEF)
5. "Gold Hill Waltz" (BCFGH)
6. "Down Among the Budded Roses" (ACDF)
7. "Alabama Gals" (CDF)

Tape and accompanying notes. 1982. Submitted by the National Council for the Traditional Arts to the Heritage Awards Panel, National Endowment for the Arts. The notes state: "This supporting tape is an attempt to show Albert [Hash] as a teacher and storyteller as well as a musician. As we all know, students are subject to many influences, but in this case I believe it is appropriate to present some of the older students who learned both instrument making and most of their music from Albert Hash."

1. "Rake and Rambling Boy": Thornton Spencer and Emily Spencer with the rest of Albert Hash's band. Thornton plays a fiddle he made under Albert's tutelage, and Emily sings one of Albert's favorite "Whitetop songs."
2. "Liberty": Wayne Henderson and Ray Cline play guitars Wayne made.
3. "Sally Anne": Albert Hash plays lead fiddle with his band. This is the first tune that he teaches to his fiddle students.
4. "Stories": Albert as a storyteller—three tall tales.

Winefarger's Mill. 1983. Heritage Records 046C.

Side A
1. "Winefarger's Mill"
2. "Pretty Little Indian"
3. "Dusty Miller"
4. "Sweet Fern"
5. "Soldier's Joy"
6. "Wildwood Flower"
7. "Silver Bells"
8. "Mid the Greenfields of Virginia"
9. "Spencer's Reel"

Side B
1. "When the Snowflakes Fall"
2. "Mississippi Sawyer"
3. "Old Molly Hare"
4. "Intoxicated Rat"
5. "Whistlin' Rufus"
6. "No Hiding Place Down Here"
7. "Sourwood Mountain"
8. "Great Physician"

Heritage Records has also done re-releases.

"Uncle" Dave Sturgill

Abrams, Rick. *Wild Goose.* Audiotape. 1987. Dave Sturgill plays fiddle for one number, the tune "Wild Goose."

Creed, Kyle. *New River Jam. Record album.* 1976. Dave Sturgill and his band, the "Skyland Strings," play on this album.

Sturgill, Dave. *Echoes from the Hills: Old-time Mountain Music by 'Uncle' Dave Sturgill, the Banjo Man.* 1981. Privately produced.

Side A: Clawhammer banjo and guitar

1. "Cumberland Gap"
2. "John Henry"
3. "Cotton Eyed Joe"
4. "Old Time Cindy"
5. "Lonesome Road"
6. "Bear Tracks"
7. "Pig in a Pen"
8. "Sugar Hill"

Side B: Clawhammer banjo and fiddle

1. "Arkansas Traveler"
2. "Mississippi Sawyer"
3. "Wild Goose"
4. "Sail Away Ladies"
5. "Love Somebody"
6. "Shady Grove"
7. "Mole in the Ground"
8. "Danny Boy" (violin)
9. "Red Wing" (guitar)
10. "Amazing Grace" (violin)

Sturgill, Dave. *Dave Sturgill Playing Old-Time Mountain Music on Different Handmade Instruments.* Audiotape. Privately produced, 1983.

Side A: Banjo

1. "Cluck Old Hen"
2. "Sourwood Mountain"
3. "Cumberland Gap"
4. "Fire in the Mountain"
5. "Wreck of the Old Ninety-Seven"
6. "Jesse James"

7. "Sugar Hill"

8. "Mississippi Sawyer"

9. "Sally Ann"

10. "Lonesome Road"

11. "Cindy"

Side B: Fiddle

1. "Raggedy Ann"

2. "Sally Ann"

3. "Wild Goose"

4. "Danny Boy"

5. "Fraulein"

6. "Wabash Cannon Ball"

Side B: Mandolin

7. "Fireball Mail"

8. "The Devil in a Briar Patch"

9. "Lonesome"

10. "Wreck of Old Number Nine"

11. "Amazing Grace"

Side B: Guitar

12. "Black Mountain Rag"

13. "Kentucky Waltz"

Sturgill, Dave. *Uncle Dave Sturgill: A One-man Band.* Audiotape. 1985. Produced by Dave Sturgill.

Sturgill, Dave. *Here and There with Skyland Strings.* Audiotape. 1990. Produced by Dave Sturgill.

Virgil Sturgill

Archive of Folk Song, Library of Congress, Washington, D.C.:

There is no record of commercial recordings by Virgil Sturgill. However, unpublished recordings of ballads and songs collected and sung by Virgil Sturgill form part of the holdings of the Archive of Folk Song, Library of Congress, Washington, D.C. There were two sittings for these recordings, one (LWO 1821) in June 1951 and the other (LWO 2586) on July 31, 1957. In addition to playing music, Virgil gave an introduction and discussed playing the dulcimer. Below is a combined list of all the songs in these two recordings.

1. "Ashland Tragedy"

2. "Bury Me Beneath the Willow"

3. "Down in a Willow Garden"

4. "In the Pines"

5. "Jackie's Gone A-Sailing"

6. "Jesus Lover of My Soul"

7. "London Bridge"

8. "Lord Lovel and Lady Nancy"

9. "On Top of Clinch Mountain"

10. "Pearl Bryan"

11. "Pretty Mohee"

12. "The Soldier and the Lady"

13. "Tap Each Other on the Shoulder"

14. "The Two Ravens"

15. "Wayfaring Stranger"

16. "Whalie, Whalie"

17. "William-A-Trimmy-Toe"

Dean Sturgill

Riding the Lost Train. Audiotape. 1992. Features Dean Sturgill and the "Grayson Highlands Band." Dean Sturgill, fiddle; Dee Dee Price, banjo; Max Henderson, mandolin; JoAnne Andrews Redd, autoharp; Freel Taylor, bass; Jerry Smith, guitar.

Side A

1. "Train 45"

2. "Sailor on the Deep Blue Sea"

3. "Freight Train"

4. "Orange Blossom Special"

5. "Rubber Dolly"

6. "Lost Train Blues"

Side B

1. "John Brown's Dream"

2. "Whoa Mule Whoa"

3. "Tennessee Wagoner"

4. "Dance All Night With a Bottle in Your Hand"

5. "Somebody Stole My Old Coon Dog"

6. "Sugar Hill"

7. "Scotland"

8. "Old-time Picking"

Just Trotting Along. Audiotape. 1993. Produced by Jerry Smith and Max Henderson, Jefferson, North Carolina. Recorded and mixed by Jim Poe. Features Dean Sturgill and the "Grayson Highlands Band." Dean Sturgill, fiddle; Dee Dee Price, banjo; Max Henderson, mandolin; JoAnne Andrews Redd, autoharp; Freel Taylor, bass; Jerry Smith, guitar.

Side A

1. "Gray Eagle"

2. "Ride Old Buck to Water"

3. "Bringing in the Georgia Mail"

4. "Poor Polly Ann"

5. "Trot Along"

6. "High Country"

7. "Jenny Ling"

Side B

1. "Katy Hill"

2. "Ebenezer"

3. "Shout Little Lulu"

4. "Cotton Eyed Joe"

5. "I'm So Lonesome I Could Cry"

6. "Cacklin' Hen"

7. "Bells of Saint Mary"

Wayne Henderson and Gerald Anderson

Appalwood—Handpicked. 1988. Heritage Records, Galax, Va. Gerald Anderson, Wayne Henderson, and others.

1. "Devilish Mary"

2. "Pretty Polly"

3. "Redwing" (Gerald featured)

4. "Carter Family Medley" (Wayne featured)

5. "Black Jack Davy"

6. "Banks of the Ohio"

7. "Saddle Up the Grey" (Wayne featured)

8. "Star the County Down"

9. "Lisa Jane Medley"

10. "Handsome Molly" (Wayne featured)

Contest Favorites. Record and audiotape. 1989. Flying Cloud Records. Produced by Doug Rorrer, Eden, N.C. Features Wayne Henderson and Robin Kessinger.

<u>Side A</u>

1. "Leather Britches"

2. "Little Rock Getaway"

3. "Ragtime Annie"

4. "Fisher's Hornpipe"

5. "Cherokee Shuffle"

6. "Mississippi Sawyer"

<u>Side B</u>

1. "Forked Deer"

2. "Sweet Georgia Brown"

3. "Turkey in the Straw"

4. "East Tennessee Blues"

5. "Temperance Reel"

6. "Flop-eared Mule"

My Window Faces the South. Audiotape. 1992. Warehouse Records, Galax, Va. C-5654. Gerald Anderson, solo guitarist.

<u>Side A</u>

1. "My Window Faces the South"

2. "Leather Britches"

3. "Can't Take It With You"

4. "Going Home"

5. "Streamline Cannonball"

<u>Side B</u>

1. "Blue Ridge Mountain Blues"

2. "Forked Deer"

3. "I Am a Pilgrim"

4. "I'll Get Over You"

Four of a Kind. Compact disc and audiotape. 1993. Warehouse Records, Galax, Va. 24333. C-5741. Gerald Anderson, Wayne Henderson, Glenn Bolick, and Roger Hicks.

<u>Side A</u>

1. "Speedin' West"

2. "New River Train"

3. "Old Joe Clark"

4. "Georgia"

5. "Blackberry Blossom"

6. "Will the Circle Be Unbroken"

Side B

1. "Tennessee Waltz"

2. "Dandelion Wine"

3. "John Henry"

4. "Florida Blues"

5. "Eight More Miles to Louisville"

6. "Battle Hymn of the Republic"

Wayne C. Henderson and Company. Compact disc and audiotape. 1994. Hay Holler Harvest, Inc., Blacksburg, Virginia. HHH-C-107. Features Wayne Henderson, Gerald Anderson, Carson Cooper, Randy Greer, David Holt, Kevin Jackson, Herb Key, Tim Lewis, Jeff Little, Butch Robins, Katy Taylor, Tony Testerman, Doc Watson, Helen White. Liner notes by Joseph T. Wilson.

Side A

1. "Hey Good-looking"

2. "Hangman's Reel"

3. "Saint Anne's Reel"

4. "Whistlin' Rufus"

5. "Handsome Molly"

6. "Bill Bailey"

7. "Billy in the Lowground"

8. "Carter Family Medley"

9. "Spinning Wheel"

Side B

1. "The Cat Came Back"

2. "Salty"

3. "Alabama Jubilee"

4. "Sweet Fern"

5. "Whiskey Before Breakfast"

6. "Back Up and Push"

7. "Sweet Sunny South"

8. "Peace in the Valley"

Flatridge Boys

Home to Kentucky. Compact disc. 1991. Frontier Productions. Recorded at Heritage Studio, Galax, Va. Produced by the Flatridge Boys, Flatridge, Virginia, Post Office of Troutdale, Virginia. Wayne Osborne, guitar, lead vocal; Elmer Russell, guitar, tenor, lead vocal; Ron Russell, autoharp, vocal, bass vocal; Gary Shepherd, bass, vocal. Bobby Patterson, banjo.

1. "Home to Kentucky"
2. "Little Cabin Home On the Hill"
3. "I Miss You All the Time"
4. "I Overlooked An Orchid While Looking for a Rose"
5. "Little Ole Log Cabin in the Lane"
6. "I Heard the Bluebirds Sing"
7. "Molly Darlin'"
8. "Tombstone Every Mile"
9. "Be Nobody's Darlin'"
10. "Smoke Along the Track"
11. "Truck Driving Man"
12. "When You and I Were Young, Maggie"
13. "Don't Turn Around"
14. "Remember Me"
15. "I Don't Care If Tomorrow Never Comes"
16. "Let's Say Good-bye Like We Said Hello"
17. "Maple on the Hill"
18. "You are My Flower"

Where No One Stands Alone. Audiotape. 1992. Recorded at Heritage Studio, Galax, Va. 24333. Elmer Russell, rhythm guitar, lead guitar, and tenor vocals; Ron Russell, autoharp, harmonica, lead and bass vocals; Gary Shepherd, bass guitar; Carol Russell Frenza, lead guitar, mandolin, and vocals. Dedicated to a special friend and cousin, Johnny Russell.

Side A

1. "Where No-one Stands Alone"
2. "There's Going to be a Payday"
3. "I'd Rather Be an Old-Time Christian"
4. "O Come Angel Band"
5. "Beautiful Star of Bethlehem"
6. "Lord, Lead Me On"

Side B

1. "Farther Along"

2. "I'll Meet You in the Morning"

3. "In the Garden"

4. "An Empty Mansion"

5. "Just a Little Talk With Jesus"

6. "Supper Time"

Standing on the Solid Rock. Audiotape. 1992. Recorded at Heritage Studio, Galax, Va. 24333. Wayne Osborne, guitar and lead vocals; Elmer Russell, guitar and tenor vocals; Ron Russell, autoharp, harmonica, bass, and lead vocals; Gary Shepherd, bass, vocal. Dedicated to Calvin Cornett.

Side A

1. "In His Arms"

2. "Whispering Hope"

3. "If Jesus Came to Your House"

4. "Amazing Grace"

5. "Precious Memories"

6. "Mother's Bible"

Side B

1. "Who Will Sing For Me?"

2. "God Sent An Angel"

3. "Life's Railway to Heaven"

4. "Standing on the Solid Rock"

5. "Old Brush Arbor"

6. "Flowers for Mama"

Konnarock Critters

Old Favorites. Cassette tape. 1994. Heritage Records, Galax, Va. HRC-C-113. Brian Grim, fiddle; Debbie Grim, banjo; Jim Lloyd, guitar and autoharp. Guest artists: Wayne Henderson on bass and Blanche Nichols on guitar. All except Wayne Henderson do vocals. Liner notes by Bobby Patterson.

Side A

1. "Cumberland Gap"

2. "Sally Ann"

3. "Crook Brothers Breakdown"

4. "Shady Grove"

5. "Old Sport"

6. "Wild Bill Jones"

Side B

1. "Jimmy Sutton"
2. "Lonesome Road Blues"
3. "Old-Time John Henry"
4. "Let Me Fall"
5. "Reuben"
6. "Ducks on the Millpond"
7. "Black Mountain Blues"